The Liar

The Liar

An Essay on Truth and Circularity

Jon Barwise and John Etchemendy

Stanford University

New York Oxford

Oxford University Press

1987

Oxford University Press
Oxford   New York   Toronto
Delhi   Bombay   Calcutta   Madras   Karachi
Petaling Jaya   Singapore   Hong Kong   Tokyo
Nairobi   Dar es Salaam   Cape Town
Melbourne   Auckland
and associated companies in
Beirut   Berlin   Ibadan   Nicosia

Library of Congress Cataloging-in-Publication Data
Barwise, Jon.
    The liar: an essay on truth and circularity.

    Bibliography: p.
Includes index.
1. Liar paradox.   I. Etchemendy, John, 1952-
II. Title. BC199.P2B37   1987   165   86-31260
ISBN 0-19-505072-X (alk. paper)

Printing (last digit): 9 8 7 6 5 4 3 2

Printed in the United States of America
on acid-free paper

For John Perry
teacher, colleague, and friend

Preface

Historically, the set-theoretic and semantic paradoxes have had an enormous impact in logic. On the one hand, the set-theoretic paradoxes discovered in the early twentieth century created a climate in which work in logic, metamathematics, and foundations could flourish, and led directly to many of our present day concerns. On the other hand, diagonal constructions similar to those involved in several of the paradoxes provided us with one of the most basic tools of logic. Examples come readily to mind: diagonal constructions gave us Cantor's Theorem in set theory, the undecidability of the halting problem in recursion theory, and Gödel's Incompleteness Theorems in proof theory.

It is striking, though, that in one branch of logic, model theory, the impact of the paradoxes has been almost entirely negative. The Liar paradox, by convincing the founding fathers that languages containing their own truth predicate and allowing circular reference were incoherent, has led to the exclusion of such languages from mainstream logic. Given the fruitfulness of diagonal arguments in the rest of logic, one wonders whether the path followed in model theory was really the most productive reaction to the paradox. In this book, we present an account of the Liar that shows it to be a true diagonal argument, one with profound consequences for our understanding of the most basic semantical mechanisms found in ordinary language. Indeed, we think the Liar is every bit as significant for the foundations of semantics as the set-theoretic paradoxes were for the foundations of set theory.

We have tried to make this book largely self-contained. In particular, we haven't presupposed familiarity with any of the other approaches to the semantical paradoxes. We have described two of the best known treatments, those of Tarski and Kripke, in sufficient detail for the reader to see how ours differs, and why. But many other interesting approaches have been explored in recent years which we've only mentioned in passing, if at all. We hope that after reading this book, the reader will want to compare our account with some of these others. We recommend the volume *Recent Essays on Truth and the Liar Paradox*, edited by R.M. Martin, as an excellent place to start. Several of the works referred to in what follows, including Kripke's, are reprinted in Martin's collection. We call particular attention to the accounts of Parsons (1974) and Burge (1979). While their approaches are quite different from each other, and also from ours, each has significant points of similarity with the account we end up arguing for here.

This book is meant to be accessible to anyone with a working knowledge of first-order logic and the basics of Zermelo-Fraenkel set theory. We hope that the results and techniques introduced here will be of use and interest to a fairly wide audience, including logicians, linguists, computer scientists, and philosophers of language, and so have tried to make the book accessible to all these groups. Writing for such a diverse audience has naturally been somewhat difficult. While the content has forced us into a rather mathematical style of exposition, we have tried, expositorily and organizationally, to make the book of use to this entire range of readers. Readers less interested in the technical details of our account may well want to skip the proofs of more complicated theorems. The more involved proofs begin with a description of the main idea, and this will suffice for most purposes. The simple proofs, though, should be read and understood, since they often bring out crucial features of the account.

To help the reader understand and get comfortable with the more technical side of the material, we've included a wide range of exercises, from very simple to quite difficult. These exercises should at least be read, even if not fully worked out, since they are relevant to the flow of the book. We hope that the exercises, plus the division of the book into thirteen short chapters, will make it a useful text to work through in a seminar setting. We have also included some open problems for the more adventuresome.

One chapter of the book is devoted entirely to an exposition of Peter Aczel's set theory, ZFC/AFA, and its universe of hypersets, which we use in giving our account. We have found ZFC/AFA to be an extremely convenient theory in which to model the sorts of circularity involved in the Liar, and are convinced that it is an important new mathematical tool that will find increasingly wide application. Even readers who do not find our treatment of the Liar to their liking should find the techniques made available by Aczel's hypersets to be worth the effort involved in working through the book.

Acknowledgments

The work reported in this book was made possible by an award from the System Development Foundation, and was also partially supported by grant NSF DCR-8403573. It was written at the Center for the Study of Language and Information on computer equipment provided by the Xerox Corporation and the Digital Equipment Corporation. The stimulus provided by the CSLI environment, a place where people from diverse disciplines and with radically different backgrounds and perspectives share a common subject matter, has been crucial to the development of this book, both in its form and content. We would like to thank all our colleagues at CSLI, and especially our collaborators in the STASS project,[1] for their intellectual stimulation and encouragement.

An early version of the work in Part III was presented at the 1985 summer meeting of the Association for Symbolic Logic at Stanford University. Later versions where presented at a number of colloquia and seminars during the past year. Our thinking has profited greatly from the feedback we received on these occasions, and we thank all the participants. We are particularly grateful to the participants in the AFA seminar held at CSLI last spring, who carefully worked their way through the first complete draft of the book, and to Dag Westerståhl for organizing the seminar. We also want to thank readers of the penultimate draft of the book, both anonymous and otherwise, for pointing out a number of remaining problems. We should especially mention Peter Aczel

---

[1] Curtis Abbott, Mark Gawron, Joseph Goguen, Kris Halvorsen, David Israel, Pepe Meseguer, John Perry, Stanley Peters, Carl Pollard, Ken Olson, Mats Rooth, Brian Smith, and Susan Stucky.

and Robin Cooper, who prevented us from making a couple of real blunders, as well as Mark Crimmins, Greg O'Hair, and Godehard Link, who gave us very helpful and timely suggestions for last minute improvements.

We prepared the book using LaTeX, the document preparation system created by Leslie Lamport as a special version of Donald Knuth's TeX. Ingrid Deiwiks proofread the manuscript, while Emma Pease and Dikran Karagueuzian prepared the final document to obtain a camera-ready manuscript. Nancy Etchemendy drew the figures. We thank all of them for their excellent help.

As is apparent from the book, we owe a special debt to Peter Aczel, whose work on AFA was presented during an extended visit to CSLI during the winter of 1984–85, and was in fact what initially attracted us to the topic. By providing a powerful and elegant method for modeling various sorts of circular phenomena, Aczel's work freed us from certain older ways of thinking about the topics we address in the book. Indeed, tackling the Liar with the new tools provided by AFA, and by the general perspective of situation semantics, has been both exciting and fun; we almost hate to see the project come to its natural conclusion. But we hope that readers will be able to share the enjoyment we've had working through these ideas and playing with the new mathematical tools, and that some will even go on to extend the framework presented here, or to apply AFA to other sorts of problems.

However much fun this project has been for us, we can't say the pleasure was shared by our wives. We are very grateful to Mary Ellen and Nancy for putting up with the many weekends and evenings that we've spent working together during the past year and a half. Finally, a special acknowledgment is in order to other parts of our families. Specifically, we must thank Claire Barwise and Max Etchemendy, both two years of age, for serving as the unwitting source of our examples. They are even more fun than AFA.

Stanford, California   J. B.
September, 1986   J. E.

Contents

Part I

Introduction

1

The Liar

Some background

Logicians, it is said, abhor ambiguity but love paradox. Perhaps
that is why they are so inclined to give formal prescriptions for
avoiding the famous Liar paradox, but so loathe to diagnose the
underlying problem that gives rise to it. Despite its antiquity, and
its genuine importance, no adequate analysis of it has ever been
given, or so we feel. Since it clearly involves the most basic semantical notions—truth, reference, and negation, and little else—this
lack of understanding calls into question the very foundations of
the semantical enterprise.

   The Liar paradox gets its name from formulations in which a
speaker asserts, directly or indirectly, that his own assertion is a
lie. The simplest such assertion would be one of the form "I am
now lying." Usually, though, the paradox is not discussed in this
form, since lying introduces various extraneous issues, such as the
speaker's intent to deceive, that aren't essential to the paradox.
Instead, it's more traditional to treat the paradox in one of the
following, distilled versions.

   1. What I am now saying is false.

   2. This assertion is not true.

   3. The third sentence in this list is not true.

The problem with the above assertions strikes us as soon as we try
to decide whether they are true or false. For it seems that such

claims are true if and only if they are not true. But of course that is a contradiction, and so something has gone seriously wrong.

On first encounter, it's hard not to consider assertions of this sort as jokes, hardly matters of serious intellectual inquiry. But when one's subject matter involves the notion of truth in a central way, for example when studying the semantic properties of a language, the jokes take on a new air of seriousness: they become genuine paradoxes. And one of the important lessons of twentieth century science, in fields as diverse as set theory, physics, and semantics, is that paradoxes matter. The significance of a paradox is never the paradox itself, but what it is a symptom of. For a paradox demonstrates that our understanding of some basic concept or cluster of concepts is crucially flawed, that the concepts break down in limiting cases. And although the limiting cases may strike us as odd or unlikely, or even amusing, the flaw itself is a feature of the concepts, not the limiting cases that bring it to the fore. If the concepts are important ones, this is no laughing matter.

An adequate analysis of a paradox must diagnose the source of the problem the paradox reveals, and thereby help us refine the concepts involved, making them truly coherent. But it should do so in such a way that in normal situations business can proceed as usual. This is what has happened, for example, in set theory and relativity theory. But it has not yet happened in the case of the semantical paradoxes, or so we will claim.

The traditional wisdom about the Liar paradox goes back to Tarski's important monograph, *The Concept of Truth in Formalized Languages*.[1] Tarski's was by no means the first serious attempt to solve the paradox—indeed, the Liar has been a continuing topic of concern to philosophers and logicians since the middle ages—but it was the first carefully worked out treatment that brought to bear the tools of modern logic and set theory. Largely because of its formal detail and precision, Tarski's treatment was for many years considered adequate, if not as a genuine solution to the paradox, at least as a general way to avoid it without abandoning the notion of truth entirely.

Tarski's concern was with the consistency of scientific and mathematical discourse. He recognized that in such discourse we frequently use the notion of truth in ways not easily avoided. For

---

[1] Tarski (1933), (1935), (1956).

example when, in logic, we talk about all statements of a given form being true, or about the truth of all the premises of some unspecified argument, it's hard to see how we could say the same things without employing the notion of truth. But if our ordinary concept of truth is somehow incoherent, as the paradox suggests, this raises the question of whether the same incoherence infects the mathematical and scientific discourse that presupposes the intuitive notion. It is this worry that Tarski set out to address.

What Tarski showed in his monograph is that in a wide variety of cases, if we begin with a fixed "object language" $\mathcal{L}$, it will be possible to give, in an enriched "metalanguage" $\mathcal{L}'$, an explicit, eliminable definition of a predicate $True_{\mathcal{L}}$ that applies to exactly the true sentences of the original language. To apply Tarski's technique, the metalanguage must be capable of expressing everything expressible in the original object language, must contain simple devices for describing its syntax, and finally, must have set-theoretic resources that go beyond those in the original language. Since the defined predicate applies to all and only the true sentences of $\mathcal{L}$, it will allow us to say, in the metalanguage, many of the things we wanted to say using the intuitive notion of truth, at least when our attributions of truth are restricted to sentences of the original language. And assuming the coherence of the syntactic and set-theoretic notions involved in our definition, these attributions will never lead to paradox. Of course, the defined predicate is inadequate when it comes to sentences in other languages, and in particular cannot coincide with the notion of truth for the metalanguage $\mathcal{L}'$: for that we have to define a new predicate in a *metametalanguage* $\mathcal{L}''$ that stands in the same relation to $\mathcal{L}'$ as $\mathcal{L}'$ stood to $\mathcal{L}$.

Tarski realized that his solution would not apply to natural languages, or to the notion of truth expressible in natural languages, at least without adopting radical and artificial revisions of those languages. The solution depends on the possibility of regimenting scientific language into a hierarchy of levels, from object language, to metalanguage, to metametalanguage, and so forth. If this regimentation could be carried out, then it's clear that sentences like (1) through (3) would not be expressible in the resulting, stratified system of languages. For a given language in the hierarchy could only talk about the truth of sentences in earlier languages, but not about the truth of its own claims, let alone claims that become expressible further out in the hierarchy. In this way, Tarski hoped to sidestep the paradox by employing what was admittedly an artificial device.

Despite the tremendous influence Tarski's treatment of the Liar has had, there are many reasons for dissatisfaction with it. Saul Kripke is largely responsible for convincing a substantial number of philosophers and logicians of the impossibility of extending the Tarskian approach to ordinary uses of the notion of truth.[2] In his famous paper "Outline of a theory of truth,"[3] Kripke did two things. First, he showed that circular reference of the sort involved in the Liar is not only a much more common phenomenon than had been supposed, but also that whether a given utterance is paradoxical may well depend on nonlinguistic, empirical facts. Consider, for example, the following pair of sentences from Kripke's paper.

(1.1)   Most of Nixon's assertions about Watergate are false.

(1.2)   Everything Jones says about Watergate is true.

Now there is nothing intrinsically paradoxical about these sentences. It is easy to imagine all kinds of situations where either or both could be truly uttered. But Kripke observed that there are also circumstances in which they *would* be paradoxical: for example, if 1.1 is asserted by Jones, and it is in fact his only assertion about Watergate, while Nixon asserts 1.2, and the rest of Nixon's assertions about Watergate are evenly balanced between the true and the false. Such examples show, as Kripke puts it, that "there can be no syntactic or semantic 'sieve' that will winnow out the 'bad' cases while preserving the 'good' ones."[4] In particular, the sort of linguistic stratification suggested by Tarski would have to

---

[2]There are problems with Tarski's treatment even if we limit it to uses of the concept of truth in scientific enterprises. Since Tarski gives an *eliminable* definition of $True_\mathcal{L}$, that is, one which allows the systematic elimination of all occurrences of the defined predicate, one can see his result as showing that many of the things we say using the notion of truth can be said without it if we bring in sufficient syntactic and set-theoretic machinery. One serious problem with this approach, though, is that the defined notion does not yield a concept of truth adequate to do semantics, and so the semanticist, at least, cannot appeal to a Tarskian treatment of the paradox. For an elaboration of this point, see Etchemendy (1987).

[3]Kripke (1975).

[4]Kripke (1975), 692.

rule out sentences like these, in spite of the fact that they also have perfectly innocuous, nonparadoxical uses.

Kripke's second contribution was equally important. There have been critics of Tarski's treatment since its first presentation, but Kripke did much more than criticize the standard treatment. He went on to present a well worked out theory of truth for a language that both allowed circular reference and contained its own truth predicate. In doing this he convinced people that the problem presented by the Liar in ordinary language was not intrinsically intractable, and so inspired a resurgence of interest in this perennial problem. Many authors who have taken exception to particular features of Kripke's solution have followed his general approach. We will discuss this approach at some length in Chapter 5. While we do not find Kripke's positive account of truth compelling, we do agree entirely with the first part of his argument: Tarski's treatment of the paradox does not get to the heart of the matter, it does not provide a genuine diagnosis of the paradox.

Diagnosing a paradox

A treatment of the Liar all too often takes the following form. First, various intuitively plausible principles are set out and motivated by a discussion of the commonsense notions involved. Then a contradiction is shown to follow from these intuitive principles. At this point the discussion turns directly to the question of which principles can be kept and which must be abandoned: the goal, of course, is to arrive at a consistent set of principles describing the commonsense notions, but a set immune to the paradox. But in a sense, the paradox remains paradoxical, despite the treatment. For the Liar has forced us to abandon intuitively plausible semantic principles without giving us reason, beyond the paradox itself, to suspect their falsehood. We see *that* they are false, without understanding *why*.

By calling for a diagnosis[5] of the paradox, we have in mind a rather different approach. Natural languages do provide us with various complex devices and mechanisms, such as the ability to refer to almost anything, and the ability to express propositions

---

[5]For further discussion of the difference between diagnosing a paradox and simply treating it, see Chihara (1979).

about anything referred to. And among the things we can refer
to are sentences, statements, and propositions; among the things
we can say about them are that they are true or not. Clearly,
the principles commonly introduced in treatments of the paradox
are based on our native intuitions about the way such important
mechanisms work. The obvious lesson taught by the Liar is that
our semantic intuitions, though doubtless generally sound, need
refinement. But the process of refining our intuitions requires a
better understanding of the linguistic mechanisms themselves, and
of how they interact, not just an assessment of the faulty principles
that describe our untutored intuitions.

This difference in approach has been appreciated in the case of
the set-theoretic paradoxes. Naive set theory was based on generally sound intuitions about set existence and set membership.
It turned out that these intuitions were faulty. But purely formal
treatments of these paradoxes found little favor compared with the
treatment based on new, refined intuitions about sets that grew out
of Zermelo's conception of the cumulative hierarchy. This conception sheds light on a whole raft of set-theoretic paradoxes, and similarly, an improved understanding of semantic mechanisms should
illuminate the various semantical paradoxes surrounding the Liar.

Though we would hardly claim to have an entirely new conception of the semantic mechanisms at work in the Liar, we do hope to
bring new tools to bear in the analysis of certain older, neglected
conceptions. And in so doing, we hope to expose the basic problems
that give rise to Liar-like paradoxes. The first tool is the notion
of a partial situation (and the related notion of a fact) borrowed
from situation semantics.[6] The second tool is an elegant new set-
theoretic framework developed by Peter Aczel. Aczel's motivation
in developing this framework was to model circular (and other nonwellfounded) computational processes, but it is equally suited to
model circular propositions and other nonwellfounded semantical
objects. We think the absence of such a set-theoretic framework
has limited prior treatments of the Liar, since it is tempting to
assume that what cannot be directly modeled in set theory simply
cannot *be*.

Our goal in this book will be to provide a rigorous, set-theoretic
model of the semantic mechanisms involved in the Liar, a model

---

[6]See Barwise and Perry (1983).

that preserves as many of our naive intuitions about such mechanisms as possible. Because of this, we will be rethinking several issues that contemporary treatments of the Liar tend to presuppose answers to, such as the question of what truth is really a property of. Some of our answers will seem nonstandard to many logicians and philosophers, but we think this is at least partly because the logical and philosophical communities have strayed away from various pretheoretic intuitions concerning the devices and mechanisms at work in the Liar.

In the end, we think our account provides much more than a solution to the paradox of the Liar. It provides an explanation of how the paradox comes about, and of exactly which of our untutored intuitions come in conflict. One thing the diagnosis reveals is a striking parallel between this semantic paradox and the familiar set-theoretic paradoxes, a parallel which has always been vaguely perceived but which has never clearly emerged in formal accounts of the Liar.

Some basic decisions

Before we can begin our diagnosis, we must make some very basic decisions, decisions about how to treat the three fundamental mechanisms of truth, reference, and negation. With each of these come subtleties that require attention if we are to carry out a rigorous semantical analysis. And with each it is all too easy to go astray, to oversimplify in ways that don't matter in most circumstances, but which can prove disastrous when we combine the three.

The bearers of truth

First and foremost, we must decide what truth is a property of: sentences, or the things expressed when people use sentences. The tradition in logic throughout most of this century has been to take sentences as the bearers of truth. As long as we imagine ourselves working with something like eternal sentences, sentences whose content is independent of the circumstances of use, the decision is largely a matter of convenience: under these assumptions sentences are more convenient, since they provide fairly concrete and structured objects to use in defining satisfaction and truth, and thus allow us to avoid issues about the structural properties of the things expressed when people use sentences.

Truth, as we ordinarily understand the notion, is a property of things like claims, testimony, assertions, beliefs, statements, or propositions. It is not a property of sentences. But the decision to use sentences as the bearers of truth has proven to be a useful fiction, a good way of getting a certain amount of logic done without bogging down in extralogical questions about the nature of the bearers of truth. But the fiction is harmless only in cases where we can unambiguously associate a claim about the world with each sentence, or where the slippage between different claims made by different uses of a sentence is negligible for the purpose at hand.

In many situations, the slippage between a sentence and what it expresses can be ignored. For example, given the stability of the solar system, any use of

(∗) Earth is the third planet from the sun

expresses pretty much the same thing, or at any rate something with the same truth value. However, if we take a superficially similar sentence, say,

(∗∗) Earl is the third person in the line

we see that what it expresses is highly dependent on the circumstances in which it is used. Which Earl is being referred to, and which line? And even if we fix an Earl and a line, (∗∗) may be true one moment, false the next. After all, with any luck, Earl is moving forward in line. With examples like this, it obviously makes no sense to assign a truth value to the sentence itself, as opposed to what a given use of the sentence happens to express.

Are the sentences that give rise to the Liar paradox more like (∗) or (∗∗)? Is the slippage between such sentences and what they express negligible or not? That remains to be seen.[7] The point we want to make here is that we risk prejudging a crucial issue if

---

[7]Certainly some distinguished writers have thought that it was not negligible. For example, Charles Parsons (1974) and Tyler Burge (1979) argue that the Liar involves some sort of context dependence. There is certainly a *prima facie* case for thinking this. For the paradox involves an *argument*, and in this argument there are repeated references to the Liar. If for some reason these different uses of the Liar actually express different propositions, it may be that there is no paradox at all. This is basically the line taken by Parsons. He argues that between the Liar sentence and what it expresses

we decide to assign truth values to sentences. As long as there is even a possibility that what the Liar sentence expresses depends on things other than the sentence itself, we should give up the fiction that sentences are the primary bearers of truth.

Once we abandon sentences as the bearers of truth, we must replace them with something else. The most natural candidates are *statements* or *propositions*. By a *statement* we will understand certain sorts of datable events, those where a speaker asserts or attempts to assert something using a declarative sentence. In contrast, we take a *proposition* to be a claim about the world, the kind of thing that is asserted by a successful statement. Some writers use the term "statement" the way we are using the word "proposition," but we find the present terminology more convenient, and arguably more in line with common usage.

We are going to work with both statements and propositions, but we will take truth to be fundamentally a property of propositions and derivatively a property of statements. There are two considerations that motivate this choice: considerations of grain and the possible lack of truth value. Statements are much more fine-grained than propositions. If I now say "I am tired," I express the same thing that you express by saying now, of me, "He is tired." We have made different statements, statements with many different properties: most obvious is that they involved different speakers using different sentences. But they have the same truth value. And intuitively, they have the same truth value *because* they express the very same proposition, *because* they make the very same claim. This makes it natural to view propositions rather than statements as the primary bearers of truth.

Another intuitive difference between statements and propositions is that the former can go wrong in ways the latter cannot. In particular, I may make a statement that fails to have a truth value, perhaps because the statement presupposes something that is not the case. For example, if I point at an empty tabletop and say "That card is not the ace of spades," then my statement fails in a different way than if I had been pointing at the ace of spades. We will say that it fails to express a proposition because of the failure of the presupposition—that I am pointing to a card—and that for

___

there is an implicit quantification, and that the range of quantification shifts during the course of the argument. Burge, on the other hand, argues that it is the extension of the truth predicate that varies with shifts in context.

this reason the statement has no truth value. As we understand the terms, statements are the sorts of things that may have presuppositions; propositions are not, but rather are the claims made by statements whose presuppositions are fulfilled.

Both of these considerations suggest that taking truth as fundamentally a property of propositions, with the truth value of a statement in some sense "derivative," is the appropriate choice to make in studying the Liar. As we will see, it's a choice that forces us to confront difficult issues about truth head on, rather than avoid the paradox in an *ad hoc* manner. At any rate, these considerations are the main reasons we have chosen propositions as the basic semantical objects in this study.

Of course, once this decision is made, we are immediately faced with three formidable tasks. First, we must give some account of the nature of propositions, at least enough of an account to say when a proposition is true. Second, we must give such an account of truth for propositions. And third, we must give an account of the relation between sentences and the propositions they can express.

We will actually tackle these tasks twice over. We will develop and compare two distinct, competing accounts of propositions, one due to Russell, the other derived from Austin. Each of these comes with its own account of truth and of the relation between sentences and the propositions they express. It will turn out that on the Russellian analysis, the Liar *sentence*

(λ) This proposition is not true

does express a unique proposition, f, which we call the Liar *proposition*. However, on the Austinian analysis there will be many different propositions that can be expressed using λ.

Once we admit propositions and take truth to be a genuine property propositions may have or fail to have, we must abandon anything like the redundancy theory of truth. If "(∗)" refers to the sentence so labeled above, then admittedly (∗) and

(∗′) The proposition expressed by (∗) is true

have a pretty intimate connection. In particular, it seems that neither of the claims made by (∗) and (∗′) can be true unless the other is as well. Still, they are importantly different claims. For there is a clear shift of subject matter: one is a claim about the earth, the other a claim about a proposition.

Intuitively, the intimate connection between the above pair of sentences is a consequence of the meaning of "true," and is closely related to Tarski's famous "T-schema." When truth is taken as a property of propositions, rather than sentences, then the T-schema presumably takes something like the following form.

(T) The proposition that ... is true iff ....

Here the two occurrences of "..." can be filled in by any sentence that expresses a proposition, as long as it expresses the same proposition both times. It turns out that the strict counterparts of this schema come out valid on both accounts we consider, though a related schema must be given up in the Russellian treatment.

Before we turn to the other mechanisms involved in the Liar, it is important to note one significant consequence of our decision to treat truth as a property of propositions rather than of sentences or statements. Sentences or statements may well fail to express a proposition, and so fail to have a truth value. Which is to say, a sentence or statement might *not* be true, but not because it makes a *false* claim about the world. In contrast, it's not clear what it could mean for a proposition to be false except for it simply not to be true. For once we arrive at the proposition, a genuine claim about the world, only two possibilities seem to remain: either the claim is right or it's not. With propositions, then, it seems that being false is nothing more nor less than failing to be true.[8]

This consequence obviously has an important effect on any treatment of the Liar. To date, most treatments of the paradox have dealt with sentences, and many have employed the notions of a truth value gap or a third value. These accounts declare the Liar sentence to be neither true nor false. But from our perspective, assigning a truth value gap to the Liar sentence is tantamount

---

[8]We are setting aside issues of time and tense in this book, and so do not need to take a stand on propositions about the future, say the proposition that there will be a nuclear war before the year 2025. If we had to take a stand we would say that such claims either are true or not, but note that it might not now be determinate which is the case. Perhaps only in the year 2025 could one look back and see whether that proposition is (and so was) true, and what events between now and then contributed to its truth or falsity. But, as we say, such a stand is not forced on us. We just think it is right.

to saying it does not express a proposition, since gaps are never associated with propositions. Thus if this option is pursued, one owes an explanation of *why* such sentences cannot express propositions. This is a major defect in most accounts that appeal to gaps: they offer no accompanying explanation for the failure of the Liar sentence to express a claim, one that is either true or not. An adequate explanation of this alleged feature of the Liar sentence must say more than that assuming otherwise would lead to paradox, for that explains nothing. Similarly, simply asserting that the Liar sentence cannot express a proposition due to its "vicious circularity" is no explanation, as has been emphasized by Kripke. For many perfectly acceptable claims involve similar kinds of circularity.

This defect in accounts that employ gaps or third values generally comes back to haunt them in the form of so-called *strengthened* Liars. If we've given no explanation of why a Liar sentence like

(λ_S) This sentence is false

fails to express a genuine claim, but have simply assigned it a gap, then nothing stands in the way of reintroducing the paradox in slightly altered guise:

(λ'_S) This sentence is either false or "gappy."

If we had a convincing account of why λ_S should fail to express a proposition, then that same account would presumably transfer over to λ'_S as well, or even, for that matter, to

(λ''_S) This sentence is either false or fails to express any claim at all.

In the absence of such an account, though, sentences like the latter two seem intuitively to make perfectly understandable claims. But they turn out to be paradoxical, even if we grant the original "solution" applied to λ_S.

The fact that the paradox can be reintroduced in the form of a Strengthened Liar is sure indication that an account fails on precisely this point. Thus we see one final reason for explicitly introducing propositions, and for insisting on the simple point that they are either true or not. By so doing we force ourselves to confront the issue of whether Liar sentences make genuine claims, and if we decide they do not, to explain exactly why this should be so. Thus it does not limit our options, though it does force us to be forthright in the treatment of any presumed "gaps."

Referring to propositions

Truth comes first, because it is to bearers of truth we must refer
if we are to say things like "... is true." Once we have settled
on propositions, the next question is: what propositions can one
refer to? Our answer is the simplest possible one: you can refer
to any proposition whatsoever. More generally, there seems to
be no particular reason to doubt that one can refer to absolutely
anything at all, using some pronoun or other, or by giving it a
name, at least as long as that thing can be described, pointed at,
or in some other way made salient. Propositions are no different
in this respect from anything else.

Of course this doesn't tell us what propositions there are to
be referred to. In particular, it does not answer the question of
whether there are circular propositions of the sort that seem to be
expressed by Liar-like sentences. Sentences like "This proposition
is expressible in English using fewer than twelve words," as well as
the examples of Kripke discussed earlier, seem to show that there
is nothing wrong in principle with circular propositions, or with
sentences that refer to the very proposition they express. This
does not show that the Liar sentence itself expresses a proposition,
but it does argue against any simple-minded ban on circularity, on
propositions that are directly or indirectly about themselves. Our
policy will be to take the most liberal stance on this issue, and so
build into both of our models the assumption that one can always
use the phrase "this proposition" to refer to something, and that
that something can be the very proposition the embedding sentence
is used to express. Thus if the Liar sentence does not express a
proposition, it is not because of a general prohibition against self-
reference or circularity.[9]

Once we decide that we can refer to any proposition at all, we
must still decide how the various linguistic mechanisms for referring
work. In this book we are going to follow tradition by treating
names as uniquely referring expressions. That is, we are going to
assume, contrary to fact, that a name like "Max" picks out a single

---

[9]We prefer the term circularity to self-reference since referring is something
speakers do, and so the object of an act of self-reference should be the
speaker, not a sentence, statement, or proposition. This point has usually
been set to one side, and since sentences are syntactically wellfounded, and
so can't contain themselves as proper parts, traditional sentential treatments
of the Liar have taken self-reference to be the phenomenon at issue.

individual. This counterfactual assumption does not prejudice our
study of the Liar, since we will not be using a version where the Liar
is referred to by a name.[10] Rather, we will use demonstratives such
as "this proposition" and "that proposition," and so should say
something about how these work. As for "this proposition," we will
treat it as semantically reflexive, that is, as always referring to the
proposition expressed by a sentence of which it is a part. This is a
slight regimentation of ordinary English, where "this proposition"
can also be used demonstratively, to refer to some other proposition
immediately at hand. Thus, for example, if we are in a department
meeting discussing a proposal to change the graduate requirements,
one might say, "This proposition will improve the program in three
ways." Here there is no temptation to take "this proposition" as
referring to the proposition expressed by the speaker, but rather,
to the proposition on the floor at the moment. We will return to
this point below. As for "that proposition," we will assume it can
be used to refer to any proposition at all.

In the Austinian account, we will see that reference enters the
picture in another way as well, since the theory supposes that
statements are always made with an implicit reference to some actual situation. So the question will arise: which situations can one
say something about? The most liberal answer, and so the most
attractive initially, is again the simplest: you can say something
about any actual situation. We will begin with this assumption,
but will find reasons for supposing it to be too liberal. Indeed, we
will suggest restrictions on which actual situations a speaker may
legitimately refer to without being subject to a charge of quibbling.

Negation and denial

Finally, let us consider negation. Some students of language have
accused logicians of overlooking an important distinction, the distinction between negation and denial. There is some intuitive
support for such a distinction. An assertion, even if it contains
a negative element, stakes out a claim about the world, whereas

---

[10]Note, however, that this counterfactual assumption certainly does infect
any treatment of the paradoxes which deals with sentences, and which also
uses names for sentences, as in:

(μ) μ is not true.

intuitively, a denial rejects some claim that has already been raised. Thus denials presuppose the salience of the proposition to be denied.

Let's distinguish verb phrase negation from sentence negation, where verb phrase negation involves a negative element in the verb phrase (as in the verb phrase "doesn't have the ace of spades") and sentence negation is expressed in sentences beginning with "It is not the case that ... ." Other things being equal, verb phrase negation is more likely to be used to assert a negative claim than sentence negation. In contrast, a denial will probably be expressed using sentence negation or, more likely, a sentence that exploits the salience of the proposition in question, such as "That's not the case" or "That's not true."

Unfortunately, syntactic structure alone does not settle the question of whether the utterance is an assertion or a denial. For example, said with the right intonation, sentences involving verb phrase negation can take on the same presupposition as those involving sentence negation. Thus, a sentence containing a negative verb phrase can be used in either way, to assert a proposition or to deny some presupposed proposition.

Whether this pragmatic ambiguity is important in understanding the semantics of the Liar remains to be seen, but again, as long as there is a chance that it is, we should keep the distinction between acts of assertion and acts of denial in mind. For this is just the sort of subtlety that could emerge as important in extreme cases like those involving the Liar. Traditional logic, by focusing on sentence negation alone, has given itself no mechanism for keeping these distinct sorts of activities apart.

For the most part, we are going to focus on assertions in this book. In particular, just as our main interpretation of sentences like

The ace of clubs is not red

will be as assertions, so too our main interpretation of sentences like

Proposition p is not true

will be as *asserting* a proposition about p, that p is not true, rather than as a denial of either the proposition p or the proposition that

p is true. In particular, we will primarily treat the Liar as an assertion about itself, the assertion that it is not true. However, on both of our analyses of propositions, the distinction between assertions and denials will, in different ways, play an important role. In Chapter 12 we will discuss how the ambiguity between assertion and denial plays a significant role in the Liar.[11]

We saw earlier that the T-schema describes the intuitive relation between a proposition p and the proposition that p is true. We expect a dual relation to obtain between p and the proposition that p is *not* true, namely:

(F) The proposition that . . . is not true iff ¬ . . . .

In this case the initial occurrence of ". . ." is to be replaced by a sentence expressing a proposition. But what about "¬ . . ."? Should it be replaced by a sentence asserting the negated proposition, or should it be interpreted as an embedded denial? It will turn out that these are vastly different conditions.

Plan of the book

Having argued that the propositional version of the Liar prejudges fewer potentially important issues, we can now describe in more detail the form our analysis will take. In broadest outline, our methods are the standard ones of model theory: we use set theory to construct models of sentences, propositions, and worlds, and of the various relations among these. The most basic relations we will have to account for are, first, the relation between sentences and the propositions they express, and second, the tripartite relation between propositions, the property of truth, and the world. In detail, though, the methods we use differ in various ways from more traditional treatments.

Perhaps the most striking difference is the set theory we use. Since the semantic phenomena that concern us involve circularity of various sorts, standard set theories, all of which assume the axiom of foundation, are quite awkward in that they foreclose the most natural ways of modeling these phenomena. Because of this, we have turned to an elegant alternative due to Peter Aczel. In this theory the axiom of foundation is replaced with an

---

[11]For another discussion of the role of denial in the paradoxes, see Terry Parsons (1984).

"anti-foundation" axiom, called AFA. This axiom is based on an extremely intuitive alternative to the cumulative conception of sets, and guarantees the existence of a rich class of circular objects with which to model the circular phenomena involved. We present a self-contained introduction to this theory in Chapter 3.

As we indicated earlier, we will develop two distinct accounts, one based on a fairly common, Russellian conception of the relation between language and the world, the other based on an Austinian conception. In both, propositions are taken as the primary bearers of truth. Where the accounts differ is in their view of the nature of propositions, the mechanisms whereby sentences can be used to express propositions, and the nature of truth. In neither account do we use the most familiar, "possible worlds" technique for modeling propositions, where propositions are modeled as subsets of an indexed set of first-order structures.[12] In both of our approaches, we use structured, set-theoretic objects which code up the claim made by a proposition to represent that proposition. The specific structure of these set-theoretic representatives is not meant to signify that propositions themselves display the same or similar structure, or even that they are necessarily structured objects at all. Rather, the structure is there to facilitate our characterization of the two basic relations mentioned above.

We present these two models side by side, the Russellian account in Part II and the Austinian account in Part III, making the best case we can for each. Ultimately, we argue that the Austinian treatment provides a far superior account, one that preserves vir-

---

[12]We have avoided the possible worlds approach for several reasons, but mainly because it prejudges a number of crucial issues that the Liar forces us to rethink. In particular, the approach does not treat the truth of propositions on a par with other properties, but instead reduces it to the membership of the "actual world" in the proposition in question. This makes it difficult, if not impossible, to distinguish sensibly between a proposition p and the proposition that p is true, or between the negation of p and the proposition that p is false. Other problems arise due to the "coarse-grainedness" of this representation of propositions: on this approach, logically equivalent propositions are represented by the same set. For reasons related to this, it turns out that there is no way to indicate what a proposition is about, and hence no way to indicate which propositions are circular, i.e., about themselves. Finally, as will become clear in Part II, the intuitive conception of propositions underlying the possible worlds approach, which is in relevant respects similar to the Russellian, is actually at odds with the assumption that worlds are total, i.e., that they settle all issues.

tually all of our pretheoretic intuitions about truth and the world, while at the same time more accurately reflecting the enormous flexibility of language. But the Russellian account is not simply presented as a foil, since what we learn in the Russellian account takes on deeper significance viewed from the Austinian perspective. Indeed, there is a certain sense in which the Russellian account can be embedded in the Austinian framework. Doing so illuminates both accounts, while also spotlighting those pretheoretic intuitions about language that lead to paradox. The relation between these accounts is discussed in detail in Chapter 11, as well as in the conclusion.

A budget of Liar-like paradoxes

We said earlier that a genuine diagnosis of the Liar paradox should provide an understanding of a host of related phenomena. In this section we collect together several examples of paradoxical propositions, and of others that, while not paradoxical, are related to those that are in obvious ways.

The Liar: Our framework will allow us to consider the relation between sentences and the various propositions they can express, and, in particular, the relation between the *Liar sentence*

(λ) This proposition is not true.

and the propositions, if any, that it can express.

Just for the record, let us run through the intuitive reasoning that shows λ to be paradoxical.

1. It seems clear that λ can be used to express a proposition about any proposition p that we can successfully refer to with the expression "this proposition," namely, the proposition that p is not true.

2. Thus, it seems plausible that λ can be used to express a proposition, call it f, about itself, namely, the proposition that f is not true.

3. If f were true, then what it claims would have to be the case, and so f would not be true. So f cannot be true.

4. But if f is not true, then what f claims to be the case is in fact the case, so f must be true, which is a contradiction.

At first blush, it does seem as though (2) may be the most vulnerable link in this reasoning, and many attempted solutions to the paradox have drawn the line at this point. For example Russell's ban on "vicious circles" took just this line, as did Tarski's insistence on a strict language/metalanguage hierarchy. The problem with such treatments, as has been recognized by many authors, is that they also exclude from consideration perfectly understandable and nonproblematic propositions, like this one.

We have already indicated that our general methodological concerns lead us to avoid such ad hoc strictures, unless, of course, they turn out not to be ad hoc: unless a careful analysis of the relation between reference and propositions shows the restriction to be an upshot of the general mechanisms involved. At first sight, this just seems false, since there are many nonparadoxical propositions, both true and false, that are about themselves. And indeed, in each of the models we present, there are legitimate propositions about themselves that can be expressed by λ. So we will have to locate the problem elsewhere.

The above reasoning is closely related to the T-schema. Applied to the Liar, the T-schema yields:

> The proposition that (this proposition is not true) is true if and only if (this proposition is not true).[13]

But this is not, in and of itself, a flat-out contradiction. To arrive at one, we need to get from the above instance to the result of replacing the second occurrence of "this proposition" with "the proposition that (this proposition is not true)." This substitution gives us:

> The proposition that (this proposition is not true) is true if and only if the proposition that (this proposition is not true) is not true.

This substitution is justified by (2). And of course, the above is indeed a flat-out contradiction. The "only if" direction corresponds to step (3) of our reasoning, the "if" direction to step (4).

---

[13]The purpose of the parentheses is to make clear that the "this" refers to the proposition expressed by the sentence within parentheses, not some larger sentence. In our formal language $\mathcal{L}$ introduced below, where parentheses are used as usual, this particular function will be carried out with a scope indicator symbol $\downarrow$.

The Truth-teller: Closely related to the Liar is the *Truth-teller*, the proposition that claims of itself that it is true. It is expressed by the sentence

(τ) This proposition is true.

Here the basic intuition is that the proposition expressed by τ is not paradoxical, but rather that its truth value is "up for grabs." That is, we seem to be able to assume either that it is true or that it is false, without any contradiction arising, and completely independent of whatever "brute," non-semantical facts there are.

Liar Cycles: Another sort of example is the so-called *Liar cycle*, which combines features of both the Liar and the Truth-teller. We might imagine several people $A_1, A_2, \ldots, A_n, B$ making claims, each one about the claim made by the next person, and the last, B, about the claim made by the first, A_1.

(α_1)   The proposition expressed by α_2 is true.
(α_2)   The proposition expressed by α_3 is true.

$$\vdots$$

(α_n)   The proposition expressed by β is true.
(β)   The proposition expressed by α_1 is false.

Each α_i claims that the proposition expressed by the next sentence is true, while β claims that α_1's claim is false. Again, as in the case of the Liar, there seems to be no assignment of truth values consistent with these claims.

Contingent Liars: Next consider an example of a *Contingent Liar* like the following.

(γ) Max has the three of clubs and this proposition is false.

If Max does not have the three of clubs, then it would seem that this proposition is simply false. However, if Max does have the three of clubs, then the proposition becomes paradoxical, or so it would seem.

Contingent Liar Cycles: Kripke's examples discussed earlier (1.1 and 1.2) combine features of the Liar cycle and the Contingent Liar. A simpler version of the same phenomenon is given by the following. We will have Nixon assert both α_1 and α_2, and Jones assert β.

(α_1)   Max has the three of clubs.
(α_2)   The proposition expressed by β is true.
(β)   At least one of the propositions expressed by α_1 and by α_2 is false.

Again, if Max does not have the three of clubs, there's no problem here. Nixon is wrong both times, and Jones is right. But if Max does have the three of clubs, then there is no consistent way to assign truth values to the propositions expressed by either α_2 or β.

Löb's Paradox: Closely related to the Contingent Liar is *Löb's Paradox.*[14] Consider the following sentence.

(δ)   If this proposition is true, then Max has the three of clubs.

This example seems to allow you to prove, using only modus ponens and conditional proof, that Max has the three of clubs. The argument goes as follows. Assume the antecedent of δ, that is, that the proposition expressed by δ is true. But then we have both the proposition expressed by δ and its antecedent. In which case, by modus ponens, it follows that Max has the three of clubs. Thus we have shown that if the antecedent of δ is true, Max has the three of clubs, and by conditional proof we have established the truth of δ. One last application of modus ponens then gives us that Max has the three of clubs.

Gupta's Puzzle: Next consider an example, due to Anil Gupta,[15] of an interesting sort of circularity. Imagine two people, R and P, who make the following claims about a card game between Claire and Max, a game in which Claire has the ace of clubs (and so ρ_1, the first claim made by R, is false, while π_1 is true).

R's claims: (ρ_1)   Max has the ace of clubs.
                  (ρ_2)   All of the claims made by P are true.
                  (ρ_3)   At least one of the claims made by P is false.

P's claims: (π_1)   Claire has the ace of clubs.
                  (π_2)   At most one of the claims made by R is true.

---

[14]We are grateful to Dag Westerståhl for bringing this fascinating example to our attention. It is closely related to Löb's Theorem in proof theory, the result which shows that the sentence of arithmetic which "asserts its own provability" is provable. For a discussion of the two, see Boolos and Jeffrey (1980), 186.

[15]Gupta (1982), example (3) in part IV.

Gupta points out that we naturally reason about this case in the following way. First, we note that ρ_2 and ρ_3 contradict each other, and so at most one of these claims can be true. Since the claim made by ρ_1 is false, the one made by π_2 must be true. So ρ_2 expresses a truth while ρ_3 does not.

Gupta introduces this nonparadoxical case of circularity as a counterexample to one treatment of the Liar discussed by Kripke. Kripke's "least fixed point" account would render this simple reasoning invalid, though it seems perfectly legitimate.[16]   We will discuss Kripke's treatment in more detail in Chapter 5. We list the example here because the failure of this reasoning on many accounts makes it an important test for any competing treatment.

Strengthened Liar: For our final example, let's return to the Liar again. Only this time, consider two people, one of whom asserts the Liar, while the second, a logician, comments on the proposition expressed by the first:

(λ_1)   This proposition is not true.
(λ_2)   That proposition is not true.

The interesting thing here is that there is nothing obviously circular about the second claim. Furthermore, since it seems clear that the proposition expressed by λ_1 cannot be true, it would seem reasonable to assume that the proposition expressed by λ_2 is unproblematically true. But if that's the case, doesn't the same reasoning show that the Liar itself is true? If we can step back and recognize that the Liar cannot be true, why isn't this same recognition exactly what is expressed by the Liar itself? As we have already noted, a dilemma of this sort has plagued many treatments of the paradox, and indeed has led many to claim that one simply cannot speak of the truth of the Liar.

---

[16]We refer here to the least fixed point generated by the Strong Kleene evaluation scheme, the treatment Kripke discusses in greatest detail. Kripke is not committed to this particular evaluation scheme, or to the least fixed point. In maximal fixed points of the Strong Kleene scheme, the sentences receive the appropriate truth values. Kripke has also observed that there are alternative valuation schemes which validate the reasoning even in the corresponding minimal fixed points.

Exercise 1 Consider the example: "This proposition is true and it is not true." Does the proposition expressed seem to be true, false, up for grabs, or paradoxical?

Exercise 2 Consider the example: "This proposition is true or it is not true." Does the proposition expressed seem to be true, false, up for grabs, or paradoxical? Contrast this with the proposition expressed by "The Liar is true or it is not true."

Exercise 3 Consider the examples: "Max has or doesn't have the three of clubs, or this whole proposition is false," and "Max both has and doesn't have the three of clubs, or this whole proposition is false." Do these seem true, false, up for grabs, or paradoxical?

Exercise 4 Contrast the Liar with the proposition expressed by "The Truth-teller is false." Show that the truth value of the proposition expressed by the latter is up for grabs, and so it must be a different proposition from the Liar.

2

Sentences, Statements, and Propositions

In the previous chapter, we argued that in order to prejudge as few issues as possible, we should treat truth as a property of propositions, where these are thought of as objective claims about the world, and only derivatively as a property of statements or sentences. To model propositions we'll have to delve a bit into questions about the nature of a proposition, as well as questions about the relations between sentences, statements, and the propositions they express. We will discuss two distinct views: a rather orthodox view, which we call the Russellian view, and a less familiar account due to Austin.

Russellian propositions

Of the two conceptions we'll consider, the Russellian view is the simpler and more naive. By calling it "naive," though, we don't mean to denegrate it; other things being equal, this is a strong point in its favor. According to the Russellian view, sentences are used to express propositions, claims about the world, and these claims are true just in case the world is as it is claimed to be. These propositions are thought of as having constituents corresponding to the subject matter of the claim. For example, a statement made with the sentence "Claire has the ace of hearts" expresses a proposition about Claire, the ace of hearts, and the relation of

having, a claim that is true if the facts that make up the world
include Claire's having the ace of hearts.[1] In the simplest possible
case, a Russellian proposition will have one object and one property
as constituents, and will constitute the claim that that very object
has that very property. The proposition will be true just in case it is
a fact that the object has the property. In particular, a proposition
that some proposition p has some property or other, say is true, or
interesting, or expressible in English using at most ten words, has
the proposition p and the corresponding property, as constituents.
It is true just in case the world is such that the proposition has the
property.

By calling these propositions Russellian, we do not mean to
make a substantive historical claim about Russell. Indeed, it would
be foolhardy to claim that Russell held any *single* view of propositions. The nature of true and false propositions was a problem
Russell struggled with throughout his life. His theories were driven
by the paradoxes, by the view that true propositions are made true
by the facts, and by the certainty that there were no such things as
"false facts" to make false propositions false. Indeed, Russell frequently identified true propositions with the facts that make them
true, and for this reason found it hard to give an account of false
propositions.

Our treatment of Russellian propositions will model them and
facts with appropriately structured set-theoretic objects. We will
define a basic relation that holds between a set of facts and a Russellian proposition just in case the facts make the proposition true.
Then a Russellian proposition will be true just in case there is a set
of facts that makes it true, and false just in case there is no such set.
Our model will admit propositions that make claims about themselves, and hence propositions that are constituents of themselves,
and also collections of propositions that are about each other in circular ways. In this respect our model is a liberalization of Russell's
own view, which simply banned "vicious circles" of this sort.

In modeling this conception of a proposition, we will adopt
the most straightforward technique for coding up the claim made
by a proposition. Thus, for example, the proposition that Claire
has the ace of hearts will be represented by a set-theoretic ob-

---

[1]If we weren't setting aside issues of time and tense in this book, the Russellian proposition would also have as a constituent some particular time, a
time determined by the context of the statement.

ject containing among its constituents three objects: Claire, the ace of hearts, and the relation of having. The set-theoretic representative of this proposition will also need something to indicate that it represents a proposition and to distinguish it from the representative of the negative proposition that Claire *doesn't* have the ace of hearts. For example, we could use the 5-tuple $\langle Prop, \text{Having}, \text{Claire}, A\heartsuit, 1 \rangle$, where *Prop* is some distinguished atom and the number 1 indicates that the proposition is positive. In order not to bog the reader down with irrelevant coding details, we will just write [Claire H $A\heartsuit$] for this representative, and $[\overline{\text{Claire } H \text{ } A\heartsuit}]$ for the 5-tuple $\langle Prop, \text{Having}, \text{Claire}, A\heartsuit, 0 \rangle$, the representative of the negative proposition.

Although in describing the Russellian conception of propositions we have emphasized the fact that they contain their subject matter as constituents, this particular feature of Russell's view will turn out to be inessential to our treatment of the Liar. What is mainly relevant is that the truth of a proposition is arbitrated by the world as a whole. In this important respect the Russellian view agrees with many other conceptions of propositions, including that embodied in possible worlds semantics. Indeed we could equally well consider our set-theoretic representatives as standing for propositions under a conception where they do not have any constituents at all, or where their constituents are something other than their intuitive subject matter. The moral that we draw from Part II of the book is intended to apply equally to these other conceptions.

Austinian statements and propositions

Austin, in his famous paper "Truth,"[2] gives a strikingly original view of the property of truth. On his view speakers use sentences to do a variety of things, among them to make statements. According to Austin, a legitimate statement A provides two things: a historical (or actual) situation s_A, and a type of situation T_A. The former is just some limited portion of the real world; the speaker refers to it using what Austin calls "demonstrative conventions." The latter is, roughly speaking, a property of situations determined from the statement by means of "descriptive conventions" associ-

---

[2]Austin (1950).

ated with the language. The statement A is true if s_A is of type T_A; otherwise it is false.

Consider a simple example. If the sentence "Claire has the ace of hearts" is used to describe a particular poker hand, then on the Austinian view the speaker has made a claim that the relevant situation is of the type in which Claire has the ace of hearts. Notice that such a claim could fail simply because Claire wasn't present, even if Claire had the ace of hearts in a card game across town. By contrast, on the Russellian view the claim would be true.

While Austin did not use the term "proposition," it seems in the spirit of his account to identify what we will call the *Austinian proposition* expressed by A with the claim that s_A is of type T_A, and to individuate such a proposition by its two components, the situation referred to and the type of situation it is claimed to be. We call the first component the situation the proposition is about, $About(p)$, and the second component the proposition's constituent type, $Type(p)$. In the second of our two accounts, we will provide a simple set-theoretic model of Austinian propositions and show that in this model every Austinian proposition, including those expressed by the Liar sentence λ, are either true or false (and not both).

The move from the Russellian view to the Austinian involves a significant shift in our conception of statements and propositions. The most obvious change is that on the Austinian view all propositions contain an additional contextually determined feature, namely, the situation they are about. Of course the Russellian admits that contextual elements of the statement play an important role in getting you from the sentence to the proposition, in particular when the sentence involves indexical elements like "I," "you," "now," and "that." However, on the Austinian view the very act of making a statement always brings in another feature, one not tied to any explicit indexical element in the sentence.

If Austinian propositions are about situations, how can they be about other things as well, things like Claire and Max or statements and propositions? And how could they ever be about themselves?[3]

---

[3] Austin himself thought that they could not be, and gave as his reason the idea that the situation the statement was about had to exist independent of the statement. On the one hand, this constraint seems just as ad hoc as Russell's vicious circle principle, and for the same reasons. But as we'll see, it also doesn't preclude circularity, as Austin seemed to think.

Austin does not directly address this question, but there would seem to be two ways an Austinian statement might be said to be about, say, Max, one having to do with the demonstrative conventions, the other with the descriptive conventions.

The demonstrative conventions require that a statement be about a situation, and situations are portions of the world. As such they have constituents, things that actually have properties and stand in relations in those situations. We will model the world as a collection of facts, where we model facts with tuples $\langle R, a_1, \ldots, a_n, i \rangle$ consisting of an n-ary relation (for some n), an n-tuple of objects, and a polarity $i \in \{1, 0\}$, representing the having ($i = 1$) or not having ($i = 0$) of the relation. Since situations are portions of the world, we will model them with subsets of the collection of all facts. The a_i are constituents of the fact, and so of any situation in which the fact holds. When we express a proposition about (in Austin's sense) some situation in which Max is a constituent, then in one respect we make a statement about Max.

The descriptive conventions give us types of situations, and these types are themselves much like Russellian propositions. As such they may contain objects as constituents. For example, a use of the sentence "Max has the three of clubs" says, according to Austin, that the situation described is of the type in which Max has the three of clubs. Here, the statement is intuitively about Max, not because of the situation the statement is about, but because Max is involved in the type determined by the descriptive conventions of English. If the statement is true, then Max will also have to be a constituent of the situation, and so the proposition will be about Max in both respects.

Thus, although we have defined *About(p)* to be the situation described by p, there are two ways in which Austinian propositions can be about objects other than situations. And so it makes sense to ask whether on this conception there is a genuine Liar proposition, one that is about itself, and claims of itself that it is false. And of course if there is, we must then ask whether that proposition is true or false under the Austinian analysis.

A formal language

Before constructing models of Russellian and Austinian propositions, we will define a simple formal language $\mathcal{L}$ that we can then use to illustrate some of the essential features of English, and to facilitate the comparison of our two accounts. The language gives us mechanisms for referring to various things, including propositions, and mechanisms for expressing propositions about the things we can refer to. In particular, it will allow us to express the propositions presented in Chapter 1. We have decided to omit quantification, since getting a clear, convincing account of reference, truth, and negation, the semantical mechanisms that give rise to the Liar, is hard enough. First things first.

Ultimately, we will give two semantic interpretations for our language, one using Russellian propositions, one using Austinian propositions. The language is designed for talking about a card game involving Claire and Max, and about propositions about this game. We throw in the relation of belief, which we take to hold between players and propositions, mainly to add variety, to allow some simple statements about propositions over and above those involving truth.

We assume that our formal language $\mathcal{L}$ has the following basic resources:

- *Constant symbols:* **Claire, Max, 2♣, 3♣,..., K♠, A♠**

- *(Propositional) Demonstratives:* **this, that$_1$, that$_2$,...**

- *A 2-ary relation symbol:* **Has**

- *A 2-ary relation symbol:* **Believes**

- *A 1-ary relation symbol:* **True**

- *Logical connectives:* $\wedge, \vee, \neg$

- *A scope indicator:* $\downarrow$

There are three sorts of atomic formulas:

- Those of the form **(a Has c)** where **a** is one of the names **Max, Claire** and where **c** is a name of one of the cards.

- Those of the form **(a Believes th)** where **th** is a propositional demonstrative.

- Those of the form **True(th)**.

The class of $\mathcal{L}$-formulas is the smallest collection containing the atomic formulas and closed under the following formation rules:

- If φ and ψ are formulas, so are $(\varphi \wedge \psi), (\varphi \vee \psi)$, and $\neg\varphi$.

- If φ is a formula, so is (**True** φ) and (**a Believes** φ), where **a** is either **Claire** or **Max**.[4]

- If φ is a formula, so is $\downarrow\varphi$.

A word of explanation is in order about the scope symbol "$\downarrow$". When we provide semantics for $\mathcal{L}$, we will ensure that **this** automatically refers to the proposition expressed by the sentence in which it occurs. Thus it will be our formal analogue of the English expression "this proposition," when that phrase is used reflexively. But even in its reflexive use, this expression is ambiguous. The ambiguity emerges in cases like the following.

(2.1)   Max has the three of clubs or this proposition is true.

We think the most natural reading here is one in which "this proposition" refers to the proposition expressed by the whole of 2.1. However, we can also imagine it being used to refer to the proposition expressed by the second disjunct alone, in which case it would refer to the ordinary Truth-teller proposition. The two readings give quite different propositions, with different truth-conditions. In the first case, we will say that the scope of "this" is the entire sentence; in the second case, its scope is just the second disjunct. In our formal language, the two would be disambiguated as follows.

(2.2)   (**Max Has 3♣**) $\vee$ **True(this)**

(2.3)   (**Max Has 3♣**) $\vee$ $\downarrow$**True(this)**

Thus, the scope symbol $\downarrow$ in $\downarrow\varphi$ indicates that the "loose" occurrences of **this** within the formula φ refer to the proposition expressed by φ. With no scope indication, as in 2.2, it is assumed that **this** refers to the proposition expressed by the whole sentence. Thus 2.2 and 2.4 express the same proposition.

---

[4]In what follows we will usually refer to formulas of these forms as atomic formulas, reserving the designation *nonatomic* for sentences with $\wedge$, $\vee$ or $\neg$ as a main connective.

(2.4) $\downarrow((\textbf{Max Has 3\clubsuit}) \vee \textbf{True(this)})$

To formalize all this, we define the notion of a formula containing a *loose* occurrence of **this** by the obvious recursion, with the crucial clauses being: **this** is loose in **True(this)** and **(a Believes this)**; **this** is loose in, say, $\varphi \wedge \psi$ just in case it is loose in either; and **this** is not loose in $\downarrow\varphi$. By a *sentence* of $\mathcal{L}$ we mean a formula with no loose occurrence of **this**.

We will frequently omit the outermost occurrence of the scope indicator $\downarrow$. Thus when we display a formula φ which is not a sentence and refer to it as a sentence, we mean the closure $\downarrow\varphi$. For example, if we were to refer to 2.2 as a sentence, we would really mean the sentence 2.4. This accords with our convention that in a formula with a loose **this,** the demonstrative should refer to the proposition expressed by the whole, not by some proper part. We will also occasionally use the notation $\varphi(\textbf{this}/\psi)$ for the result of replacing all loose occurrences of **this** in a formula $\varphi(\textbf{this})$ with the formula ψ.

A final word about the scope symbol. We could obviously have dispensed with it, always opting for the widest possible interpretation. However, the language is clearly much more expressive with it. For example, without the scope symbol there would be no direct way to express the proposition expressed by $\neg\downarrow\textbf{True(this)}$. But the real reason we have introduced it is that it makes the resulting language much better behaved, so that it is far easier to prove the various results below than it would be with the more impoverished language.

Exercise 5 Find $\mathcal{L}$ versions of the English sentences from the exercises given at the end of the previous chapter. Which seem to depend crucially on the presence of the scope operator? (Of course we cannot prove any of this until we define a semantics for $\mathcal{L}$.)

Exercise 6 Explain how the claims made by the following sentences differ.

1. $\neg\downarrow\textbf{True(this)}$
2. $\downarrow\neg\textbf{True(this)}$

Is either claim paradoxical? Are both?

3

The Universe of Hypersets

Set theory from Z to A

In both of our analyses of the paradox we take seriously the intuition that the propositions involved are genuinely circular. Since we are going to model propositions, situations, and facts with set-theoretic objects, it is extremely inconvenient to adopt a set-theoretic framework that precludes circular or nonwellfounded objects. The source of this inconvenience is simple. By far the most natural way to model a proposition about a given object is to use some set-theoretic construct containing that object (or its representative) as a constituent, that is, where the object appears in the construct's hereditary membership relation. But if we carry out this straightforward approach in a set theory based on Zermelo's cumulative hierarchy, we find ourselves inadvertently excluding the possibility of circular propositions. For the model of a proposition about another *proposition* will have to contain the latter's representative as a constituent, and the model of a circular proposition, one directly or indirectly about itself, will have to contain itself as a constituent. But the axiom of regularity, or foundation, bans sets that are members of themselves, or pairs of sets that are members of each other, and so forth, and so would block us from using such natural techniques of modeling propositions.[1]

---

[1]The axiom of foundation asserts that the membership relation is well-founded, that is, that any nonempty collection Y of sets has a member $y \in Y$ which is disjoint from Y. This follows from the iterative conception by chosing any $y \in Y$ of "least rank," that is, a y that occurs as early in

There are various ways we could sidestep this problem within standard set theory, but they would involve us in complexities of considerable magnitude, ones completely irrelevant to the task at hand. Of course if worse came to worse, we could just give up set theory entirely as our working theory. If there had been no coherent alternative to the Zermelo conception of sets, one that admits circularity, we would probably have done just that. But Peter Aczel has recently developed an appealing alternative conception of sets, and with it a consistent axiomatic theory tailor-made for our purposes. Aczel's theory, based on an extremely natural extension of the Zermelo conception, is quite easy to learn and, once learned, lets us bring to bear all of the familiar set-theoretic techniques to the problem of modeling circular phenomena. We devote this chapter to an exposition of Aczel's theory, one that will allow the reader to follow the details of the rest of the book, as well as apply the theory in other domains.

To appreciate the intuitive appeal of Aczel's conception, let's first rehearse a common way of picturing ordinary sets. Consider, for example, the set $c_0 = \{a_0, b_0\}$ where $a_0 = \{$Claire, Max$\}$ and $b_0 = \{a_0,$ Max$\}$. There are many ways to picture this set, but one natural and unambiguous way is with the labeled graph shown in Figure 1. In this graph each nonterminal node represents a nonempty set, the set containing the objects represented by the nodes below it. For example the top node in the graph represents the set c_0, a set whose only members are the sets a_0 and b_0, and these latter sets are in turn represented by the nodes immediately below the top node. Note that the set represented by a node need not itself *be* the node, and indeed in Figure 1 we find two different nodes that each depict, and so are labeled by, the single set a_0. The bottom nodes in this example represent Max and Claire, neither of whom have elements, and so there are no nodes below them. The idea of such a graph, of course, is that the arrows represent the converse membership relation: an arrow from node x to node y indicates that the set (or atom) represented by y is a member of the set represented by x.

Notice that one and the same set may well be depicted by many different graphs. Consider, for example, the graphs in Figure 2.

---

the cumulative hierarchy as any other member of Y. This rules out circularity. For example, note that if $a \in a$ then the set $Y = \{a\}$ violates this assumption.

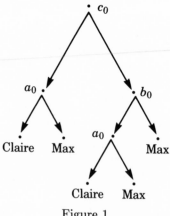

Figure 1

These are clearly different graphs since they have different graph-theoretic properties. For example, the three graphs have different numbers of nodes, and the first is a tree while the others are not. Still, as we've indicated by the labeling, they all depict the same set, the von Neumann ordinal three. Similarly, Figure 3 gives a different, and more economical depiction of our original set c_0. The differences among these graphs, for our purposes, amount to little more than the relative economy of nodes: Figure 3 has four fewer nodes than Figure 1, but it gives us a picture of exactly the same set.

In the same way, any set can be depicted by a graph. One canonical way to build a graph is to start with the desired set a and consider all of its "hereditary" members (members, members of members, members of members of members, and so on) as

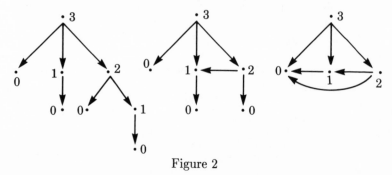

Figure 2

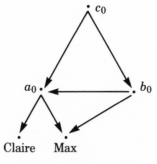

Figure 3

nodes of a graph. Then draw an edge from any set to each of its members. The resulting graph will depict the given set a (and in this case, the nodes actually *are* the sets depicted). This construction allows us to build a canonical graph for any set whatsoever. (And note that this does not presuppose that we are dealing with sets under the cumulative conception. Under any conception, sets give rise to graphs in this way.)

Exercise 7 Draw two graphs that represent the von Neumann ordinal four. Make the first graph a tree (on the model of the first graph in Figure 2), and make the second as economical as possible (on the model of the third graph in Figure 2).

Aczel's conception of a set arises directly out of the intuition that a set is a collection of things whose (hereditary) membership relation can be depicted, unambiguously, by graphs of this sort. The liberating element is that we allow arbitrary graphs, including graphs that contain proper cycles. Of course graphs with cycles cannot depict sets in the wellfounded universe.[2] Thus, for example, in Aczel's universe there is a set $\Omega = \{\Omega\}$, simply because we can picture the membership relation on Ω by means of the graph G_Ω shown in Figure 4. Furthermore, on Aczel's conception this graph *unambiguously* depicts a set; that is, there is only one set with G_Ω as its graph. Consequently, there is only one set in Aczel's universe equal to its own singleton.

---

[2]To see this, suppose we have a graph with a proper cycle. Take Y to be the set containing all the sets depicted by nodes that occur in the cycle. It is clear that no member of Y is disjoint from Y, thus violating the axiom of foundation.

$$\Omega = \{\Omega\}$$

Figure 4

To take another example, let's consider the set $c = \{a, b\}$ where $a = \{\text{Claire, Max, } b\}$ and $b = \{\text{Max, } a\}$. The only difference between this set and our set c_0 above, is that b is an element of a, while b_0 is not an element of a_0 (and could not be, according to the cumulative conception). To get a graph of c, we can simply modify a graph of c_0, say the one given in Figure 3. Here, we need only add an edge from the node that represents a_0 to the node that represents b_0. The result, in Figure 5, is a graph of c.

The sets we get on Aczel's conception include all those in the traditional, wellfounded universe. But in addition to these, we get a rich class of nonwellfounded sets, or as we will sometimes call them, *hyper*sets. As we'll see, these sets behave in many respects just like the ordinary, wellfounded variety. But they permit the use of straightforward modeling techniques even when the phenomena modeled involve circularity.

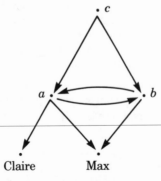

Figure 5

AFA

Let's flesh out Aczel's idea in more detail and describe the axiomatic theory explicitly. Actually, we will describe a variant of Aczel's theory that allows a collection $\mathcal{A}$ of "atoms" like Max and Claire, instead of just pure sets. This theory, then, will consist of all the usual axioms of ZFC set theory (modified in the usual way to admit atoms), except that the axiom of regularity is replaced by a strong form of its negation, called AFA, for (Aczel's) Anti-Foundation Axiom (with Atoms).

We said that on Aczel's conception a set is any collection of objects whose hereditary membership relation can be pictured by a graph. More precisely, a *graph* G is a set of nodes and directed edges, as usual. (Any set X can be a set of nodes, and any set $R \subseteq X \times X$ of ordered pairs from X can be used to represent the directed edges of a graph G. It is customary to write $x \to y$ to indicate that the graph contains an edge pointing from node x to node y.) If there is an edge $x \to y$ from node x to node y, then y is said to be a *child* of x. A node with no arrow starting from it is said to be *childless*. So, for example, in Figure 3 there are two childless nodes and three "parent" nodes, that is, nodes with children. In Figure 4, on the other hand, there is only one node, and it is a child of itself.

A *tagged graph* is a graph in which each childless node x has been "tagged" by an object $tag(x)$, which is either an atom or the empty set. Think of tagging as the process of simply writing the name of an atom or the empty set next to each childless node to indicate what it represents. More formally, a tagged graph is a graph G together with a function tag mapping the childless nodes of G into $\mathcal{A} \cup \{\emptyset\}$. (Note that if G has no childless nodes, as with Figure 4, then the totally undefined function suffices to tag the graph.) Aczel's basic idea is that once we have a tagged graph, we can use the nodes and edges of the graph to picture sets and set membership. To make this notion precise, we bring in the concept of a decoration for a tagged graph.

A *decoration* for a tagged graph is a function $\mathcal{D}$ defined on the nodes of the graph such that for each node x, if x has no children, then $\mathcal{D}(x) = tag(x)$, whereas if x has children, then

$$\mathcal{D}(x) = \{\mathcal{D}(y) \mid y \text{ is a child of } x\}.$$

Each node x of G that has children is said to *picture* the set $\mathcal{D}(x)$. Thus we can think of the process of decorating a graph as simply continuing the process started by tagging the graph: we write next to each parent node a name of the set it depicts. We have in fact decorated all of the above graphs in just this way.

AFA can now be stated quite simply: it asserts that *every tagged graph has a unique decoration*. It is clear that this axiom conflicts with the Zermelo conception since, for example, the graphs in Figures 4 and 5 cannot be decorated with sets from the cumulative hierarchy. For example to decorate the graph in Figure 4, $\mathcal{D}$ would have to assign to the single node some set that contains itself. But there is no such set among the wellfounded sets.

There are two parts to AFA, existence and uniqueness. That is, part of what AFA asserts is that every tagged graph has a decoration. This guarantees the existence of all the sets we consider. However, equally important in applications is the uniqueness half, the assertion that no graph has more than one decoration. It is this part of the axiom that gives us a useful handle on the identity of nonwellfounded sets.

Consider, for example, the sets $a = \{\text{Max}, a\}$ and $b = \{\text{Max}, b\}$. Does $a = b$? The usual axiom of extensionality is useless in answering this question, for it asserts only that $a = b$ if a and b have the same members, which boils down to the assertion that $a = b$ if $a = b$. However, on Aczel's conception, it turns out that a is indeed equal to b since they are depicted by exactly the same graphs. To see this in detail, suppose we have a tagged graph G and a decoration $\mathcal{D}$ that assigns a to a node x of G, $\mathcal{D}(x) = a$. Consider the decoration $\mathcal{D}'$ just like $\mathcal{D}$ except that $\mathcal{D}'(x) = b$. A second's thought shows that $\mathcal{D}'$ must also be a decoration for G. But by the uniqueness part of AFA, we must have $\mathcal{D} = \mathcal{D}'$ and so $\mathcal{D}(x) = \mathcal{D}'(x)$; i.e., $a = b$.

On Aczel's conception, then, for two sets to be distinct there must be a genuine structural difference between them, one that prevents them from being depicted by the same tagged graph. This will be important in what follows, since the identity conditions on sets give rise to identity conditions on the various set-theoretic models that we construct below.

It's fairly easy to see which graphs can be decorated with wellfounded sets. Say that a graph G is *wellfounded* if for each nonempty subset Y of the nodes of G, some node in Y has no

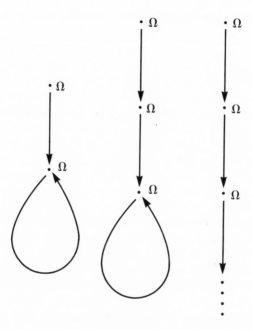

Figure 6

child in Y. Only wellfounded graphs can have decorations in the Zermelo universe; indeed the claim that no nonwellfounded graph can be decorated is just a reformulation of the axiom of foundation. Further, Mostowski's Collapsing Lemma[3] tells us that *every* wellfounded tagged graph has a unique decoration in the universe of wellfounded sets. So we can think of Aczel's axiom as extending this natural relationship between graphs and sets beyond the wellfounded.

It should once again be noted that under either conception, a set can in general be depicted by many different graphs. Figure 2 presented three different graphs of a wellfounded set, the von Neumann ordinal three. Similarly, Figure 6 gives a few additional graphs of the nonwellfounded set Ω. In this case, to see that each of these graphs depicts Ω, we need only note that all the nodes *can* be decorated with Ω, and so by AFA *must* be, the decoration being unique.

---

[3]See, for example, Kunen (1980), 105.

While Aczel's is quite a different conception from Zermelo's, it turns out that all the usual axioms of ZFC are true under this conception, except, of course, the axiom of foundation. This means that we can use all the familiar set-theoretic operations (intersection, union, power set, ordered pairs, and so forth) without any change whatsoever. Only when the axiom of foundation enters (as with inductive definitions, which we discuss in the last section of this chapter) do we need to rethink things.

Let's look at one more example, this time a bit more relevant for our purposes. Consider the English sentence

(ϵ) This proposition is not expressible in English using ten words

and the various propositions it can express. Let us use an atom E to represent the property that holds of a proposition just in case it is expressible in English using ten words. Suppose we were to model the proposition that p has the property E with the triple $\langle E, p, 1 \rangle$, and the proposition that p does not have E with the triple $\langle E, p, 0 \rangle$.[4] Recall that in set theory triples $\langle x, y, z \rangle$ are taken to be pairs of pairs $\langle x, \langle y, z \rangle \rangle$, that an ordered pair $\langle y, z \rangle$ is construed as the set $\{\{y\}, \{y, z\}\}$, and that 0 is represented by the empty set. Then we can see that a graph of our model of the proposition that p does not have E and a graph G_p of p are related as in Figure 7.

Suppose we want to represent the (intuitively false) circular proposition expressed by (ϵ) when "this proposition" is given the reflexive reading. This will be the proposition q that claims, of itself, that E does not hold. That is, we want $q = \langle E, q, 0 \rangle$. By what we have just said, it suffices to take the special case of Figure 7 where the graph G_p is the whole graph. This is shown in Figure 8. Thus, the proposition we are after is modeled by the set assigned to the top node in Figure 8. There is exactly one such set in the universe of hypersets.

Exercise 8 Label the unlabeled nodes of the graphs in Figures 7 and 8.

Exercise 9 Show that Ω is depicted by all the graphs in Figure 9.

---

[4]To keep the graph simple, we are suppressing the atom *Prop* introduced in Chapter 2, page 28.

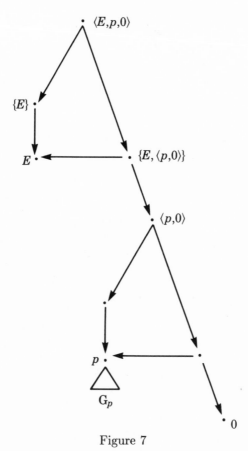

Figure 7

Exercise 10 Using AFA, show that there is a unique set a satisfying the equation

$$a = \{a, \emptyset\}.$$

Show that $a \neq \Omega$.

Exercise 11 Show that the graph shown in Figure 5 is nonwellfounded. That is, find a nonempty set Y of nodes of the graph such that every member of Y has a child in Y.

Exercise 12 Say that a graph is transitive if for each pair of edges $x \rightarrow y$ and $y \rightarrow z$ there is an edge $x \rightarrow z$. Similarly, say that a set a is transitive if $c \in b \in a$ implies $c \in a$. Show that a set is transitive if and only if it can be depicted by a transitive graph.

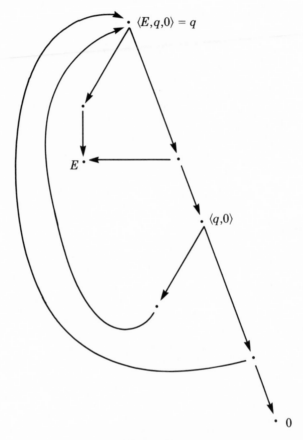

Figure 8

The transitive closure of a set a is the smallest transitive set containing a as a subset. Suppose that a node x of a graph pictures the set a. Show that the transitive closure of a is the set of all decorations of nodes appearing "below" x. (By "y is below x" we here mean that there is a path of arrows from x to y.)

The consistency of ZFC/AFA

There were really two sorts of set-theoretic paradoxes that threatened early, intuitive set theory: paradoxes of size and paradoxes like those engendered by the Russell set, the set z of all sets that

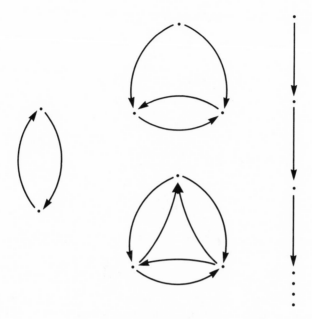

Figure 9

are not members of themselves. The Zermelo conception killed
two birds with one stone. On the one hand, it gave us a way to
conceptualize classes that are never collected into sets, and, on the
other, it ruled out sets that are members of themselves. But as a
reaction to the paradoxes, this latter move was really unnecessary.
On Zermelo's conception the Russell "set" is actually the universe
of all sets. And since this is a proper class, not a set at all, the
familiar reasoning that derives a contradiction from the definition
of z is blocked. But the set/class distinction is the key here, not
the banning of self-membership.

On Aczel's conception, we still have the set/class distinction,
only now there is a proper class of sets that *do* contain themselves,
as well as a proper class that *do not*. (See Exercise 14.) In both
cases there is no Russell set, only a Russell class. To obtain sets
using the Russellian definition, the comprehension schema does not
allow the earlier definition of z:

$$z = \{x \mid x \notin x\}$$

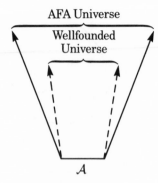

Figure 10

but rather requires that we introduce a parametric version of the definition:

$$z_a = \{x \in a \mid x \notin x\}.$$

What the Russell argument now shows is just that z_a can never be in the set a, whether or not a is wellfounded. The set z_a is said to "diagonalize out" of the set a.

Since we are working in the realm of the paradoxes, both set-theoretic and semantic, it is obviously important to be sure that our metatheory, ZFC/AFA, is consistent. Aczel has shown that it is.[5] Indeed, he has shown more. Working in ZFC⁻ (ZFC without the axiom of foundation), Aczel shows how to canonically embed the universe of wellfounded sets into a universe satisfying ZFC/AFA, what we have been calling the universe of hypersets. We call this result the Embedding Theorem. Since the construction yields a model of ZFC/AFA, it shows that the theory is consistent, assuming of course that ZFC is. But it also shows that we can think of the universe of hypersets as a mathematical enrichment of the universe of wellfounded sets. Thus we can depict the relationship between the two as in Figure 10.

The situation here is entirely analogous to any number of similar cases in mathematics. For example, consider the relation between the real numbers and the complex numbers. The familiar model of the complex numbers as equivalence classes of pairs of reals yields a consistency proof of the theory of complex numbers

---

[5]See Aczel (1987).

relative to the theory of real numbers. But it also does something more: it shows us that the complex numbers can be thought of as an expansion of the reals.

The proof of the Embedding Theorem, while a bit tricky in detail, is simple enough to describe. First Aczel isolates an equivalence relation $\equiv_A$ on graphs which holds between two graphs just in case they represent the same set. For example, all the graphs in Figure 2 are $\equiv_A$, as are the four graphs from Figures 4 and 6. This allows each set in Aczel's universe to be represented by an equivalence class of graphs from the wellfounded universe. There is a slight hitch, though, since each set is actually depicted by a proper class of graphs, and to carry out the proof in ZFC$^-$ one has to work with sets. To do this Aczel borrows a trick of Dana Scott's, and represents each set b by the *set* G_b of those graphs of minimal rank in the cumulative hierarchy that depict it. Since every graph is, by the axiom of choice, isomorphic to a graph on some set of ordinals, G_b will always be nonempty.[6] Then, using the class of sets of the form $G_b/\equiv_A$, Aczel is able to show (1) that all the axioms of ZFC/AFA are true (using the natural interpretation of membership), and (2) that every wellfounded set is uniquely represented in the resulting model.

Aczel's proof shows that there is a sense in which AFA does not give rise to any new mathematical structures. One could always replace talk of the nonwellfounded sets in the AFA universe with talk of the structures $G_b/\equiv_A$, just as one could replace talk of complex numbers with talk of equivalence classes of pairs of real numbers, or replace talk of real numbers with talk of equivalence classes of Cauchy sequences of rationals. You could do any of these in principle, but it would be completely impractical, and ultimately misguided. As mathematical objects, the complexes are as legitimate as the reals, and the AFA universe is as legitimate as the universe of wellfounded sets. The fact that we can model one with the other does not make the latter more basic or more legitimate than the former.

Exercise 13 Recall the definition of the parametric Russell set z_a given above. What is z_Ω? Let c be the nonwellfounded set

---

[6]Notice that this observation also shows that we get the same AFA universe whether our graphs are drawn from the wellfounded universe or from the full AFA universe.

depicted in Figure 5, page 38. What is z_c? Let a be the set defined in Exercise 10, page 43. What is z_a?

Exercise 14 Show that for any set a, there is a set $b = \{a, b\}$. Show that distinct sets a thereby give rise to distinct sets b. Conclude that there is a proper class of sets which are members of themselves.

Solving equations

In addition to standard set-theoretic facts from ZFC, there is one simple consequence of AFA that we will use over and over in what follows, a result that allows us to assert that various sets exist without first depicting them with graphs.

Consider an "indeterminate" **x** and the equation

$$\mathbf{x} = \{\mathbf{x}\}.$$

This equation has a solution[7] in the universe of hypersets, namely Ω. Furthermore, since any solution to this equation would be depicted by the graph G_Ω, this equation has a unique solution in the universe.

Similarly, consider the following three equations in the indeterminates **x**, **y**, and **z**.

$$\mathbf{x} = \{\text{Claire}, \text{Max}, \mathbf{y}\}$$
$$\mathbf{y} = \{\text{Max}, \mathbf{x}\}$$
$$\mathbf{z} = \{\mathbf{x}, \mathbf{y}\}$$

AFA tells us that these equations have a unique solution in the hyperuniverse, the sets $\mathbf{x} = a, \mathbf{y} = b$, and $\mathbf{z} = c$ pictured in Figure 5, page 38.

Aczel has a general result which allows us to find, for any system of equations in indeterminates $\mathbf{x}, \mathbf{y}, \mathbf{z}, \ldots$, say,

$$\mathbf{x} = a(\mathbf{x}, \mathbf{y}, \ldots)$$
$$\mathbf{y} = b(\mathbf{x}, \mathbf{y}, \ldots)$$
$$\vdots$$

---

[7]We use the term "solution" in exactly the same way as it's used in algebra. Below we will represent a solution to a system of equations as a function that assigns objects to each indeterminate and satisfies all the equations in the system.

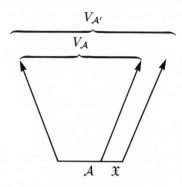

Figure 11

a unique solution in the universe of hypersets. This result, which we call the "Solution Lemma," is used repeatedly throughout the book. The remainder of this section (to page 51) is devoted to a precise formulation of this lemma, and can be skipped by anyone who finds the formulation just given precise enough.

Given a collection $\mathcal{A}$ of atoms, let us write $V_{\mathcal{A}}$ for the hyperuniverse of all sets with atoms from $\mathcal{A}$, assuming ZFC/AFA, of course. Given some larger collection $\mathcal{A}' \supseteq \mathcal{A}$ of atoms, we may also consider the hyperuniverse $V_{\mathcal{A}'}$ of all sets with atoms from $\mathcal{A}'$. Since the sets in $V_{\mathcal{A}}$ are those depicted by arbitrary graphs with tags chosen from $\mathcal{A}$, and likewise for $V_{\mathcal{A}'}$ and $\mathcal{A}'$, it is clear that $V_{\mathcal{A}} \subseteq V_{\mathcal{A}'}$. (See Figure 11.)

Let us write $\mathfrak{X} = \mathcal{A}' - \mathcal{A}$ and call the elements $\mathbf{x} \in \mathfrak{X}$ *indeterminates* over $V_{\mathcal{A}}$. Think of these indeterminates as unknowns ranging over the hyperuniverse $V_{\mathcal{A}}$. By analogy with ring theory, we write $V_{\mathcal{A}'} = V_{\mathcal{A}}[\mathfrak{X}]$. Then given any set $a \in V_{\mathcal{A}}[\mathfrak{X}]$, we can construe it as a "term" in the indeterminates that occur in its transitive closure, that is, the indeterminates in $a \cup (\bigcup a) \cup (\bigcup \bigcup a) \ldots$. By an *equation in* $\mathfrak{X}$ we mean an "expression" of the form

$$\mathbf{x} = a$$

where $\mathbf{x} \in \mathfrak{X}$ and $a \in V_{\mathcal{A}}[\mathfrak{X}]$. By a *system of equations in* $\mathfrak{X}$ we mean a family of equations $\{\, \mathbf{x} = a_{\mathbf{x}} \mid \mathbf{x} \in \mathfrak{X} \,\}$, exactly one equation for each indeterminate $\mathbf{x} \in \mathfrak{X}$.

In the first of the examples above, we considered $\mathfrak{X} = \{\mathbf{x}\}$ and the system of equations was simply the single equation

$$\mathbf{x} = \{\mathbf{x}\}.$$

In the second example, we had $\mathfrak{X} = \{\mathbf{x}, \mathbf{y}, \mathbf{z}\}$ and the following three equations.

$$\mathbf{x} = \{\text{Claire}, \text{Max}, \mathbf{y}\}$$
$$\mathbf{y} = \{\text{Max}, \mathbf{x}\}$$
$$\mathbf{z} = \{\mathbf{x}, \mathbf{y}\}$$

In both of these examples, the sets on the right-hand side of the equations are actually wellfounded, but we could also consider equations like

$$\mathbf{x} = \langle \Omega, \mathbf{x} \rangle$$

where the nonwellfounded set $\langle \Omega, \mathbf{x} \rangle$ occurs on the right-hand side.

We next define what we mean by a solution to a family of equations, in the natural way. By an *assignment* for $\mathfrak{X}$ in V_A we mean a function $f : \mathfrak{X} \to V_A$ which assigns an element $f(\mathbf{x})$ of V_A to each indeterminate $\mathbf{x} \in \mathfrak{X}$. Any such assignment f extends in a natural way to a function $\hat{f} : V_A[\mathfrak{X}] \to V_A$. Intuitively, given some $a \in V_A[\mathfrak{X}]$ one simply replaces each $\mathbf{x} \in \mathfrak{X}$ by its value $f(\mathbf{x})$. (To make this rigorous, one has to work with a canonical graph depicting a, replacing any childless nodes tagged by an indeterminate $\mathbf{x} \in \mathfrak{X}$ with a graph depicting the set $f(\mathbf{x})$.) Rather than write $\hat{f}(a)$, we write $a[f]$, or even more informally, $a(\mathbf{x}, \mathbf{y}, \ldots)$ and $a(f(\mathbf{x}), f(\mathbf{y}), \ldots)$.

An assignment f is a *solution of an equation* $\mathbf{x} = a(\mathbf{x}, \mathbf{y}, \ldots)$ if

$$f(\mathbf{x}) = a(f(\mathbf{x}), f(\mathbf{y}), \ldots).$$

More generally, f is a *solution of a system of equations in* $\mathfrak{X}$ if it is a solution of each equation in the system.

Theorem 1 (Solution Lemma) *Every system of equations in a collection $\mathfrak{X}$ of indeterminates over V_A has a unique solution.*

This lemma is illustrated in Figure 12. Again, we stress that the lemma has two aspects, existence and uniqueness, both of which are crucial to what follows. The proof, while not difficult, is somewhat tedious, largely for notational reasons. It can be found in Aczel (1987). The following example, though, will illustrate the main idea.

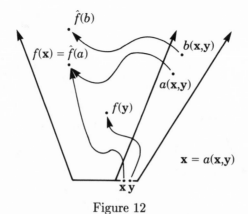

Figure 12

Example 1 Let $\mathfrak{X} = \{\mathbf{x}, \mathbf{y}\}$ consist of two indeterminates and consider the following equations.

$$\mathbf{x} = \{\Omega, \{\mathbf{x}\}\}$$
$$\mathbf{y} = \{\text{Max}, \mathbf{x}, \mathbf{y}\}$$

The sets on the right-hand side of the equations are depicted in Figure 13. To depict the solutions to the equations, we simply alter these graphs by replacing all edges terminating in a node tagged with $\mathbf{x}$ by an edge terminating in the top node of $G_{\mathbf{x}}$, and similarly for $\mathbf{y}$ and $G_{\mathbf{y}}$. This gives us the graphs in Figure 14.

By AFA, these graphs have unique decorations, and the sets assigned to the top nodes are solutions of our equations. Further-

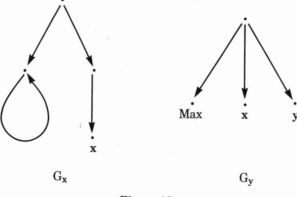

Figure 13

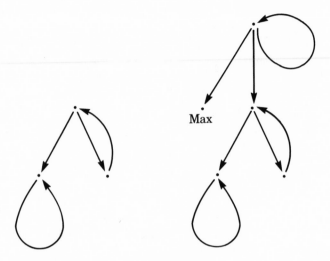

Figure 14

more, any solutions of the equations would give rise to a decoration of these graphs, so there is only one solution.

Exercise 15 Show that in the above example, the unique solution is just the assignment $f(\mathbf{x}) = \Omega$ and $f(\mathbf{y}) = a$, where a is the set depicted in Figure 15.

Exercise 16 Construct a graph depicting the set $f(\mathbf{x})$ where f is the solution of the following system of equations.

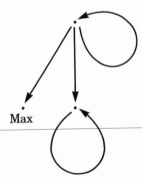

Figure 15

$$\mathbf{x} = \{\text{Claire}, \mathbf{y}\}$$
$$\mathbf{y} = \{\text{Claire}, \mathbf{z}\}$$
$$\mathbf{z} = \{\text{Max}, \mathbf{x}\}$$

Show that $f(\mathbf{x}) \neq f(\mathbf{y})$. In contrast, show that if the third equation had been

$$\mathbf{z} = \{\text{Claire}, \mathbf{x}\}$$

we would have $f(\mathbf{x}) = f(\mathbf{y}) = f(\mathbf{z})$.

Exercise 17 Working in ZFC$^-$ (i.e., without AFA or the axiom of foundation), show that the Solution Lemma implies AFA. Thus, in the presence of the other axioms, the Solution Lemma is really a restatement of AFA.

Inductive and coinductive definitions

One final matter before we apply ZFC/AFA to model circular propositions. In set theory, a frequent technique for defining a set or class is to take the desired class to be the unique fixed point of some "monotone operator."[8] But when we work with ZFC/AFA, it often happens that there is no longer a unique fixed point, but rather many. For reasons closely connected with the Solution Lemma, it is usually the largest fixed point that is needed.

Let's look at a very simple example. Assume for simplicity that our collection $\mathcal{A}$ of atoms is finite, and consider the operator Γ that assigns to each set X the set $\Gamma(X)$ of all its finite subsets. Then if our set theory incorporates the axiom of foundation, there is a unique fixed point for this operator, the set HF of all hereditarily finite sets. That is, if we assume foundation, then HF is the unique set such that $\Gamma(X) = X$. However, in the hyperuniverse of sets, there will be many distinct fixed points, a smallest, a largest, and others in between.

The smallest fixed point HF_0 can be characterized as the smallest set satisfying the condition:

- If $a \subseteq HF_0 \cup \mathcal{A}$ and a is finite, then $a \in HF_0$.

The above is called an *inductive* definition of HF_0. By contrast, the largest fixed point HF_1 can be characterized as the largest set satisfying the converse condition:

---

[8]An operator Γ is *monotone* if $X \subseteq Y$ implies $\Gamma(X) \subseteq \Gamma(Y)$. X is a *fixed point* for Γ if $\Gamma(X) = X$.

- If $a \in HF_1$, then $a \subseteq HF_1 \cup \mathcal{A}$ and a is finite.

This is called a *coinductive* definition of HF_1. It is obvious from these definitions that $HF_0 \subseteq HF_1$. But in the hyperuniverse, the converse does not hold.

Exercise 18 Prove that every member of HF_0 is wellfounded. In particular, $\Omega \notin HF_0$.

Exercise 19 Prove that $\Omega \in HF_1$.

Since it seems that Ω should certainly count as a hereditarily finite set, this suggests that the coinductive definition will be the more natural one to use when working with hypersets. And indeed it is. HF_1 is just the set of those sets which can be pictured by at least one finitely branching graph. It will contain Ω and all the other examples we have given.

This is a typical phenomenon in working with hypersets. A pair of inductive and coinductive definitions which characterize the same set or class in the universe of wellfounded sets often yield distinct collections in the universe of hypersets. The smallest fixed point, specified by the inductive definition, usually consists of the wellfounded members of the largest fixed point, specified by the coinductive definition. It is usually the latter that is needed in applications.

Aczel has a theorem, the Special Final Coalgebra Theorem, which explains why coinductive definitions are so important. While the formulation of this theorem is too technical to present in detail here, we can explain the basic idea. We begin with a couple of examples to illustrate the main feature of the result.

In ZFC/AFA the Solution Lemma frequently takes the place of the Recursion Theorem of ZFC, the theorem which lets one define some operation by $\in$-recursion. To do this same sort of thing in ZFC/AFA, you show that some operation F on sets is well-defined by obtaining it as the solution to a system of equations. But then you want to know that certain properties of the equations carry over to their solutions. As long as these properties are defined by coinductive definitions, this usually works out. For example, we have the following.[9]

---

[9] We number theorems, propositions, and lemmas with a single numbering scheme, restarting the numbers in each of the three parts of the book.

Proposition 2 *Suppose that $\mathcal{E}$ is a finite system of equations of the form*
$$\mathbf{x} = a_\mathbf{x}(\mathbf{x}, \mathbf{y}, \ldots)$$
where each $a_\mathbf{x}$ is in HF_1. If f is the unique solution to this system, then for each indeterminate $\mathbf{x}$, $f(\mathbf{x}) \in HF_1$.

Proof: The basic idea is that if you eliminate the indeterminates from a finite set of finitary equations, in the way suggested by the proof of the Solution Lemma, you end up with a finite graph, which must then depict a set in HF_1. To do this in detail, first note that by introducing more indeterminates, we can assume each equation is of one of the following simple forms:

- $\mathbf{x} = \emptyset$,

- $\mathbf{x} = a$ (for some atom $a \in \mathcal{A}$),

- $\mathbf{x} = \{\mathbf{y}_1, \ldots, \mathbf{y}_n\}$, where the $\mathbf{y}_i$ are other indeterminates with their own equations in the system.

Let f be the solution. Since it is obvious that $HF_1 \cup rng(f)$ still satisfies the defining equation of HF_1, $dom(f) \subseteq HF_1$, as desired. $\Box$

Exercise 20 Use the above proposition to show that the unique set $a = \langle a, a \rangle$ is in HF_1.

Exercise 21 Assume the axiom of foundation, and show that $HF_0 = HF_1$. (Hint: Prove by induction on the rank of the well-founded set a that if $a \in HF_1$ then $a \in HF_0$.)

To give a second illustration of the basic notion, let's use hypersets to provide a model of what are called "streams" in computer science. The basic idea is that a stream is a possibly infinite sequence of elements. But rather than think of streams as functions from natural numbers to elements, the computer scientist thinks of them as ordered pairs, the first element of which is an atom, the second a stream. So for example, the following would be a stream.

$$\langle \text{Max}, \langle \text{Claire}, \langle \text{Max}, \langle \text{Claire}, \ldots \rangle \rangle \rangle \rangle$$

To provide an interesting illustration of the Special Final Coalgebra Theorem, let's model not just streams but arbitrary nested sequences. Given some set A atoms, let A_* be defined inductively as the smallest set containing A and closed under the rule: if $x, y \in A_*$ then $\langle x, y \rangle \in A_*$. Similarly, let A^* be defined coinductively as the largest set every member of which is either a member of A, or else of the form $\langle x, y \rangle$, where $x, y \in A^*$. We will call the members of A^* *nested sequences* on A, and the members of A_* the finite nested sequences on A.

Exercise 22   1. Show that the axiom of foundation implies that $A_* = A^*$.

2. Show that AFA implies that A_* is a proper subset of A^*. Then, show in particular that there is a nested sequence $\langle 1, \langle 2, \langle 3, \ldots \rangle \rangle \rangle$ on the set of natural numbers.

3. Show that the unique solution to the following equations yields elements of $A^* - A_*$. Give an intuitive description of those elements.

$$\mathbf{x} = \langle \text{Max}, \mathbf{y} \rangle$$
$$\mathbf{y} = \langle \text{Claire}, \mathbf{x} \rangle$$

To illustrate the Special Final Coalgebra Theorem once more, we present an analogue of Proposition 2 for nested sequences. Let $\mathfrak{X}$ be a collection of indeterminates, and consider the class of nested sequences on $A \cup \mathfrak{X}$. That is, we allow elements of $\mathfrak{X}$ as well as elements of A as basis elements in the definition. Thinking of these indeterminates as parameters, we call the nested sequences on $A \cup \mathfrak{X}$ *parametric nested sequences on* A. The Special Final Coalgebra Theorem shows that if we use parametric nested sequences in the Solution Lemma, then the resulting solutions are themselves nested sequences.

Proposition 3   Suppose $\mathcal{E}$ is a system of equations of the form

$$\mathbf{x} = a_{\mathbf{x}}(\mathbf{x}, \mathbf{y}, \ldots)$$

for $\mathbf{x} \in \mathfrak{X}$, where each $a_{\mathbf{x}}$ is a parametric nested sequence on A. Let F be the unique solution of this set of equations. Then for each $x \in \mathfrak{X}$, $F(\mathbf{x})$ is a nested sequence on A.

Exercise 23   Prove Proposition 3.

The general case of Aczel's Special Final Coalgebra Theorem goes roughly as follows. Suppose we are given some monotone operator Γ. We can use Γ to define a largest fixed point in the universe V_A. Call this collection the collection of Γ-objects. However, we can also use Γ to define the largest fixed point in the universe $V_A[\mathfrak{X}]$, where we adjoin indeterminates. Call this the collection of parametric Γ-objects. Aczel's Theorem shows that under very general conditions on Γ, equations involving parametric Γ-objects have Γ-objects as their unique solutions. While the general formulation of Aczel's result is somewhat complicated, the proof of this consequence in any particular case is quite straightforward. We will not use the general theorem, though we will have occasion to prove special cases of it in what follows.

A final remark on Aczel's terminology, just for the curious. From the point of view of category theory, a system of equations is dual to the notion of an algebra, and hence is called a coalgebra. Final coalgebras are final in the sense of category theory, and exist under very general conditions. AFA shows that these can often be taken to be largest fixed points of monotone operators.

Exercise 24 Consider the smallest class $B_\circ$ containing Max as an element and closed under the rule: if $x \in B_\circ$ then $\{x\} \in B_\circ$. Similarly, define the largest class B° satisfying: if $x \in B^\circ$, then x is Max or $x = \{y\}$ for some $y \in B$.

1. Show that the axiom of foundation implies that $B_\circ = B^\circ$.

2. Show that $\Omega \in B^\circ$.

3. Formulate and prove a version of the Special Final Coalgebra Theorem for B°.

Exercise 25 Inductive definitions are used to define classes as well as sets. For example, the class of (wellfounded) ordinals can be defined inductively as the smallest class ON such that

1. $\emptyset \in ON$,

2. if $\alpha \in ON$ then $\alpha \cup \{\alpha\} \in ON$, and

3. if $a \subseteq ON$ then $(\bigcup a) \in ON$.

Give a corresponding coinductive definition of a largest fixed point ON^* and show that $\Omega \in ON^*$. Thus one might consider the set Ω a hyperordinal. However, this is a good example of a case where one would want to use the inductive definition, since the point of defining the ordinals is as representatives of well-orderings. Hyperordinals like Ω are of no use for such purposes. Formulate and prove a version of the Special Final Coalgebra Theorem for hyperordinals.

Historical Remark: The history of AFA, and other work on non-wellfounded sets, is far more complicated than we have suggested. In particular, the axiom AFA was studied independently, and earlier, by Forti and Honsell, who called it axiom X_1. Other axioms have been proposed by Finsler, Scott, and Boffa, among others. Also, the proof of consistency of ZFC/AFA is not original with Aczel, but goes back to Forti and Honsell, Gordeev, and others. The reader is invited to consult Aczel (1987) for the history of this work. We have presented it in the way we have since, to our knowledge, Aczel was the first to see that AFA could be obtained from a coherent, intuitive conception of set, rather than just being a formally consistent axiom, and to demonstrate that it is an important mathematical tool for the modeling of various kinds of real-world circularity, not just a mathematical curiosity.

The introduction of a new sort of mathematical object has always met with considerable resistance, including such now mundane objects as zero, the negative numbers, the irrationals, the imaginary numbers and infinitesimals. We realize that some set theorists feel a similar reluctance to admit hypersets as legitimate mathematical objects. While this reluctance is perhaps understandable, it is also somewhat ironic. After all, many set theorists prior to Zermelo were working with a conception which admitted circularity, as is apparent from the formulation of Russell's paradox. Furthermore, the axiom of foundation has played almost no role in mathematics outside of set theory itself. We must admit, though, that we initially shared this reluctance, having been raised within the Zermelo tradition. But our own experience has convinced us that those who take the trouble to master the techniques provided by AFA will quickly feel at home in the universe of hypersets, and find important and interesting applications.

Part II

Russellian Propositions
and the Liar

4

Modeling Russellian Propositions

Basic definitions

In this chapter we begin modeling the Russellian conception of a proposition and of the way sentences express propositions; in the next chapter we will turn to the accompanying conception of truth and the relation between propositions and the world they describe. Our approach to modeling Russellian propositions is the simplest one possible. At the atomic level, such propositions assert of one or more objects that they stand in some relation or other. To represent these atomic claims, we use complex set-theoretic objects built out of Max, Claire, the 52 cards, and three additional atoms, *H*, *Bel*, *Tr*, representing the relations of *having*, *believing*, and the property of *truth*. Among the things a proposition *p* can be about, though, are propositions, including the very proposition *p* itself. This fact will be captured in our definition.

To carry this out, we begin by defining a class *PrePROP* that properly contains the propositions we're actually interested in. We will single out a class *PROP* below, after motivating an additional restriction on propositions. Our definition takes the form of a coinductive definition.

Definition 1 Let *PrePROP* be the largest class such that if $p \in$ *PrePROP* then *p* is of one of the following forms:

1. $[a \; H \; c]$ or $[\overline{a \; H \; c}]$, where *a* is Claire or Max, *c* is a card; or

2. $[a \; Bel \; p]$ or $[\overline{a \; Bel \; p}]$ where a is Claire or Max and $p \in$ *PrePROP*; or

3. $[Tr \; p]$ or $[\overline{Tr \; p}]$, where $p \in$ *PrePROP*; or

4. $[\bigwedge X]$ or $[\bigvee X]$, where X is a subset of *PrePROP*.

The pairs of propositions in (1), (2), and (3) are said to be *negations* of one another. More generally, we will define the *negation* of any proposition by taking $[\overline{\bigwedge X}] = [\bigvee \{ \overline{p} \mid p \in X \}], [\overline{\bigvee X}] = [\bigwedge \{ \overline{p} \mid p \in X \}]$, and $\overline{\overline{p}} = p$. We will write $[Fa \; p]$ as short for $[\overline{Tr \; p}]$.

A few things should be said about Definition 1, some trivial and some significant. On the trivial side, note that we are simply assuming some technique for systematically representing distinct objects by distinct sets. We are not concerned with exactly how elements of *PrePROP* are distinguished from elements of other classes that we will introduce below, except that they should be so distinguished. We mentioned one possibility in Chapter 2. Anyone familiar with the use of ZFC set theory as a framework for developing model theory will be used to these sorts of assumptions. Our notation is designed to reflect the fact that different sorts of objects are represented in different ways. Thus, we use $[a \; H \; c]$ for that set-theoretic object which represents the proposition that a has c, a proposition completely determined by the player a, the relation having, and the card c. Exactly how these are represented by sets doesn't really matter, and burdening our definitions with the inessential detail would just obscure matters. We will assume as a general feature of our coding, though, that the objects referred to in naming the set-theoretic representative are members of its transitive closure.[1] Thus we assume that a is in the transitive closure of $[a \; H \; c]$.

The second point is more important. We have given a coinductive definition of *PrePROP*, taking it to be the *largest* collection satisfying the various clauses. It may take a moment's thought to see that there is such a unique largest class. But there is, and the fact that there is follows easily from the general considerations discussed in Chapter 3. On a more intuitive level, though, the way to understand the above definition is to note that every object that *can* be included in the class *is* so included. Instead of working from the bottom up, asking which objects are *forced into* the

---

[1]For a definition of transitive closure, see Exercise 12, page 43.

defined class, we work from the top down, asking which objects are legitimately *excluded*. This feature guarantees that circular members of *PrePROP* are not excluded.

The third point has to do with our allowing arbitrary infinite conjunctions and disjunctions to count as propositions. There is a sense in which this introduces a gratuitous generality, since our sample language $\mathcal{L}$ has no devices for expressing these propositions. We could well restrict ourselves to finite combinations, or combinations of sets of size smaller than some fixed regular cardinal κ. Such a restriction would simplify things a bit, since we wouldn't then have a proper class of propositions to cope with, and as a result, the models of the world defined in the next chapter would also be sets rather than classes. Other than that, nothing whatsoever would change, and those who are squeamish about classes might be more comfortable assuming this modification. We haven't taken this course for two reasons: first, cardinality restrictions really have nothing to do with what we are up to, and second, we feel that by allowing arbitrary infinite combinations, it is clearer that the account extends to a language that allows quantification.[2]

The final point has to do with our definition of the negation of a proposition. If we had built *PrePROP* up from below, by a standard inductive characterization, then the definition of the operation that takes propositions to their negations would follow this recursion, and the usual considerations would show it to be well defined. But since *PrePROP* contains nonwellfounded objects (see the examples below), this method is not available. So how do we know that this operation is well defined? The answer lies in the Solution Lemma, our replacement for ∈-recursion.

We will treat this first use of the Solution Lemma in some detail, since it is a method that will be quite important in this book. There is no problem about negating atomic propositions, since their negations are explicitly introduced in (1)–(3) of Definition 1. The problem has to do with $\bigwedge$ and $\bigvee$.

---

[2]Although the use of infinitary conjunction and disjunction suggests a natural and rather standard extension to a quantified language, we would in fact not favor the suggested extension. Once one admits properties and facts into the semantics, the most natural treatment of quantified claims is as descriptions of a separate kind of "higher order" fact. See Barwise and Perry (1985), 146. Without some such treatment, many of the theorems in this book could not themselves be expressed in the language, especially those in Part III that quantify over all situations.

Lemma 1 *There is a unique operation* − *which assigns to each $p \in$ PrePROP an element $\overline{p} \in$ PrePROP which satisfies the following conditions.*

1. *If p is atomic, then $\overline{p}$ is its negation.*
2. $[\overline{\bigwedge X}] = [\bigvee \{\, \overline{p} \mid p \in X \}]$.
3. $[\overline{\bigvee X}] = [\bigwedge \{\, \overline{p} \mid p \in X \}]$.

Proof: The basic idea will be to generate a system of equations from conditions (1)-(3), and then apply the Solution Lemma. To do this, introduce an indeterminate $\mathbf{x}_p$ for each $p \in$ *PrePROP*, and consider the system of equations:

$\mathbf{x}_p = \overline{p}$, if p is an atomic proposition
$\mathbf{x}_p = [\bigvee \{\, \mathbf{x}_q \mid q \in X \}]$, if $p = [\bigwedge X] \in$ *PrePROP*
$\mathbf{x}_p = [\bigwedge \{\, \mathbf{x}_q \mid q \in X \}]$, if $p = [\bigvee X] \in$ *PrePROP*.

By the Solution Lemma, there is a unique solution F to this family of equations. The set assigned to $\mathbf{x}_p$ by F is the desired negation $\overline{p}$. We need to make sure that $\overline{p} \in$ *PrePROP*, but this follows from the maximality of *PrePROP*. That is, the collection *PrePROP* $\cup \{\, \overline{p} \mid p \in$ *PrePROP* $\}$ satisfies the defining conditions, and so is just *PrePROP*. Thus the operation is defined by

$$\overline{p} = F(\mathbf{x}_p). \quad \square$$

Let's now consider a few examples of propositions in the class *PrePROP*. Note that, except for the first example, all of these would have been excluded had we used a standard inductive definition rather than the coinductive definition.

Example 1 The *PrePROP* [Claire H 3♣] will be construed as the proposition that Claire has the three of clubs; its negation, [$\overline{\text{Claire } H \text{ 3♣}}$], will be the proposition that she does not.

Example 2 (Russellian Liar) There is a unique member of *Pre-PROP* satisfying the equation

$$f = [Fa\ f].$$

To see that this is the case, note that AFA guarantees a set with this structure, and if we "add" it to *PrePROP*, the resulting collection still satisfies the defining clauses. So $f \in$ *PrePROP*, by maximality. This proposition is directly about itself, and says of itself that it is false. We will call it the Russellian Liar. Note that since $f = [Fa\ f]$, we also have, by substitution, $f = [Fa\ [Fa\ f]]$, and so on.

Example 3 We also have a Truth-teller proposition satisfying the equation

$$t = [Tr\ t].$$

Note that the Truth-teller is not the negation of the Liar. The negation of the Liar is the proposition $[Tr\ f]$ that claims the Liar is true.

Example 4 There are arbitrarily long Liar cycles, $p_1, \ldots, p_n, q$, where each proposition claims that the next one is true, except for q, which claims that p_1 is false:

$$p_1 = [Tr\ p_2]$$
$$\vdots$$
$$p_n = [Tr\ q]$$
$$q = [Fa\ p_1].$$

Example 5 There is a unique proposition p satisfying

$$p = [\text{Max } Bel\ p] \wedge [Fa\ p].^3$$

This proposition also seems Liar-like in character. It will be true only if Max has a belief that that very belief is false.

Example 6 There is a unique (pre-)proposition:

$$p = [a\ H\ 3\clubsuit] \vee p$$

and its negation $q = \bar{p}$, the unique proposition satisfying:

$$q = \overline{[a\ H\ 3\clubsuit]} \wedge q.$$

If we were to define truth for pre-propositions in the natural way, it would turn out that if a did not have the three of clubs, then both

---

[3]Note that we are using the obvious abbreviation for the conjunction:

$$\bigwedge \{[\text{Max } Bel\ p], [Fa\ p]\}.$$

of these propositions would be true.[4] For an even more bizarre example of such pre-propositions, consider:

$$p = [p \land p]$$

and its negation:

$$q = [q \lor q].$$

It is really atomic propositions that make basic claims about the world, even if they are atomic propositions involving propositions (which may involve circularity, of course, as in the case of the Liar). The reason for this is pretty clear. To make a basic claim about something, we must assert that that thing has a property or stands in a relation to some other thing, and properties and relations only come in at the level of atomic propositions. These last examples show that there is a problem with our definition of *PrePROP* in that it allows cycles and other descending sequences of propositions which never get around to making a substantive claim, which never "pass through" an atomic proposition. The next definition allows us to throw out these nonsubstantive propositions.

Definition 2

1. A set $X \subseteq$ *PrePROP* is *nonsubstantive* if X contains no atomic propositions and every member of X has an immediate constituent that is also a member of X.

---

[4]To see this, the reader might want to reflect back on these examples after considering the definition of truth in the next chapter. The situation is quite different with the superficially similar proposition:

$$p' = [a \; H \; 3\clubsuit] \lor [Tr \; p']$$

and its negation q' given by:

$$q' = \overline{[a \; H \; 3\clubsuit]} \land [Fa \; p'].$$

No set of facts would make both of these true on any reasonable definition of truth.

It is significant that both p' and q' are expressible in English, while the propositions given in Example 6 are not. The reason for this is that English provides us with no sentential analogue of "this proposition," no expression which behaves grammatically like a sentence but which expresses exactly the proposition expressed by the entire sentence in which it is a constituent. To our knowledge, no natural language contains such an expression, and apparently for good reason.

2. A proposition p is *nonsubstantive* if it is a member of some nonsubstantive set of propositions. Otherwise p is *substantive*.

3. The class *PROP* is the largest subclass of *PrePROP* such that if $p \in PROP$, then p is substantive and every immediate constituent of p is in *PROP*.

We will call the members of *PROP Russellian propositions*. There is an obvious analogy between the restriction we've built into the above definition and the axiom of foundation. But it should be emphasized that we have not excluded circular propositions from the class *PROP*. Indeed, all of the propositions discussed in Examples 1 through 5 remain, though those in Example 6 do not.

At this point, a word is in order about the identity conditions of Russellian propositions, as we've modeled them. Whenever one uses sets to model something else, the identity conditions on sets impose identity conditions on the models, and so, indirectly, on objects modeled. As we've seen, AFA gives us identity conditions on sets by telling us that two distinct sets can never decorate a single graph. This has ramifications concerning the adequacy of our models of propositions. In order for (pretheoretic) propositions to be modeled by distinct sets, there must be some difference that comes to be reflected in a structural difference in the sets that model them. So, for example, the negation of the Liar, $[Tr\ f]$, is distinct from the Truth-teller, $[Tr\ t]$, since the former is a proposition with the Liar as a constituent, while the latter has the Truth-teller as a constituent, and these are structurally distinguishable. However, the proposition $[Fa\ f]$ is the same proposition as $[Fa\ [Fa\ f]]$, since $f = [Fa\ f]$, and so both are just the Liar f.

Propositions as modeled here are far finer-grained than when modeled as sets of possible worlds. Besides admitting circularity, they permit us to distinguish the following propositions, for example.

$$[\text{Max } H\ 3\clubsuit]$$

$$[\text{Max } H\ 3\clubsuit] \wedge [[\text{Claire } H\ 3\diamondsuit] \vee [\overline{\text{Claire } H\ 3\diamondsuit}]]$$

Still, there is an issue as to whether the identity conditions imposed by our model are still too coarse-grained, forcing us to identify intuitively distinct propositions. This is an issue we will return to in Chapter 6.

Exercise 26 Using equations in the indeterminates **p** and **q**, specify the negation $\overline{f}$ of the Liar proposition f. Contrast this with the single equation in the indeterminate **p** whose solution is the Truth-teller.

Exercise 27 Show that if $p \in PROP$, then its negation $\overline{p}$ is also in *PROP*.

Exercise 28 In this exercise we will give a characterization of the class *PROP* that does not detour through the class *PrePROP*. First define the propositional closure $\Gamma(X)$ of X to be the *smallest* collection containing X and closed under the above infinitary conjunction and disjunction operations. Then define the collection *AtPROP* of atomic propositions to be the largest class such that if $p \in AtPROP$, then p is of one of the following forms:

1. $[a\ H\ c]$ or $\overline{[a\ H\ c]}$, where a is Claire or Max, c is a card; or

2. $[a\ Bel\ q]$ or $\overline{[a\ Bel\ q]}$ where a is Claire or Max and $q \in \Gamma(AtPROP)$; or

3. $[Tr\ q]$ or $\overline{[Tr\ q]}$, where $q \in \Gamma(AtPROP)$.

Show that $PROP = \Gamma(AtPROP)$.

A Russellian semantics for $\mathcal{L}$

We will now show how Russellian propositions, including circular propositions, can be the semantic values of the (wellfounded) sentences of our language $\mathcal{L}$. The basic intuition we must capture is this: given any sentence $\varphi(\textbf{this},\ \textbf{that}_1,\dots,\textbf{that}_n)$, and any assignment $q_1,\dots,q_n$ of propositions to the demonstratives $\textbf{that}_1,\dots,\textbf{that}_n$, one can use φ to express a proposition p while simultaneously using the demonstrative **this** to refer to that very same proposition.

To avoid bogging down in side issues, let's temporarily restrict our attention to the case of a formula $\varphi(\textbf{this})$, where **this** may occur in φ but where φ does not contain any of the other demonstratives $\textbf{that}_i$. Now imagine that we could go around pointing at propositions and using **this** to refer to them. Then, intuitively, just what proposition p is expressed by our use of $\varphi(\textbf{this})$ will be a function F_φ of the proposition q that we refer to:

$$p = F_\varphi(q).$$

What we want, to capture the reflexive use of **this**, is the proposition p that is the fixed point of this equation:

$$p = F_\varphi(p).$$

This suggests that we use the Solution Lemma. To invoke the lemma in our semantics, we will represent the function F_φ as a set $g(\mathbf{p})$ which is just like a proposition except that it has an indeterminate $\mathbf{p}$ standing in place of a proposition. We will call such things *parametric propositions*, or sometimes, following Russell, *propositional functions*.

With this for motivation, let's go back to the general case. Introduce special *propositional indeterminates* $\mathbf{p}, \mathbf{q}_1, \mathbf{q}_2, \ldots$ corresponding to the demonstratives **this**, **that**$_1$, **that**$_2$, and so forth. Next, generalize the definition of the class *PROP* of propositions to the class *ParPROP* of parametric propositions, by allowing additional atomic propositions of the following forms, where $\mathbf{z}$ is one of the indeterminates.

$$[a \; Bel \; \mathbf{z}] \quad \overline{[a \; Bel \; \mathbf{z}]}$$
$$[Tr \; \mathbf{z}] \quad \overline{[Tr \; \mathbf{z}]}$$

We will leave the details of this simple extension to the reader, but for those familiar with the procedure, we note the analogy with forming a ring of polynomials in given indeterminates.

Our semantics for $\mathcal{L}$ will now proceed in two stages. First we define a function *Val* that assigns a parametric proposition to each formula φ of $\mathcal{L}$. In general, $Val(\varphi)$ will contain the parameters $\mathbf{p}$ and, for each **that**$_i$ occurring in φ, $\mathbf{q}_i$. If φ is a sentence, though, $Val(\varphi)$ will only contain the parameters $\mathbf{q}_i$, and the proposition expressed by φ will be determined by a context c that fixes the referents of the demonstratives **that**$_i$ occurring in φ. Since this is the only role contexts play in the Russellian account, it will suffice to model them with functions that assign propositions to the **that**$_i$. Thus the second step will be to define a function *Exp* which gives us, for any sentence φ and context c, the proposition $Exp(\varphi, c)$ expressed by φ in c.

Definition 3 We define the function *Val* which assigns to each formula $\varphi(\textbf{this}, \textbf{that}_1, \ldots, \textbf{that}_n)$ a parametric proposition $Val(\varphi)$ in the indeterminates $\mathbf{p}, \mathbf{q}_1, \ldots, \mathbf{q}_n$, as follows:

1. $Val(\mathbf{a\ Has\ c}) = [a\ H\ c]$
2. $Val(\mathbf{a\ Believes\ that}_i) = [a\ Bel\ \mathbf{q}_i]$
3. $Val(\mathbf{a\ Believes\ this}) = [a\ Bel\ \mathbf{p}]$
4. $Val(\mathbf{a\ Believes}\ \varphi) = [a\ Bel\ Val(\varphi)]$
5. $Val(\mathbf{True\ that}_i) = [Tr\ \mathbf{q}_i]$
6. $Val(\mathbf{True\ this}) = [Tr\ \mathbf{p}]$
7. $Val(\mathbf{True}\ \varphi) = [Tr\ Val(\varphi)]$
8. $Val(\varphi_1 \wedge \varphi_2) = [\bigwedge\{Val(\varphi_1),\ Val(\varphi_2)\}]$
   $Val(\varphi_1 \vee \varphi_2) = [\bigvee\{Val(\varphi_1),\ Val(\varphi_2)\}]$
9. $Val(\neg\varphi) = \overline{Val(\varphi)}$
10. $Val(\downarrow\varphi) =$ the unique solution $p \in ParPROP$ to the equation

$$\mathbf{p} = Val(\varphi)(\mathbf{p}, \mathbf{q}_1, \ldots).$$

Lemma 2 $Val(\varphi)$ *is a parametric proposition in the parameters* $\mathbf{q}_i$, *where* $\mathbf{that}_i$ *occurs in* φ, *and the additional parameter* $\mathbf{p}$ *if* **this** *is loose in* φ.

Proof: This is a routine induction on formulas. Only clause (10) is of any interest, and it follows directly from the Solution Lemma. $\square$

Let's return for a moment to the special case $\varphi(\mathbf{this})$ considered above. Since φ does not contain any of the demonstratives $\mathbf{that}_i$, the preceding lemma tells us that the parametric proposition $g(\mathbf{p}) = Val(\varphi)$ has at most a single parameter, $\mathbf{p}$. What's more, if we use the Solution Lemma to obtain the unique solution $p = g(p)$, as we would to find $Val(\downarrow\varphi)$, we are guaranteed, by the maximality of $PROP$, that p is a proposition. Indeed, it follows quite generally from the above that if φ is a sentence, and hence contains no loose occurrences of **this**, then $Val(\varphi)$ is a proposition. We call this the proposition expressed by the sentence φ, denoted $Exp(\varphi)$.

To deal with the general case, where we have sentences containing some $\mathbf{that}_i$'s, we define a *Russellian context* for a sentence $\varphi(\mathbf{that}_1, \ldots, \mathbf{that}_n)$ to be a function c defined on all the propositional demonstratives $\mathbf{that}_1, \ldots, \mathbf{that}_n$ of φ, and taking propositions $q_1, \ldots, q_n$ as values. Such a context c gives us a natural assignment to the propositional indeterminates $\mathbf{q}_1, \ldots, \mathbf{q}_n$ of $Val(\varphi)$.

Thus, we can define the proposition expressed by sentence φ in context c, $Exp(\varphi, c)$, to be the proposition:

$$Val(\varphi)(q_1, \ldots, q_n).$$

This is just the proposition that results from replacing each indeterminate $\mathbf{q}_i$ with the corresponding proposition q_i determined by the context.

Example 7 The Liar sentence of $\mathcal{L}$ is the following sentence λ.[5]

(λ) $\neg\mathbf{True(this)}$

According to the above definition, this sentence expresses the unique proposition $p = [Fa\ p]$. But this is just the Liar proposition f presented in Example 2, page 64.

The above definition gives us what we want in the case of a proposition expressed by a single sentence in isolation, but some of the examples we discussed in Chapter 1 involved multiple sentences referring to the propositions expressed by each other in various ways. The remainder of this section will be devoted to extending our semantics to handle cases of this sort, and could be skipped on a first reading.

To establish the connection between sequences of statements and sequences of propositions about each other, we modify the semantics as follows. We will model examples involving multiple sentences with sequences $\varphi_1, \ldots, \varphi_n$ of sentences, and alter the semantics so that the demonstrative $\mathbf{that}_i$ refers automatically to the proposition expressed by φ_i, for $i \leq n$. For other demonstratives ($\mathbf{that}_i$ for $i > n$), though, we still carry along a context. Thus, by a context c for a *sequence* $\varphi_1, \ldots, \varphi_n$ of sentences, we will mean an assignment that is defined on all propositional demonstratives appearing in the sequence except for the demonstratives $\mathbf{this}, \mathbf{that}_1, \ldots, \mathbf{that}_n$. Given such a context c and propositions $q_1, \ldots, q_n$, we write $(q_1, \ldots, q_n, c)$ for the extension of c that assigns q_i to $\mathbf{that}_i$. Thus $(q_1, \ldots, q_n, c)$ will be a context (in the earlier sense) for each of the single sentences φ_i.

---

[5]Recall our convention of dropping the initial occurrence of $\downarrow$.

Theorem 3 *Given any sequence $\varphi_1, \ldots, \varphi_n$ of sentences and a context c for the sequence, there is a unique sequence $q_1, \ldots, q_n$ of propositions such that, for each $i \leq n$,*

$$Exp(\varphi_i, (q_1, \ldots, q_n, c)) = q_i.$$

That is, q_i is the proposition expressed by φ_i in the expanded context $(q_1, \ldots, q_n, c)$.

Proof: This is again a simple application of the Solution Lemma. Given the definition of the function *Exp* in terms of the function *Val*, what we want is a unique sequence $q_1, \ldots, q_n$ of propositions satisfying the following equations.

$$q_1 = Val(\varphi_1)(q_1, \ldots, q_n, c)$$
$$q_2 = Val(\varphi_2)(q_1, \ldots, q_n, c)$$
$$\vdots$$
$$q_n = Val(\varphi_n)(q_1, \ldots, q_n, c)$$

That there is such a sequence follows immediately from the Solution Lemma, as expected. □

Using these results, it is easy to verify that all of the propositions discussed in the previous section are indeed expressed by the obvious $\mathcal{L}$-analogues of the English sentences that express those propositions. We give just one example, using the obvious extension of the notational conventions used above.

Example 8 Consider the following sequence of sentences φ_1, φ_2, φ_3.

$$\textbf{True}(\textbf{that}_2)$$
$$\textbf{True}(\textbf{that}_3)$$
$$\neg\textbf{True}(\textbf{that}_1)$$

Then $Exp(\varphi_1, \varphi_2, \varphi_3)$ is the unique sequence p_1, p_2, p_3 of propositions satisfying the following equations.

$$p_1 = [Tr\ p_2]$$
$$p_2 = [Tr\ p_3]$$
$$p_3 = [Fa\ p_1]$$

This is just the Liar cycle of length three.

Exercise 29 There are only four distinct propositions expressed by the following eight sentences. They are the Truth-teller t, the Liar f, and their negations, $\bar{t}$ and $\bar{f}$. Determine which sentences express which of these propositions.

1. **True(this)**
2. **True(True(this))**
3. **True($\downarrow$True(this))**
4. **¬True(this)**
5. **¬ $\downarrow$True(this)**
6. **¬True(¬True(this))**
7. **¬ (¬True(this))**
8. **¬ ($\downarrow$¬True(this))**

Exercise 30 Identify the propositions expressed by the following sentences. What are your intuitions regarding the truth or falsity of these propositions? Which seem paradoxical? We will return to them in a later exercise, where we can compare these intuitions with the predictions made by the Russellian and Austinian accounts.

1. **((Claire Has 5♡) ∧ ¬(True(this)))**
2. **((Claire Has 5♡) ∨ ¬(True(this)))**
3. **((Claire Has 5♡) ∧ ¬(Claire Has 5♡)) ∧ ¬True(this)**
4. **((Claire Has 5♡) ∧ (Max Has 5♡)) ∧ ¬True(this)**
5. **((Claire Has 5♡) ∨ ¬(Claire Has 5♡)) ∨ ¬True(this)**
6. **((Claire Has 5♡) ∨ ¬(Claire Has 5♡)) ∧ ¬True(this)**
7. **¬True(this) ∨ $\downarrow$True(this)**
8. **¬True(this) ∨ True(this)**
9. **¬True(this) ∧ $\downarrow$True(this)**
10. **¬True(this) ∧ True(this)**
11. **¬True(¬True(this))**
12. **True(¬True(¬True(this)))**
13. **¬True(True(¬True(this)))**
14. **¬True(True($\downarrow$¬True(this)))**

Exercise 31 Consider the two following propositions.

$$p = \overline{[[\mathit{Tr}\ p] \wedge [\mathit{Tr}\ q]]}$$
$$q = [[\mathit{Tr}\ p] \wedge [\mathit{Tr}\ q]]$$

1. Show that these propositions cannot be expressed in $\mathcal{L}$ without using the demonstratives **that**$_i$.

2. Extend the language by allowing two scope indicators in such a way that p is expressed by the following sentence.

$$\downarrow_1 \neg \downarrow_2 (\mathbf{True}(\mathbf{this}_1) \wedge \mathbf{True}(\mathbf{this}_2))$$

Exercise 32 Give a general graph-theoretic characterization of those propositions that can be expressed in $\mathcal{L}$ without using the demonstratives **that**$_i$.

5

Truth of Russellian Propositions

Truth and the world

We now turn to the definition of truth for Russellian propositions. The basic idea is that a Russellian proposition is true just in case there are facts that make it true, not true just in case there are no such facts. Facts, however, are relative to the actual world, so we will eventually fix some model $\mathfrak{M}$ of the world and let any subset of $\mathfrak{M}$ count as a set of facts. Until we have such a model, we talk about states of affairs, not facts, and about what it would be for a set of states of affairs (a "situation") to make a proposition true.

Definition 4 Let *SOA* and *SIT* be defined as follows:

- $\sigma \in SOA$ if and only if σ is of one of the following forms:
    - $\langle H, a, c; i \rangle$, or
    - $\langle Tr, p; i \rangle$, or
    - $\langle Bel, a, p; i \rangle$,

  where H, Tr, and Bel are distinct atoms, a is Claire or Max, c is one of the standard cards, p is in *PROP*, and i is either 0 or 1.

- $s \in SIT$ if and only if s is a subset of *SOA*.

We will call the members of *SOA* *states of affairs* (or *soa*'s, for short). *Situations*, the members of *SIT*, are sets (not classes) of these. If $\langle H, a, c; 1 \rangle$ is in situation s, this will be taken to represent person a's having card c in s; if $\langle H, a, c; 0 \rangle$ is in s, then this represents a's not having card c in s. If neither, then s does not determine whether or not a has c. We call $\langle H, a, c; 1\rangle$ and $\langle H, a, c; 0\rangle$ *duals* of one another (and similarly for states of affairs involving Tr and Bel).

Definition 5 We define the *makes true* relation to be the unique relation $\models$ contained in $SIT \times PROP$ satisfying:

- $s \models [a \; H \; c]$ if and only if $\langle H, a, c; 1\rangle \in s$.
- $s \models [\overline{a \; H \; c}]$ if and only if $\langle H, a, c; 0\rangle \in s$.
- $s \models [a \; Bel \; p]$ if and only if $\langle Bel, a, p; 1\rangle \in s$.
- $s \models [\overline{a \; Bel \; p}]$ if and only if $\langle Bel, a, p; 0\rangle \in s$.
- $s \models [Tr \; p]$ if and only if $\langle Tr, p; 1\rangle \in s$.
- $s \models [\overline{Tr \; p}]$ if and only if $\langle Tr, p; 0\rangle \in s$.
- $s \models [\bigwedge X]$ if and only if $s \models p$ for each $p \in X$.
- $s \models [\bigvee X]$ if and only if $s \models p$ for some $p \in X$.

It may not be immediately obvious that there is such a unique relation, since we have nonwellfounded propositions. Indeed, were we to attempt the same definition for the class *PrePROP*, it would fail because there would then be many relations satisfying these clauses. But they all agree on *PROP*, as the following lemma shows.

Lemma 4 *Let $\models_1 \subseteq (SIT \times PrePROP)$ be defined inductively as the smallest relation satisfying the $(\Leftarrow)$ half of the conditions in Definition 5, and let $\models_2 \subseteq (SIT \times PrePROP)$ be defined coinductively as the largest relation satisfying the $(\Rightarrow)$ half. Then we have:*

1. *$\models_1$ and $\models_2$ both satisfy the full conditions in Definition 5.*
2. *If $s \models_1 p$ then $s \models_2 p$, for all $p \in PrePROP$.*
3. *For $p \in Prop$, $s \models_1 p$ iff $s \models_2 p$.*

Proof: (1) and (2) are simply instances of general facts about inductive and coinductive definitions. To prove (3), we show that the counterexamples form a nonsubstantive collection, and so there is no counterexample in the set *PROP*.

Let X be the collection of all $p \in PrePROP$ such that for some $s \in SIT$,

$$s \models_2 p \text{ but } s \not\models_1 p.$$

Clearly X contains no atomic propositions. Suppose $p = \bigwedge Y$ is in X. Then since $s \not\models_1 p$, there is a $q \in Y$ such that $s \not\models_1 q$. But since $s \models_2 p, s \models_2 q$. Thus p has a constituent $q \in X$. The case for $p = (\bigvee Y) \in X$ is similar, and so X is a nonsubstantive collection. $\square$

A similar proof allows us to establish the following fact. We take this pair of results as showing that our trimmed down $PROP$ is a more natural class than $PrePROP$.

Lemma 5 *Let $s \in SIT$ not contain any state of affairs and its dual. Then there is no proposition $p \in PROP$ such that $s \models p$ and $s \models \bar{p}$.*

Proof: Let X be the collection of propositions $p \in PROP$ for which we have both $s \models p$ and $s \models \bar{p}$. By the assumption about s and the definition of the relation $\models$, X contains no atomic propositions. But ordinary reasoning about conjunction and disjunction shows that if some nonatomic proposition were in X, then some immediate constituent of it would have to be in X. Thus X is nonsubstantive, and so is empty by the definition of $PROP$. $\square$

Exercise 33 Let p and q be the unique members of $PrePROP$ satisfying the following equations.

$$p = [p \wedge p]$$
$$q = [q \vee q]$$

1. Show that p and q are negations, i.e., $\bar{p} = q$.

2. Show that for any s, $s \models_2 p$ and $s \models_2 q$ (using the notation from Lemma 4).

3. Show that for any s, $s \not\models_1 p$ and $s \not\models_1 q$.

To depict the role played by the actual world in determining the facts, and hence the truth of propositions, we introduce the notion of a model of the world. Basically, a model of the world will simply be a collection (set or class) of states of affairs, including states of affairs involving the property of truth. But we will impose certain coherence conditions to rule out various sorts of logical incoherence, in particular, incoherence involving the properties of truth and falsity. The kind of thing we need to insure against is models that on the one hand contain a fact $\langle Tr, p; 1 \rangle$ declaring a proposition p to be true, but on the other hand fail to make p true. We do not bother to bring in the analogous coherence conditions on the relations of believing or having (like the condition that two players cannot have the same card), since such conditions do not influence our account of truth.

Minimally, we need to impose three conditions. First, we must ensure that no state of affairs and its dual both appear in a model $\mathfrak{M}$. Second, if $\langle Tr, p; 1 \rangle$ is in $\mathfrak{M}$, then it really should be the case that p is made true by facts of $\mathfrak{M}$, that is, that there is a subset s of $\mathfrak{M}$ such that $s \models p$. Just so, and even more important, if $\langle Tr, p; 0 \rangle$ is in $\mathfrak{M}$, then we must ensure that there is no subset s of $\mathfrak{M}$ such that $s \models p$. We will begin by introducing the notion of a *weak* model of the world by imposing these very minimal coherence conditions. The notion of a (standard) model of the world will be introduced in due course, by imposing natural closure conditions on weak models.

Definition 6

1. Given a collection $\mathfrak{M}$ of soa's, a proposition p is *made true by* $\mathfrak{M}$, written $\mathfrak{M} \models p$, if there is a set $s \subseteq \mathfrak{M}$ such that $s \models p$; p is *made false by* $\mathfrak{M}$, written $\mathfrak{M} \not\models p$, if there is no such s.

2. By contrast, a proposition p is *true in* $\mathfrak{M}$, written $True_{\mathfrak{M}}(p)$, if $\langle Tr, p; 1 \rangle \in \mathfrak{M}$; *false in* $\mathfrak{M}$, written $False_{\mathfrak{M}}(p)$, if $\langle Tr, p; 0 \rangle \in \mathfrak{M}$.

3. A collection $\mathfrak{M}$ of soa's is *coherent* if no soa and its dual are in $\mathfrak{M}$.

4. A *weak model* $\mathfrak{M}$ of the world is a coherent collection of soa's satisfying:

   - If $True_{\mathfrak{M}}(p)$, then $\mathfrak{M} \models p$.
   - If $False_{\mathfrak{M}}(p)$, then $\mathfrak{M} \not\models p$.

A word of explanation about these definitions. Regarding (1) and (2), note that $\mathfrak{M} \models p$, $True_{\mathfrak{M}}(p)$, and $False_{\mathfrak{M}}(p)$ are all positive claims about $\mathfrak{M}$, claims that facts of one kind or another are present in $\mathfrak{M}$. $\mathfrak{M} \models p$ requires that the facts needed to make p true are in $\mathfrak{M}$, while $True_{\mathfrak{M}}(p)$ and $False_{\mathfrak{M}}(p)$ require that the *seman-tical* facts $\langle Tr, p; 1 \rangle$ and $\langle Tr, p; 0 \rangle$ be in $\mathfrak{M}$. By contrast, $\mathfrak{M} \not\models p$ is negative. We can think of it as denying that there are facts in $\mathfrak{M}$ that make p true. Regarding (3) and (4), these impose abso-lutely minimal conditions on weak models. Requiring coherence of a weak model simply reflects the fact that no object can both have and fail to have a given property, while the remaining demands are minimal conditions on the property of truth: it cannot be a *fact* that a proposition is true unless the world really makes it true, and if the world really makes a proposition true, it cannot be a fact that it is *not* true.

Theorem 6 *The Liar proposition $f = [Fa \; f]$ is made false by any weak model $\mathfrak{M}$, but it is not false in any such $\mathfrak{M}$. That is, the fact of its being false is not a fact in the world.*

Proof: Suppose $\mathfrak{M} \models f$. Then there is a set $s \subseteq \mathfrak{M}$ such that $s \models f$. In which case $\langle Tr, f; 0 \rangle \in s$, and so $\langle Tr, f; 0 \rangle \in \mathfrak{M}$. But then by our condition on weak models, f must be made false by $\mathfrak{M}$, which contradicts our assumption. Hence $\mathfrak{M} \not\models f$.

Now let us show that f is not false *in* $\mathfrak{M}$. Suppose it were. That is, suppose $\langle Tr, f; 0 \rangle \in \mathfrak{M}$. Let $s = \{\langle Tr, f; 0 \rangle\}$. Then s is a set of facts in $\mathfrak{M}$ and $s \models f$. So f would then be made true by $\mathfrak{M}$, which cannot be, by the preceding. $\square$

Notice that the proof of this theorem exactly parallels the rea-soning usually taken to show that the Liar is paradoxical. Indeed, if we look back at the intuitive reasoning given in Chapter 1, page 20, we see that the proof that f is made false by $\mathfrak{M}$ corresponds to step (3), while the proof that f is not false in $\mathfrak{M}$ corresponds to (4). Here, however, there is no paradox, only a somewhat puzzling moral. The moral is that on the Russellian view of propositions and truth, or at any rate on our reconstruction of it, the Liar is made false *by* the world but its falsity cannot be construed as a fact *in* the world. For adding its falsity to the world, that is, throw-ing the soa $\langle Tr, f; 0 \rangle$ into $\mathfrak{M}$, would violate the minimal coherence conditions that anchor our notions of truth and falsity in the first place. We think the significance of this moral will become clearer as we play out the consequences of the Liar in more detail.

One way to interpret Theorem 6 in line with our discussion in Chapter 1 about negation and denial might be this. What the theorem tells us is that we can deny the truth of the Liar f, but we cannot assert that f is not true, since asserting that f is not true is just asserting f. The puzzling feature of the theorem would then be the question of how these two can possibly diverge.

The T-schema and the world

In Chapter 1 we remarked that deriving a contradiction from the Liar seemed to require only the T-schema. Let us try to reconstruct this schema in the present Russellian framework in order to see what must be given up and why.

Definition 7 Let $\mathfrak{M}$ be a weak model of the world.

1. We call $\mathfrak{M}$ *T-closed* if it satisfies the condition: $True_{\mathfrak{M}}(p)$ iff $\mathfrak{M} \models p$. This can also be restated as: $\mathfrak{M} \models [Tr\ p]$ iff $\mathfrak{M} \models p$.

2. We call $\mathfrak{M}$ *F-closed* if it satisfies the condition: $False_{\mathfrak{M}}(p)$ iff $\mathfrak{M} \not\models p$. This can be restated as: $\mathfrak{M} \models [Fa\ p]$ iff $\mathfrak{M} \not\models p$.

3. We call $\mathfrak{M}$ *semantically closed* if it is both T- and F-closed.

The most direct reconstruction of the intuitive T-schema is the requirement that models be T-closed. We will see that there is no problem at all with assuming that the world is T-closed. According to Theorem 6, the Liar is made false by any model $\mathfrak{M}$, and so T-closure only guarantees that the Liar cannot be true in $\mathfrak{M}$. But this in fact was already guaranteed by our coherence conditions on weak models. This is why the distinct notion of F-closure must be introduced to capture the full intent of the T-schema.

Notice that the ($\Rightarrow$) half of T-closure is guaranteed by the definition of weak model, as is the ($\Rightarrow$) half of F-closure. Where the Liar proposition causes problems is with the ($\Leftarrow$) half of F-closure. Theorem 6 tells us that the Liar f is not made true by a model $\mathfrak{M}$, and F-closure would then demand that $[Fa\ f]$ be made true by $\mathfrak{M}$. But f and $[Fa\ f]$ are the same proposition. Consequently, we have the following corollary to Theorem 6.

Corollary 7 *No weak model is F-closed. Thus there are no semantically closed models.*

The Liar shows us that there are no F-closed, and hence no semantically closed, models. But it is possible to introduce an approximation of the notion of semantic closure. Recall that when we discussed the F-schema in Chapter 1, there was a question about whether the "¬ . . ." should be construed as a negative assertion or as some sort of "embedded denial." The notion of F-closure introduced above in effect opts for the latter, since the negation appearing on the right-hand side ($\mathfrak{M} \not\models p$) is completely external to the proposition. This suggests an alternative closure condition which, it will turn out, can indeed be satisfied.

Definition 8 Let $\mathfrak{M}$ be a weak model of the world.

1. We call $\mathfrak{M}$ *N-closed* if it satisfies the condition: $False_{\mathfrak{M}}(p)$ iff $\mathfrak{M} \models \bar{p}$. This can be restated as: $\mathfrak{M} \models [Fa\ p]$ iff $\mathfrak{M} \models \bar{p}$.

2. We call $\mathfrak{M}$ *almost semantically closed* if it is both T- and N-closed.

N-closure is weaker than F-closure in one extremely important sense: the ($\Leftarrow$) half only requires $False_{\mathfrak{M}}(p)$ for a restricted class of propositions, the ones whose negations are made true by $\mathfrak{M}$. But as long as we are dealing with the very spare notion of a weak model, there is also a sense in which N-closure is stronger than F-closure. For the ($\Rightarrow$) half requires that for any proposition that is false in $\mathfrak{M}$, there must be a set of facts that "witnesses" p's falsity by making its negation true. For future reference, we will call this ($\Rightarrow$) half of N-closure the *witnessing condition*. Thus a weak model $\mathfrak{M}$ satisfies the witnessing condition just in case $False_{\mathfrak{M}}(p)$ implies $\mathfrak{M} \models \bar{p}$.

There are many ways in which almost semantically closed models more naturally represent the behavior of truth and falsity, and hence are more natural representations of the world than weak models in general. For example, we have the following.

Proposition 8 *Let $\mathfrak{M}$ be a weak model that is almost semantically closed. Then the following hold:*

1. $\mathfrak{M} \models [Tr\ p]$ *iff* $\mathfrak{M} \models p$.
2. $\mathfrak{M} \models [Fa\ p]$ *iff* $\mathfrak{M} \models \bar{p}$.
3. $\mathfrak{M} \models [Fa\ [Fa\ p]]$ *iff* $\mathfrak{M} \models p$.
4. $\mathfrak{M} \models [Tr(\bigwedge X)]$ *iff* $\mathfrak{M} \models [Tr\ p]$ *for each* $p \in X$.
5. $\mathfrak{M} \models [Tr(\bigvee X)]$ *iff* $\mathfrak{M} \models [Tr\ p]$ *for some* $p \in X$.

6. $\mathfrak{M} \models [Fa(\bigwedge X)]$ *iff* $\mathfrak{M} \models [Fa\ p]$ *for some* $p \in X$.

7. $\mathfrak{M} \models [Fa(\bigvee X)]$ *iff* $\mathfrak{M} \models [Fa\ p]$ *for each* $p \in X$.

Proof: These are routine calculations from the above definition. $\square$

So the question is, are there almost semantically closed models? First, let's say that a *semantical fact* σ of a model $\mathfrak{M}$ is any soa $\sigma \in \mathfrak{M}$ of the form $\langle Tr, p; 1 \rangle$ or $\langle Tr, p; 0 \rangle$. Then we have the following theorem.

Theorem 9 *Let $\mathfrak{M}$ be any weak model containing no semantical facts. There is a smallest model $\mathfrak{M}^* \supseteq \mathfrak{M}$ which is almost semantically closed.*

Proof: If $\mathfrak{M}$ contains no semantical facts, then it vacuously satisfies the witnessing condition. Consequently, this theorem follows from the next, which is more general. $\square$

The preceding theorem would answer the simple question about the existence of almost semantically closed models. But there is a more general question that is worth investigating, and which will prove much more useful: which weak models can be enlarged to almost semantically closed models? The answer, suggested in the proof above, is given in the following.

Theorem 10 (Closure Theorem) *Let $\mathfrak{M}$ be a weak model satisfying the witnessing condition. Then there is a smallest almost semantically closed model $\mathfrak{M}^* \supseteq \mathfrak{M}$.*

Proof: The idea here is to define, for any such weak model $\mathfrak{M}$, another weak model $\mathfrak{M}'$ containing $\mathfrak{M}$ and one additional "level" of semantical facts needed to close $\mathfrak{M}$. We then iterate this operation.

Let $\mathfrak{M}'$ be the collection of soa's σ satisfying one of the following:

1. $\sigma \in \mathfrak{M}$, or

2. $\sigma = \langle Tr, p; 1 \rangle$ where $\mathfrak{M} \models p$, or

3. $\sigma = \langle Tr, p; 0 \rangle$ where $\mathfrak{M} \models \bar{p}$.

We first show that $\mathfrak{M}'$ is a weak model. To prove this, we need to establish the following:

1. $\mathfrak{M}'$ contains no soa and its dual.

2. If $\langle Tr, p; 1 \rangle \in \mathfrak{M}'$ then $\mathfrak{M}' \models p$.

3. If $\langle Tr, p; 0 \rangle \in \mathfrak{M}'$ then $\mathfrak{M}' \not\models p$.

To prove (1), we first note that there is no p for which $\mathfrak{M} \models p$ and $\mathfrak{M} \models \overline{p}$, since $\mathfrak{M}$ is coherent. Consequently, we have not put any soa σ and its dual in $\mathfrak{M}'$ in steps (2) and (3) in the definition of $\mathfrak{M}'$. However, we must also check to see that we have not in either of these steps thrown in the dual of some element already in $\mathfrak{M}$. This amounts to checking:

4. If $\langle Tr, p; 0 \rangle \in \mathfrak{M}$ then $\mathfrak{M} \not\models p$, and

5. If $\langle Tr, p; 1 \rangle \in \mathfrak{M}$ then $\mathfrak{M} \not\models \overline{p}$.

These are immediate consequences of the definition of weak model.

The proof of (2) is almost immediate from the definition, so we prove (3). Assume $\langle Tr, p; 0 \rangle \in \mathfrak{M}'$. Then either $\langle Tr, p; 0 \rangle \in \mathfrak{M}$, or we have added this soa in step (3) because $\mathfrak{M} \models \overline{p}$. But if $\langle Tr, p; 0 \rangle \in \mathfrak{M}$, then $\mathfrak{M} \models \overline{p}$ by the witnessing condition. Thus in either case, $\mathfrak{M} \models \overline{p}$, and so $\mathfrak{M}' \models \overline{p}$. But if $\mathfrak{M}' \models p$ as well, then there would be an $s \subseteq \mathfrak{M}'$ such that $s \models p \wedge \overline{p}$. But then s contains some soa and its dual, by Lemma 5. But this contradicts (1).

Now simply close $\mathfrak{M}$ under this operation. It is routine to check that $\mathfrak{M}^*$, the closure, is a weak model and is almost semantically closed. $\square$

The following is an immediate consequence of the Closure Theorem.

Corollary 11 *A weak model is contained in an almost semantically closed model if and only if it is contained in a weak model that satisfies the witnessing condition.*

This corollary shows the importance of weak models that satisfy the witnessing condition. We will call such weak models *closable* weak models or *cw-models*. An important example of a closable weak model is any weak model containing no semantical facts. All such weak models satisfy the witnessing condition trivially, and so are closable, as was noted in Theorem 9.

We now use the closure conditions embodied in the notion of an almost semantically closed model to define the notions of a model and a maximal model of the world. It is in maximal models that truth and falsity are represented in a way that corresponds most closely to our pretheoretic intuitions.

Definition 9 A *model of the world* is any weak model $\mathfrak{M}$ that is almost semantically closed. A *maximal* model is a model $\mathfrak{M}$ that is not properly contained in any other model $\mathfrak{N}$.

Our decision to dub the almost semantically closed models simply *models* injects a slightly confusing twist into our terminology. In particular, note that weak models and even closable weak models are not always models. But then reputed logicians aren't always logicians, either.

Theorem 9 assures us that there are models, while the Closure Theorem gives us a sufficient condition for expanding weak models to models. We have seen that models are much better behaved than weak models. Proposition 8 gave us one example of the natural behavior of models not displayed by weak models in general. The next proposition gives us the tool that is needed to show that every closable weak model can be expanded to a maximal model.

Proposition 12 *The union of an increasing chain of closable weak models is a closable weak model.*

Proof: The proof of this is routine, given the observation that if $\mathfrak{M} \subseteq \mathfrak{N}$ and $\mathfrak{M} \models p$, then $\mathfrak{N} \models p$. This fact is immediately obvious from Exercise 28, page 68, but also follows easily from the original definition of *PROP*. □

Corollary 13 *Every model can be expanded to a maximal model. More generally, any closable weak model can be expanded to a maximal model.*

Proof: We have already seen that a cw-model can be expanded to a model. From here, one proceeds in a routine way by enumerating all states of affairs in a transfinite sequence, σ_α, where α ranges over the ordinals. Given a cw-model $\mathfrak{M}_\alpha$, we take $\mathfrak{M}_{\alpha+1}$ to be a cw-model containing $\mathfrak{M}_\alpha \cup \{\sigma_\alpha\}$ if there is such a cw-model, otherwise to be $\mathfrak{M}_\alpha$. We take unions at limit ordinals, as usual. Proposition 12 assures us that these unions, as well as the final limit, are all cw-models. The final limit must be a maximal model. □

Exercise 34 Show that the union of a chain of models is not necessarily a model.

Exercise 35 By contrast with the previous exercise, show that the union of an increasing chain $\{\mathfrak{M}_\alpha \mid \alpha \text{ an ordinal}\}$ of models, where the collection is indexed by all the ordinals, is itself a model. Use this to give an alternate proof of Corollary 13.

Kripke's construction and other closure conditions

We arrived at the witnessing condition and the notions of a model and a maximal model in an attempt to salvage, within the Russellian framework, the core of the intuition underlying the T-schema. An examination of the Russellian account reveals a striking parallel with Kripke's fixed point approach to the Liar. To bring out this parallel, let's briefly review Kripke's account.

Kripke deals with sentences, not propositions. His idea is that the set of true sentences must be a "fixed point" of some monotonic evaluation scheme. He illustrates his idea in some detail by examining the evaluation scheme associated with Kleene's strong three-valued logic. To show that there are fixed points, he uses this scheme to define a process whereby one starts with a standard, first-order model and a pair $\langle T_0, F_0 \rangle$ of sets of sentences, call them the initially true and initially false. Then Kripke uses the scheme to define a transfinite sequence of pairs $\langle T_\alpha, F_\alpha \rangle$ of sets of sentences, using conditions like: if $\varphi \in T_\alpha$ then $(\mathbf{True}\ \varphi) \in T_{\alpha+1}$ and $\neg(\mathbf{True}\ \varphi) \in F_{\alpha+1}$. In general, this process is not going to give you anything reasonable. For example, if you start with the Liar sentence in either T_0 or F_0, then it is going to get tossed back and forth willy nilly. But if you start out with the pair $\langle \emptyset, \emptyset \rangle$, or with certain other pairs satisfying a condition analogous to our witnessing condition, then you will arrive, in due course, at a fixed point[1] $\langle T_\infty, F_\infty \rangle$ where the two sets are disjoint, as they ought to be. In such fixed points, sentences like the Liar will not appear in either T_∞ or F_∞, and so are simply gaps in the final distribution of truth values.

If we think of the initial model as determining the truth values of sentences not involving truth, then the process of constructing the fixed point might be seen as the step by step assignment of

---

[1] That is, a pair $\langle T_\lambda, F_\lambda \rangle$ which is equal to $\langle T_{\lambda+1}, F_{\lambda+1} \rangle$.

truth values to sentences containing the truth predicate in increasingly complicated ways. When we think about it in this way, then
the natural starting point is with the pair $\langle \emptyset, \emptyset \rangle$, since the account
suggests that a semantical sentence must get its truth value "from
below," from the truth values of sentences with fewer nestings of
the truth predicate. This starting point yields what has come to
be known as *Kripke's least fixed point*. The least fixed point of the
Kleene evaluation scheme has arguably replaced Tarski's account
as the orthodox treament of the Liar.

However, this is not Kripke's own position, though it is often
thought to be. Kripke does not commit himself to the Kleene
scheme, or to the least fixed point of any scheme. His argument
is that truth should be a fixed point of some scheme or other. In
this regard, the Russellian account agrees completely with Kripke's
actual position, though not with the common misunderstanding of
his position. Our notion of an almost semantically closed model
is just a fixed point requirement on truth, of the kind Kripke en-
dorses, and our proof of the Closure Theorem corresponds closely
to his construction of a least fixed point.

The parallel between Kripke's construction and our proof of
the Closure Theorem is this. Look at the special case of the result
presented as Theorem 9, page 82, the case where we start with
a weak model $\mathfrak{M}$ containing no semantical facts. According to
this theorem, there is a smallest model $\mathfrak{M}^*$ containing $\mathfrak{M}$. If we
set aside sentences involving **Believes**, which Kripke doesn't deal
with, and look at the distribution of truth and falsity *internal* to
this model, we will find that it corresponds exactly to the least
fixed point on the Kleene evaluation scheme. That is, $\mathfrak{M}^*$ will
contain $\langle Tr, Exp(\varphi); 1 \rangle$ if and only if $\varphi \in T_\infty$, and similarly for
falsity.

There are two interesting points to be made about this parallel.
The first point has to do with how the truth value "gaps" appear in
the two treatments. Note that on our approach, every proposition
is either made true by $\mathfrak{M}$ or false by $\mathfrak{M}$ (i.e., not made true by $\mathfrak{M}$)
for any given weak model $\mathfrak{M}$. In this sense, our logic is strictly
two-valued, and so in this sense disagrees sharply with Kripke's.
However, if we look at the class of propositions that are true or
false *in* $\mathfrak{M}$, then gaps do appear, as they do in any of Kripke's
fixed points. For example, neither $\langle Tr, f; 1 \rangle$ nor $\langle Tr, f; 0 \rangle$ can be
in a weak model $\mathfrak{M}$. Weak models that are almost semantically

closed fill in many of these internal gaps. For example, "internal" and "external" truth are coextensive in such models. On the other hand, internal and external falsity are not coextensive in any model, again due to Liar-like propositions. Now, we do not equate the pretheoretic notion of the nontruth of p (captured by $\mathfrak{M} \not\models p$) with the truth of its negation ($\mathfrak{M} \models \bar{p}$). But if we did, the inevitable internal gaps would appear as genuine truth value gaps, and, indeed, some form of three-valued logic would then hold directly in our semantics. However, the standard "undefined" interpretation of Kleene's third value would be quite unnatural in the Russellian account, since for a proposition not to be true is simply for it not to be true.

Kripke seems to suggest in footnotes that the presence of truth value gaps in his treatment might be linked to the attribution of truth to sentences rather than propositions. From this perspective, gaps would arise when a sentence fails to express a proposition, in which case the sentence would acquire neither the value true nor the value false. Such an account of truth value gaps would be committed to the claim that the Liar sentence simply cannot be used to express a proposition. As we have already observed, such an account would be incomplete without a principled explanation of why this particular sentence has this property. Needless to say, on our treatment of the Russellian Liar, the "internal" gaps cannot be chalked up to the failure of sentences to express propositions.

A point of divergence between our approach and other recent treatments concerns the question of how truth comes to be assigned as it does. Many readers of Kripke's article have come to see the problem posed by the Liar as one of finding the right evaluation scheme and the right fixed point to generate an intuitively satisfactory definition of truth. In contrast, we do not see ourselves as even aiming at a definition of truth, but rather as investigating the consequences of some very basic intuitions about the property of truth. In this way, our Russellian account is compatible with many competing conceptions of truth: indeed any that would satisfy the basic conditions in our definition of a model.

We conclude this section with some general observations about the relation between the pretheoretic T-schema and our three closure conditions, T-closure, F-closure, and N-closure, observations relevant to any comparison of the Russellian account with other accounts, including Kripke's. At first sight it seems odd that the one schema could generate three nonequivalent closure conditions. To see why this happens, we can start with the closure conditions and work back toward the intuitive schema. For ease of reference, we repeat the three conditions here.

(T) $\mathfrak{M} \models [Tr\ p]$ iff $\mathfrak{M} \models p$.

(N) $\mathfrak{M} \models [Fa\ p]$ iff $\mathfrak{M} \models \bar{p}$.

(F) $\mathfrak{M} \models [Fa\ p]$ iff $\mathfrak{M} \not\models p$.

The first thing to notice about these closure conditions is that they are conditions relating models and propositions, and so are stated at a higher ("meta") level. (Indeed, if we were dealing with sentences rather than propositions, these conditions would be expressible only in the metalanguage, but since we are dealing with propositions, the object language/metalanguage distinction is inappropriate.) To get from these conditions to their lower level correlates, to conditions not involving the notion of a model making a proposition true, we need to suppress explicit reference to the world $\mathfrak{M}$ and the relation $\models$ between world and proposition. Before making this move, though, we should also note that in their "meta" formulations, both T- and N-closure are positive conditions, in the sense that they express necessary and sufficient conditions on the positive extent of the $\models$ relation. By contrast, F-closure expresses a necessary and sufficient condition between the positive extent of $\models$, on the one hand, and the negative extent of $\models$, on the other.

The correlates of the first two closure conditions are expressed as follows, by dropping reference to $\mathfrak{M}$ and $\models$, and omitting our abbreviation "$[Fa\ p]$."

(T$_*$) $[Tr\ p]$ iff p.

(N$_*$) $\overline{[Tr\ p]}$ iff $\bar{p}$.

Formulated in this way, it would seem that N$_*$ follows from T$_*$ by simply negating each side. Since N-closure doesn't follow from T-closure, this shows that some sort of conflation has taken place in the move from the higher to the lower level versions of these conditions. However, both conditions are satisfiable, and so this fact may not seem too significant. But now consider the closest correlate of the third closure condition.

(F$_*$) $\overline{[Tr\ p]}$ iff $\bar{p}$.

F_* is the very same schema as N_*, even though N-closure is a satisfiable condition while F-closure is not. This is an extremely misleading conflation, and results from collapsing both $\mathfrak{M} \models \overline{p}$ and $\mathfrak{M} \not\models p$ to the same thing.

Again, if we were dealing with sentences rather than propositions, and if the object language contained the predicate **True**, then T_*, N_*, and F_* would be expressible in the object language, unlike the original conditions T, N, and F. This is an extremely important point, since many sentential accounts of the Liar claim to satisfy the intuitions underlying the T-schema, but then only test those intuitions against an object language version of that schema, a condition similar to T_*. Such accounts at best satisfy T-closure and N-closure; they do not satisfy the important intuition underlying F-closure, whether or not there is an adequate way to cast this condition in the object language. Frequently, this failure will emerge in the form of a Strengthened Liar: a critic, observing that the Liar is really *not* true (i.e., $\mathfrak{M} \not\models f$), can appeal to the intuition captured by F-closure, and ask why some object language version of this observation (corresponding to our $[Fa\ f]$) doesn't come out true. Of course it can't, since it would be none other than the Liar itself.

Exercise 36 In light of the above discussion, go back and reanalyze the argument on page 21 that purports to derive a contradiction directly from the propositional version of the T-schema.

Witnessing functions

Recall that one of our long-term aims in this book is to relate the two treatments, the Austinian and the Russellian, so that we can see what each has to say about sentences that express problematic propositions like the Liar. To do this right, we need to analyze those sentences that express problematic propositions, and this in turn calls for an analysis of just when a proposition is "problematic." In the Russellian case, this can be reduced to questions of when a given proposition p is true in some model $\mathfrak{M}$, or more generally, of when p is true in some extension $\mathfrak{N}$ of $\mathfrak{M}$. It turns out that the Closure Theorem allows us to formulate such a test using what we'll call witnessing functions. But the test is a bit technical, and so the reader may want to postpone this section until Chapter 11.

Prior to that, the only uses we make of witnessing functions are in the proofs of some simple results and in a few exercises. But in both cases they can be avoided fairly easily.

To understand the following definition, it helps to recall a common technique in working with ordinary propositional logic. Sometimes, rather than construct a whole truth table, one "works backwards" from a proposition and a desired truth value to see what values must be assigned to the constituents in order for the original proposition to get the target value. The notion of a witnessing function captures this idea in the present context. It is also analogous to the notion of a consistency property (sometimes called a Hintikka set) used in the model theory of infinitary logic.[2]

Definition 10

1. A *witnessing function* w is a partial function from *PROP* to *SIT* satisfying the following conditions:

   - If $p = [a \ H \ c] \in dom(w)$, then $\langle H, a, c; 1 \rangle \in w(p)$;
   - If $p = \overline{[a \ H \ c]} \in dom(w)$, then $\langle H, a, c; 0 \rangle \in w(p)$;
   - If $p = [a \ Bel \ q] \in dom(w)$, then $\langle Bel, a, q; 1 \rangle \in w(p)$;
   - If $p = \overline{[a \ Bel \ q]} \in dom(w)$, then $\langle Bel, a, q; 0 \rangle \in w(p)$;
   - If $p = [\bigwedge P] \in dom(w)$, then $P \subseteq dom(w)$ and for each $q \in P$, $w(q) \subseteq w(p)$;
   - If $p = [\bigvee P] \in dom(w)$, then for some $q \in (P \cap dom(w))$, $w(q) \subseteq w(p)$;
   - If $p = [Tr \ q] \in dom(w)$, then $q \in dom(w)$ and $w(q) \cup \{\langle Tr, q; 1 \rangle\} \subseteq w(p)$;
   - If $p = [Fa \ q] \in dom(w)$, then $\overline{q} \in dom(w)$; and $w(\overline{q}) \cup \{\langle Tr, q; 0 \rangle\} \subseteq w(p)$.

2. A witnessing function w is *coherent* if the set $\mathfrak{M} = \bigcup \{w(p) \mid p \in dom(w)\}$ is coherent. More generally, the witnessing function w is *compatible with* a set $\mathfrak{M}_0$ if the set $\mathfrak{M} = \mathfrak{M}_0 \cup \bigcup \{w(p) \mid p \in dom(w)\}$ is coherent.

3. A proposition p is *consistent* if it is in the domain of some coherent witnessing function w; it is *consistent with* $\mathfrak{M}_0$ if it is in the domain of some witnessing function that is compatible with $\mathfrak{M}_0$.

---

[2] See, e.g., Keisler (1971).

Example 9 Consider the Truth-teller $t = [\mathit{Tr}\ t]$. If we let $w_0(t) = \{\langle \mathit{Tr}, t; 1\rangle\}$, then w_0 is a coherent witnessing function for t. On the other hand, if we let $w_1(\bar{t}) = \{\langle \mathit{Tr}, t; 0\rangle\}$, then w_1 is also a coherent witnessing function for the negation of t.

Example 10 There is no coherent witnessing function w defined on either the Liar f or its negation $\bar{f}$. For example, if $w(f)$ is defined, then $\langle \mathit{Tr}, f; 0\rangle \in w(f)$ and $w(\bar{f}) \subseteq w(f)$. But $w(\bar{f})$ must contain the soa $\langle \mathit{Tr}, f; 1\rangle$.

The definition of consistent proposition is justified by the following theorem.

Theorem 14 (Model Existence Theorem) *A proposition p is consistent if and only if there is a model $\mathfrak{M}$ such that p is true in $\mathfrak{M}$. More generally, the proposition p is consistent with a model $\mathfrak{M}_0$ iff there is a model $\mathfrak{M} \supseteq \mathfrak{M}_0$ such that p is true in $\mathfrak{M}$.*

Proof: Neither half of this proof is very difficult. For the ($\Leftarrow$) half we need to show how to extract a witnessing function from a model. For the ($\Rightarrow$) half, we show how to extract a closable weak model from a witnessing function and then apply the Closure Theorem.

($\Leftarrow$) First assume that p is true in some model $\mathfrak{M} \supseteq \mathfrak{M}_0$. We can assume that $\mathfrak{M}$ is a set, without loss of generality. Let P be a set of propositions containing p and closed under the taking of constituents and the formation of negations. Let $Q = \{q \in P \mid \mathit{True}_{\mathfrak{M}}(q)\}$. Let $w(q) = \mathfrak{M}$ for all $q \in Q$. It is easy to see that this is a witnessing function which is compatible with $\mathfrak{M}_0$.

($\Rightarrow$) Assume that p is consistent with $\mathfrak{M}_0$, i.e., that there is a witnessing function w_0 defined on p and compatible with $\mathfrak{M}_0$. We can extend w_0 to a witnessing function w_1 defined on $[\mathit{Tr}\ p]$ which is also compatible with $\mathfrak{M}_0$. Let $\mathfrak{M}_1$ be the union of the range of w_1. It is easy to see that $\mathfrak{M}_1$ is a cw-model, and so contained in some model $\mathfrak{M}$. Since $\langle \mathit{Tr}, p; 1\rangle \in \mathfrak{M}$, $\mathit{True}_{\mathfrak{M}}(p)$. $\square$

Exercise 37 Construct a witnessing function for the Liar cycle p_1, p_2, q, i.e., a witnessing function with all three propositions in its domain. Show that any such witnessing function must be incoherent.

Exercise 38 Consider the proposition $p = [a \ H \ 3\clubsuit] \vee [Tr \ p]$. Use witnessing functions to show: (i) the proposition p is true in any model $\mathfrak{M}$ where a has the three of clubs; (ii) there are models $\mathfrak{N}$ where a does not have the three of clubs but the proposition p is true.

Exercise 39 (Extended Model Existence Theorem) Let us call a set P of propositions *consistent* if it is a subset of the domain of some coherent witnessing function w; it is *consistent with* $\mathfrak{M}_0$ if it is a subset of the domain of some witnessing function that is compatible with $\mathfrak{M}_0$. Show that the following is a consequence of the Model Existence Theorem:

> *A set P of propositions is consistent with a model $\mathfrak{M}_0$ iff there is a model $\mathfrak{M} \supseteq \mathfrak{M}_0$ such that each proposition in P is true in $\mathfrak{M}$.*

This result will be used below.

Saul Kripke, in private correspondence, has told us that he has independently obtained results similar to the above in his work on semantic tableaux and the Strong Kleene scheme. These will be published in due course.

Paradoxical Russellian propositions

No Russellian proposition is paradoxical in the sense of both being made true and being made false (i.e., not being made true) by a model. And so, of course, no proposition is both true in and false in any model. But propositions like the Liar still behave in a very puzzling way. Although they are made false by every model, this must somehow be treated as a second-class fact, one that is not part of the model itself. For these propositions can never have a truth value *in* a model, even in a maximal model. Following Kripke, we use this feature to define the paradoxical propositions.

Definition 11

- A proposition p is *paradoxical in* a model $\mathfrak{M}$ if for any maximal model $\mathfrak{N} \supseteq \mathfrak{M}$, neither $True_{\mathfrak{N}}(p)$ nor $False_{\mathfrak{N}}(p)$.

- By a *classical* proposition p we mean one that is not paradoxical in any model, i.e., for each maximal model $\mathfrak{M}$, either $True_{\mathfrak{M}}(p)$ or $False_{\mathfrak{M}}(p)$.

- Propositions that are paradoxical in some models but not in others are called *contingently paradoxical*.

Example 11 The Liar is intrinsically (i.e., not contingently) paradoxical. The following proposition, however, is contingently paradoxical:

$$p = [a \ H \ A\spadesuit] \vee [Fa \ p].$$

This proposition is true in those maximal models where a has the ace of spades, and paradoxical in the rest.

The following is a simple but useful reformulation of some of the notions just introduced.

Proposition 15

- *Suppose $\mathfrak{M}$ is maximal and p is not paradoxical in $\mathfrak{M}$. Then $\mathfrak{M} \not\models p$ iff $\mathfrak{M} \models \bar{p}$.*

- *A proposition p is classical iff its denial implies its negation, that is, for each maximal $\mathfrak{M}$, if $\mathfrak{M} \not\models p$, then $\mathfrak{M} \models \bar{p}$.*

Classical propositions are those for which the difference between being made true or false by a maximal model and being true or false *in* the model can be ignored. These propositions satisfy classical propositional logic in its entirety.

Theorem 16

1. *The Truth-teller is classical.*

2. *The Truth-teller is true in some maximal models, false in others.*

Proof: Let us first show (1). Let $\mathfrak{M}$ be any maximal model such that $\mathfrak{M} \not\models t$. We need to show that $\mathfrak{M} \models \bar{t}$, i.e., that $\mathfrak{M} \models [Fa \ t]$. Let w_1 be the witnessing function defined in Example 9, page 91. Since $\mathfrak{M} \not\models t$, w_1 is compatible with $\mathfrak{M}$. But then, by the Model Existence Theorem and the maximality of $\mathfrak{M}$, $\mathfrak{M} \models [Fa \ t]$, as desired. To show (2), note that both w_0 and w_1 from Example 9 are coherent, so the result follows from the Model Existence Theorem. $\square$

Part (2) of the above supports the intuition that the truth of the Truth-teller is up for grabs. Indeed, that result could be strengthened, without changing the proof, to show that if you start with any weak model containing no semantical facts, then it can be extended both to models in which t is true, and to models in which t is false.

Not only is the Truth-teller classical, so is any proposition you can build out of it using standard operations in a noncircular way. This is implied by the following closure properties that hold for classical propositions.

Proposition 17

1. *The collection of classical propositions contain all nonseman-tical atomic propositions, i.e., all atomic propositions not containing Tr as an immediate constituent.*

2. *The classical propositions are closed under* $\bigwedge, \bigvee$ *and the formation of negations.*

3. p *is classical iff* $[Tr\ p]$ *is classical, iff* $[Fa\ p]$ *is classical.*

4. *These same closure conditions hold of the propositions that are nonparadoxical in a given maximal model.*

Proof: Routine verification. $\square$

Although the Truth-teller is classical, it is also quite different from a proposition like:

$$p = [Tr\ [\text{Max } H\ 3\Diamond]].$$

While these are both propositions about propositions, the truth of the latter is automatically determined by nonsemantical facts, unlike that of the former. Using the concepts already at hand, it is easy to distinguish these two kinds of classical propositions. We will say that a proposition is *grounded over* a closable weak model $\mathfrak{M}$ if it has a truth value in the smallest model containing $\mathfrak{M}$ (in other words, it is either true in that model or false in that model). In contrast, we say that a proposition *has a determinate truth value over* $\mathfrak{M}$ if it has a single truth value in all maximal models containing $\mathfrak{M}$.[3] Notice that any proposition that is grounded over $\mathfrak{M}$ automatically has a determinate truth value over $\mathfrak{M}$, but the converse does not hold. For any closable model $\mathfrak{M}$, this gives us

---

[3]These definitions parallel those given in Kripke (1975).

a three-way classification of classical propositions: those that are grounded, those that are ungrounded but have determinate values, and those that do not have determinate truth values.

Let's look at examples of all three sorts of propositions. Let $\mathfrak{M}$ be a closable weak model containing no semantical facts. Then the Truth-teller t does not have a determinate truth value over $\mathfrak{M}$ (and so of course is not grounded over $\mathfrak{M}$, either). On the other hand, if $\mathfrak{M}$ contains an soa of the form $\langle H, \text{Max}, 3\Diamond; i\rangle$, then the proposition p above is grounded over $\mathfrak{M}$ (and so has a determinate truth value, as well). For an example of an ungrounded proposition with a determinate truth value, consider the proposition:

$$[Tr\ t] \vee [Fa\ t].$$

The fact that this proposition is ungrounded over $\mathfrak{M}$ follows from the proof of Theorem 16, since the proof shows that t will be true in some extensions of $\mathfrak{M}$ and false in others. But the proposition has a determinate truth value, namely, true, by part (1) of Theorem 16.

Finally, we should point out that there are some minor pitfalls lurking in the relation between sentences and the propositions they express, due mainly to our convention of using a formula $\varphi(\textbf{this})$, containing a loose **this**, as an abbreviation for the associated sentence $\downarrow\varphi(\textbf{this})$. For example, the sentence

(5.1)   **(Claire Has $A\spadesuit \vee$ True(this))**

expresses a classical proposition. However, there are models in which the proposition expressed by 5.1 is true, but where neither disjunct of 5.1 expresses a true proposition, that is, where neither of the following express truths.

(5.2)   **Claire Has $A\spadesuit$**

(5.3)   **True(this)**

The reason for this is the shift in scope of **this**. By contrast,

(5.4)   **(Claire Has $A\spadesuit \vee \downarrow$True(this))**

expresses a proposition which is true just in case at least one of the propositions expressed by the two disjuncts is true. In general, real sentences that express classical propositions have the expected logical behavior.

Exercise 40 The following proposition is contingently paradoxical:

$$p = \overline{[[\text{Claire } H \ A\spadesuit] \wedge [Fa \ p]]}.$$

What state of affairs is its paradoxicality contingent upon?

Exercise 41 Recall the following two propositions from Exercise 31 on page 74.

$$p = \overline{[[\ Tr \ p] \wedge [\ Tr \ q]]}$$
$$q = [[\ Tr \ p] \wedge [\ Tr \ q]]$$

Suppose $\mathfrak{M}$ is a cw-model containing no semantical facts. Are p and q grounded over $\mathfrak{M}$? Do they have determinate truth values over $\mathfrak{M}$?

6

Consequences of the Russellian Account

Further examples analyzed

It's time we examined some of the other examples given in Chapter 1, to see how they come out on this conception of propositions. Let's first look at the *Liar cycles*. This is one of the cases where things turn out differently on the Russellian and Austinian conceptions. We leave the verification of the following to the reader, since it simply uses the standard reasoning about the Liar cycle.

Proposition 18 *Let $p_1, \ldots, p_n, q$ be a Liar cycle as described in Example 4 on page 65. Then each of these propositions is intrinsically paradoxical.*

Next, consider the case in which two people each assert the following, using "that proposition" to refer to the other's claim:

This proposition is true but that proposition is false.

What we want are propositions p_0 and p_1 satisfying the following equations.

$$p_0 = [Tr\ p_0] \wedge [Fa\ p_1]$$
$$p_1 = [Tr\ p_1] \wedge [Fa\ p_0]$$

Intuitively, we would expect these to be perfectly classical propositions, akin to the Truth-teller. In a maximal model, one should be

true and the other false. Further, there should be maximal models
that go each way: there should be models in which p_0 is true (and
hence p_1 false), and others in which p_1 is true (and hence p_0 false).

Unfortunately, this isn't quite how things work out. AFA does
guarantee that there are such propositions, but it guarantees more.
Namely, it guarantees that they are the very *same* proposition.
Why? Because they have exactly the same structure, and so the
sets that model them will in fact be identical. So what we really
have is just the proposition that claims of itself that it is both true
and false—a proposition that is false in every maximal model.

There are two ways we might view this collapse. According
to one, the collapse is an artifact of our modeling process: things
that should be distinct are here modeled by the same set. This is
similar to the widely recognized problem with using sets to model
properties, where distinct properties that have the same extensions
end up being modeled by the same set. On this line, we should
really allow ourselves more freedom in modeling propositions. This
would be easy enough to arrange, say, by simply allowing ourselves
to "index" propositions. If we did this, the example would work
out just as our intuitions dictate.

We have not allowed ourselves this freedom, partly because the
single example doesn't seem important enough to complicate the
whole discussion to this extent. And in any event, a similar point
can be made by looking at a slight modification of the example,
where the propositions satisfy the following equations.

$$q_0 = [Tr \; q_0] \wedge [Fa \; q_1]$$
$$q_1 = [Tr \; Tr \; q_1] \wedge [Fa \; q_0]$$

These have distinct structure, and so are distinct. Further, they
are both classical and have opposite truth values in all maximal
models. But they do not have determinate truth values: there are
models in which q_0 is true and q_1 false, and models in which the
converse holds.

It's possible, though, that something else is going on in the
collapse of p_0 and p_1. Perhaps the collapse is not just an artifact of
the modeling, but rather indicates something important about the
nature of propositions. What, after all, gives rise to the intuition
that there are *two* propositions in this case, rather than one? Or, to
put it differently, what would the two different "indices" represent,
if we were to introduce such indices into the model? Presumably,

the intuition that there are two distinct propositions stems from the fact that there are two utterances, involving two speakers, and each speaker is claiming something that has the other person, or the other utterance, as a constituent. In other words, the index must represent something about the specific utterances that makes the propositions distinct. This way of looking at it is in fact one motivation for the Austinian view of propositions, which we will turn to soon.

Next, consider the example of Max believing that that very belief is false. This was modeled by the Russellian proposition:

$$p = [\text{Max } Bel \; p] \wedge [Fa \; p].$$

This proposition is contingently paradoxical. It is false in those maximal models where Max does not believe p, paradoxical in those where he does believe p. It would be a mistake to think that this has much at all to do with belief, though, since the observation is perfectly general. Indeed, we can bring various examples of contingently paradoxical propositions together into a single observation, one that covers both this example and Example 11 from the last chapter.

Proposition 19 *Suppose that $p = q \vee [Fa \; p]$, and that $r = q \wedge [Fa \; r]$, where q is contingent (i.e., true in some models, false in others).[1] Then p and r are contingently paradoxical. Indeed, p is true in models in which q is true, paradoxical in others, while r is false in models in which q is false, paradoxical in others.*

The reasoning used to establish this proposition is relevant to the analysis of examples like Kripke's *Contingent Liar Cycle*, described in Chapter 1. Consider the three propositions given by the following equations.

$$p_1 = [\text{Max } H \; 3\clubsuit]$$
$$p_2 = [Tr \; q]$$
$$q = [Fa \; p_1] \vee [Fa \; p_2]$$

If $\mathfrak{M}$ is a model containing the fact $\langle H, \text{Max}, 3\clubsuit; 0 \rangle$, then it's easy to see that p_1 will be false in $\mathfrak{M}$ while p_2 and q are true in $\mathfrak{M}$. However, both p_2 and q will be made false by any model that

---

[1]It may be the case that either or both of p and r are constituents of q.

contains the fact $\langle H, \text{Max}, 3\clubsuit; 1 \rangle$, but will not be false *in* any such model. Hence they are paradoxical in such models, and so are contingently paradoxical according to our definition.

While we haven't included the conditional in our treatment, we can still use Proposition 19 to shed some light on *Löb's Paradox*. Recall that this paradox involved the following sentence:

(δ) If this proposition is true, then Max has the three of clubs.

If we simply give the conditional the material reading,[2] then we end up with δ expressing the proposition:

$$p = [Fa\ p] \vee [\text{Max}\ H\ 3\clubsuit].$$

By the above result, this is contingently paradoxical; it is true if Max has the three of clubs, but paradoxical otherwise. This squares with the intuition that the proposition expressed by δ is paradoxical if Max does not have the three of clubs.

Let's see what happens with *Gupta's Puzzle*. Assume that we are in a model $\mathfrak{M}$ in which Claire has the ace of clubs and Max does not; that is, $\langle H, \text{Claire}, A\clubsuit; 1 \rangle$ and $\langle H, \text{Max}, A\clubsuit; 0 \rangle$ are in $\mathfrak{M}$. Consider the following five propositions, the first three asserted by R, the last two asserted by P.

$$R\text{'s claims:}$$
$$r_1 = [\text{Max}\ H A\clubsuit]$$
$$r_2 = [Tr\ p_1] \wedge [Tr\ p_2]$$
$$r_3 = \overline{r_2}$$

$$P\text{'s claims:}$$
$$p_1 = [\text{Claire}\ H A\clubsuit]$$
$$p_2 = [[Fa\ r_1] \wedge [Fa\ r_2]] \vee [[Fa\ r_1] \wedge [Fa\ r_3]]$$

If $\mathfrak{M}$ is maximal, then the intuitive reasoning that Gupta used to show that p_2 is true, and hence that r_2 is true and r_3 false, carries over intact. We know that r_2 and r_3 cannot both be true in $\mathfrak{M}$, since they make contradictory claims. Indeed, it's not hard to show that one or the other must be false in $\mathfrak{M}$ (see Exercise 49). In

---

[2]We don't in fact think the material reading provides an adequate treatment of the conditional. If we wanted an account that dealt more adequately with conditionals, we would adopt a treatment like that described in Barwise (1986).

which case, p_1 and p_2 are both true in $\mathfrak{M}$. Consequently, r_2 is true in $\mathfrak{M}$ while r_1 and r_3 are false in $\mathfrak{M}$. This was the result desired.

Another way to put this is that all five of the propositions have determinate truth values over any model $\mathfrak{M}$ containing the two card facts $\langle H, \text{Claire}, A\spadesuit; 1 \rangle$ and $\langle H, \text{Max}, A\spadesuit; 0 \rangle$, and that these values are the expected ones. However, they are not grounded over all such models. (See Exercise 49 for a further elaboration.)

Finally, let us return to the *Strengthened Liar*. In $\mathcal{L}$ these are expressed by the following pair of sentences, using the extended semantics.

(λ_1) ¬**True(this)**

(λ_2) ¬**True(that$_1$)**

One intuition about this case is that the second of the above sentences expresses a proposition closely related to the Liar proposition. This intuition is upheld, in that λ_2 expresses, in the Russellian semantics, the very same proposition as λ_1. Unfortunately, this also seems to involve an embarrassment for the account. For the Liar proposition is indeed not true, but there is no true proposition which expresses this fact. This expressive limitation is a serious defect in the Russellian account.

There are two things going on here that should be kept separate. One is that both λ_1 and λ_2 express the very same proposition, and so there is no way for one to be true, the other not. But this might be an artifact of our particular way of modeling propositions. The other is more serious, though. Since the Liar is only made false *by* the world, but the fact of its being false cannot be *in* the world, there can be no true proposition that expresses that the Liar is not true. This seems intrinsic to any account that adheres to anything like the basic line of the Russellian view.

Exercise 42 Recall the following sentences from Exercise 30 on page 73. Using witnessing functions, classify these propositions according to whether they are classical, contingently paradoxical, or intrinsically paradoxical. How does this square with your earlier intuitions?

1. **((Claire Has 5$\heartsuit$) $\wedge$ ¬(True(this)))**

2. **((Claire Has 5$\heartsuit$) $\vee$ ¬(True(this)))**

3. $((\mathbf{Claire\ Has\ } 5\heartsuit) \wedge \neg(\mathbf{Claire\ Has\ } 5\heartsuit)) \wedge \neg\mathbf{True(this)}$

4. $((\mathbf{Claire\ Has\ } 5\heartsuit) \wedge (\mathbf{Max\ Has\ } 5\heartsuit)) \wedge \neg\mathbf{True(this)}$

5. $((\mathbf{Claire\ Has\ } 5\heartsuit) \vee \neg(\mathbf{Claire\ Has\ } 5\heartsuit)) \vee \neg\mathbf{True(this)}$

6. $((\mathbf{Claire\ Has\ } 5\heartsuit) \vee \neg(\mathbf{Claire\ Has\ } 5\heartsuit)) \wedge \neg\mathbf{True(this)}$

7. $\neg\mathbf{True(this)} \vee {\downarrow}\mathbf{True(this)}$

8. $\neg\mathbf{True(this)} \vee \mathbf{True(this)}$

9. $\neg\mathbf{True(this)} \wedge {\downarrow}\mathbf{True(this)}$

10. $\neg\mathbf{True(this)} \wedge \mathbf{True(this)}$

11. $\neg\mathbf{True}(\neg\mathbf{True(this)})$

12. $\mathbf{True}(\neg\mathbf{True}(\neg\mathbf{True(this)}))$

13. $\neg\mathbf{True}(\mathbf{True}(\neg\mathbf{True(this)}))$

14. $\neg\mathbf{True}(\mathbf{True}({\downarrow}\neg\mathbf{True(this)}))$

Exercise 43 Consider the propositions p_1, p_2 expressed by the following sentences:

- $(\mathbf{Claire\ Has\ } 5\diamondsuit) \vee \mathbf{True(this)}$
- $(\mathbf{Claire\ Has\ } 5\diamondsuit) \vee {\downarrow}\mathbf{True(this)}$

Show that these are both classical, and that neither implies the other, in that there are maximal models $\mathfrak{M}$ in which p_1 is true, p_2 false, and maximal models $\mathfrak{N}$ in which p_2 is true, p_1 false. (Hint: Use witnessing functions.) In particular, these propositions do not have determinate truth values over all models in which Claire does not have the five of diamonds.

Exercise 44 Now consider the two propositions q_1, q_2 expressed by the following sentences:

- $(\mathbf{Claire\ Has\ } 5\diamondsuit) \vee \neg\mathbf{True(this)}$
- $(\mathbf{Claire\ Has\ } 5\diamondsuit) \vee {\downarrow}\neg\mathbf{True(this)}$

The previous exercise would suggest that there is a semantic difference between these propositions.

1. Show that q_1 and q_2 are both contingently paradoxical.

2. Show that by contrast with the previous exercise, q_1 and q_2 are true in exactly the same maximal models. This contrast suggests that a significant distinction gets lost in maximal models.

3. Show that there are cw-models $\mathfrak{M}$ *in* which q_1 is true, and where q_2 is made true, but is not true in $\mathfrak{M}$. Similarly, show that there are cw-models $\mathfrak{N}$ in which q_2 is true, but where q_1 is made true by $\mathfrak{N}$ but is not true in $\mathfrak{N}$.

Exercise 45 Each of the examples we have given of a contingently paradoxical proposition p has the following property: if $\mathfrak{M}_1$ and $\mathfrak{M}_2$ are maximal models in which p is not paradoxical, then p has the same truth value in each of $\mathfrak{M}_1$ and $\mathfrak{M}_2$, i.e., $True_{\mathfrak{M}_1}(p)$ iff $True_{\mathfrak{M}_2}(p)$. Give an example of a contingently paradoxical proposition for which this fails.

Exercise 46 The Liar proposition is made false by every weak model, but it is not true in, or false in, any weak model. By way of contrast, show that one of the intrinsically paradoxical propositions from Exercise 42, page 101, is true in some weak model. This is another reason for rejecting them as an adequate representation of the world.

Exercise 47 Show that every model is properly contained in some weak model.

Exercise 48 In Exercise 49, we will work out the details of our treatment of Gupta's Puzzle. Here we present a simpler version where it is boiled down to its basic structure.

1. Consider the following sequence of sentences.

$$\varphi_1 : \quad \textbf{True}(\textbf{that}_3)$$
$$\varphi_2 : \quad \neg\textbf{True}(\textbf{that}_3)$$
$$\varphi_3 : \quad \neg\textbf{True}(\textbf{that}_1) \vee \neg\textbf{True}(\textbf{that}_2)$$

Let r_1, r_2, p be the sequence of propositions expressed by this sequence of sentences. Give equations that describe these propositions.

2. Show that any closable weak model is compatible with the following soa's.

$$\langle Tr, r_1; 1 \rangle$$
$$\langle Tr, r_2; 0 \rangle$$
$$\langle Tr, p; 1 \rangle$$

3. Use witnessing functions to show that r_1 and p are true in any maximal model, and that r_2 is false in any maximal model. Thus, all of these propositions have determinate truth values.

4. Consider the smallest model $\mathfrak{M}_0$ containing some set of non-semantical facts. Show that r_1, r_2, and p are made false by $\mathfrak{M}_0$. Hence none of these propositions is grounded, though they have determinate truth values.

Exercise 49 This exercise will help the reader flesh out the discussion of Gupta's Puzzle. Let

$$\mathfrak{M}_0 = \{ \langle H, \text{Claire}, A\clubsuit; 1 \rangle, \langle H, \text{Max}, A\clubsuit; 0 \rangle \}.$$

1. Find a sequence of five sentences of $\mathcal{L}$ which mutually express the five propositions r_1, r_2, r_3, p_1, p_2 from the discussion of Gupta's Puzzle.

2. Show that if $\mathfrak{M}$ is a closable model containing $\mathfrak{M}_0$, then there is a witnessing function w compatible with $\mathfrak{M}$ with the following in its domain: $[Fa \ r_1], [Tr \ r_2], [Fa \ r_3], [Tr \ p_1]$, and $[Tr \ p_2]$.

3. Conclude that if $\mathfrak{M}$ is a maximal model containing $\mathfrak{M}_0$, then r_1 and r_3 are false in $\mathfrak{M}$, while r_2, p_1, and p_2 are true in $\mathfrak{M}$. Hence all these have determinate truth values over $\mathfrak{M}_0$.

4. Let $\mathfrak{M}_1$ be the smallest model containing $\mathfrak{M}_0$. Show that each of r_2, r_3, and p_2 are made false by $\mathfrak{M}_1$. Conclude that these propositions are not grounded over $\mathfrak{M}_0$.

The problem with the Russellian account

We take the various results of this chapter as showing that, within the Russellian account, maximal models are as generous as possible to our basic intuitions about truth and falsity. Further generousity leads to paradox. The Gupta Puzzle is especially relevant here, since it shows us that we need something approaching maximality to account for some very basic intuitions, in particular the intuition that propositions can have truth values even though they aren't grounded. What's more, in maximal models classical logic is perfectly legitimate as long as we restrict ourselves to classical propositions, a class that includes many circular propositions.

Still, there is something very unsatisfactory about the Russellian account. For there is one, rather deeply held intuition about the Liar that is not respected. Intuitively, one feels that once we realize that the Liar is made false by a model $\mathfrak{M}$, we ought to be able to add its falsity $\langle Tr, f; 0 \rangle$ to the model $\mathfrak{M}$. Or, to put it more poignantly, once we see that the Liar really *isn't* true, it seems that this fact should itself be a genuine feature of the world, a feature capable of influencing the truth or falsity of propositions. But of course it cannot be. For if it were, this would in turn make the Liar true, just as the intuitive reasoning predicts, and we would then have a contradiction, a violation of an even more closely held intuition.

This problem is deeply embedded in the Russellian account. In giving this account, we started out with a straightforward treatment of the relation $\models$, one that involves little more than the usual truth table semantics for propositional logic. We then placed extremely minimal conditions on weak models, our preliminary representations of the world. First, we demanded that weak models be coherent, since nothing can simultaneously have a property and fail to have it. Second, we required that they never make *positive* mistakes in their distribution of the property of truth: the facts concerning truth that they actually contain should indeed be facts supported by the $\models$ relation earlier defined. With weak models, we imposed no demands of a more stringent sort, even though further conditions are needed to fully capture our pretheoretic intuitions about truth. Yet even at this point, the die had been cast: the counterintuitive partiality of the world was a consequence of the minimal conditions already imposed.

What are we to make of this odd consequence of the Russellian account? If we take it seriously, it does indeed yield a diagnosis of the paradox, but a rather unsettling one. From this perspective, where our intuitive reasoning goes wrong is in thinking the world encompasses everything that is the case. Give up this assumption, and the paradox is avoided: the Liar is not true, but this fact cannot be a fact in the world, a fact that can be truly described. But this is a rather big assumption to give up. And, as we'll see in Part III, it is an assumption the Austinian account has no problem keeping.

7

Sentences and Russellian Propositions

In this chapter we conclude our study of the Russellian account with some material that will facilitate the comparison with the Austinian account developed in Part III. We have identified a class of paradoxical propositions within the Russellian account, but there will be no such notion in the Austinian framework. Except for some slack between sentences and the propositions they express, everything turns out to be quite straightforward from the Austinian perspective. All our basic intuitions, both about truth and about the world, are preserved. Still, there must be something special about those sentences which, on the Russellian account, express paradoxical propositions, some Austinian analogue that explains why they seem so problematic. Thus we need to examine sentences of $\mathcal{L}$ that express paradoxical Russellian propositions, so that we can determine what sorts of Austinian propositions they do in fact express.

Toward this end, we will develop "syntactic" analyses of two semantical notions, analyses that we can then use when we move to our new, Austinian semantics. First, we address the question of when two sentences express the same Russellian proposition. It turns out that the proof theory we use to answer this question is also applicable in the Austinian account, and so is useful in proving various theorems in Part III. Second, we give a syntactic characterization of when a sentence expresses a paradoxical Russellian proposition. This characterization will help us track the behavior of such sentences in the Austinian model. Both of these are interesting problems in their own right, but the reader interested in going on to the Austinian account could well postpone this chapter until the material is needed in Chapter 11.

Some proof theory

In this section we address the first question just raised, the question of when two sentences express precisely the same proposition. Notice that we are not asking when two *propositions* are equivalent, in the sense, say, of having the same truth value in all models, or in all maximal models. Nor are we asking when two sentences express propositions that are equivalent in this sense. Rather, we are asking when two sentences express the very same Russellian proposition.

Our presentation simplifies the answer to this question in one way. Our models of Russellian propositions are fairly "finegrained," in that we have chosen to reflect the conjunctive or disjunctive nature of a sentence in the structure of the proposition expressed. We will further simplify things by only considering sentences containing no propositional demonstratives other than **this**. Since the proposition expressed by such sentences does not depend on context, we write $Exp(\varphi)$ rather than $Exp(\varphi, c)$. It's not hard to extend the results below to the full language.

Example 12 First of all, note that both of the sentences

$$\textbf{True}(\textbf{this})$$

and

$$\textbf{True}(\textbf{True}(\textbf{this}))$$

express the Truth-teller t. We have seen less trivial examples in some of the exercises. For another sort of example, consider φ given by:

$$\downarrow(((\textbf{Claire Has } A\spadesuit)\wedge\textbf{True}(\textbf{this}))\vee((\textbf{Max Has } A\spadesuit)$$
$$\wedge\neg\textbf{True}(\textbf{this}))).$$

The proposition p expressed by φ is also expressed by many other sentences. For example, if we replace either or both occurrences of

this by the sentence φ itself, the new sentence will still express p, since **this** refers to what φ expresses.

Once one notices what is going on here, it is easy to generate many examples of sentences with quite different syntactic structures, but which still express the same proposition. Our aim, then, is to find a purely syntactic analysis of the semantical relation:

$$Exp(\varphi) = Exp(\psi).$$

For the purpose of giving proofs that two sentences express the same proposition, we introduce an auxiliary symbol $\rightleftharpoons$. By an *equation* we mean an expression of the form $(\varphi \rightleftharpoons \psi)$, where φ and ψ are *sentences* of $\mathcal{L}$. We will describe a proof theory which is sound and complete, in the sense that

$$\varphi \rightleftharpoons \psi \text{ is provable iff } Exp(\varphi) = Exp(\psi).$$

Our proof theory will have a set of axioms (equations of various forms) and three rules of proof: *Symmetry, Transitivity,* and *Identity of Indiscernibles*. An equation $(\varphi \rightleftharpoons \psi)$ is *provable* just in case it can be obtained from the axioms using the rules of proof, just as one would expect. The axioms and first two rules are straightforward. The third rule, Identity of Indiscernibles, is the substantive rule, and it is unusual. It reflects the fact that the only way for our propositions to be distinct is for them to have a genuine *structural* difference.

Although the $\rightleftharpoons$ symbol must be flanked by sentences, we state the four axiom schemata in terms of an arbitrary subformula φ of a sentence $\ldots\varphi\ldots$. The axioms are any $\mathcal{L}$ instances of one of the following equations.

Axioms:

1. $\ldots\neg\neg\varphi\ldots \rightleftharpoons \ldots\varphi\ldots$

2. $\ldots\neg(\varphi \wedge \psi)\ldots \rightleftharpoons \ldots(\neg\varphi \vee \neg\psi)\ldots$

3. $\ldots\neg(\varphi \vee \psi)\ldots \rightleftharpoons \ldots(\neg\varphi \wedge \neg\psi)\ldots$

4. $\ldots\downarrow\varphi\ldots \rightleftharpoons \ldots\varphi(\textbf{this}/\downarrow\varphi)\ldots$

We trust that no discussion of the first three axiom schemata is called for. As for the fourth, we first remind the reader that the notation $\varphi(\mathbf{this}/{\downarrow}\varphi)$ indicates the result of replacing all loose occurrences of **this** in φ with ${\downarrow}\varphi$. This schema is sound, since our semantics guarantees that all loose occurrences of **this** in φ refer to the proposition expressed by ${\downarrow}\varphi$, so we can replace the former by the latter without affecting the proposition expressed. Note that if φ is itself a sentence, a trivial instance of this axiom is the equation ${\downarrow}\varphi \rightleftharpoons \varphi$. Thus this axiom allows us to get rid of any vacuous occurrences of the scope indicator. More important, though, by using this axiom we can effectively move all nonvacuous scope indicators inside the scope of a relation symbol, since that is where the demonstrative **this** must occur. This will become important when we introduce the notion of normal form.

Rules of Proof:

We now list the three rules of proof, though the third one will take some explanation, which follows.

Symmetry: From $\varphi \rightleftharpoons \psi$ infer $\psi \rightleftharpoons \varphi$.

Transitivity: From $\varphi \rightleftharpoons \psi$ and $\psi \rightleftharpoons \theta$ infer $\varphi \rightleftharpoons \theta$.

Identity of Indiscernibles (I-I): If S is a finite[1] homogeneous set of equations, then for any equation $\varphi \rightleftharpoons \psi$ in S, infer $\varphi \rightleftharpoons \psi$.

We postpone the definition of the term "homogeneous" used in the rule *I-I* for a bit. In the meantime, say that an equation $\varphi \rightleftharpoons \psi$ is *patently obvious* if it follows from the axioms by means of the rules of symmetry and transitivity. We take it as obvious that all of these axioms and rules are sound.

We will say that a formula φ is in *normal form* provided: (i) the negation symbol precedes only positive atomic formulas, and (ii) every instance of the scope symbol occurs within some atomic formula.[2] The main point of the notion of patently obvious is to allow us to transform any equation into one where the sentences related are in normal form. It is important that we can do this

---

[1] The rule is both sound and complete with or without the hypothesis of finiteness.

[2] In this definition, we are considering $(\mathbf{True}\ \varphi)$ and $(\mathbf{a\ Believes}\ \varphi)$ as atomic formulas.

without using the rule *I-I*, since that rule will depend on such transformations.

Lemma 20 (Normal Form Lemma) *For each sentence φ there is a sentence φ' in normal form such that $\varphi \rightleftharpoons \varphi'$ is patently obvious.*

Proof: We first prove the following. (1) If φ is a formula in normal form and $\neg\varphi$ is a subformula of a sentence $\ldots \neg\varphi \ldots$, then there is a formula φ^* in normal form for which the equation

$$\ldots \neg\varphi \ldots \rightleftharpoons \ldots \varphi^* \ldots$$

is patently obvious. This we prove by induction on formulas φ in normal form. For example, using Axiom 2, we have

$$\ldots \neg(\varphi \wedge \psi) \ldots \rightleftharpoons \ldots \neg\varphi \vee \neg\psi \ldots.$$

Then, using the inductive hypothesis and transitivity, we obtain

$$\ldots \neg(\varphi \wedge \psi) \ldots \rightleftharpoons \ldots \varphi^* \vee \psi^* \ldots,$$

where φ^* and ψ^*, and so $\varphi^* \vee \psi^*$, are in normal form.

Next we observe (2) that if a formula φ is in normal form, then $\varphi(\mathbf{this}/\downarrow\varphi)$ is also in normal form, and further,

$$\ldots \downarrow\varphi \ldots \rightleftharpoons \ldots \varphi(\downarrow\varphi) \ldots$$

is patently obvious, by Axiom 4. Using these two facts, we can prove by induction that for any subformula φ of sentence $\ldots \varphi \ldots$, there is a φ' in normal form for which

$$\ldots \varphi \ldots \rightleftharpoons \ldots \varphi' \ldots$$

is patently obvious. The desired result is an instance of this. $\square$

The basic idea of the rule *I-I* can be understood as follows. Suppose we want to prove $\varphi \rightleftharpoons \psi$. We know that the propositions expressed by these sentences will be the same unless there is something about the sentences that generates a genuine structural difference between the propositions they express. So let us conjecture that the sentences express the very same proposition, by assuming the equation $\varphi \rightleftharpoons \psi$. We then try to demonstrate that there is no significant structural difference between the sentences by finding a "homogeneous" set of equations containing our assumption, where a homogeneous set will prove that there is no such structural difference. If we can find such a set of equations, then the original equation is valid. Before defining just what a homogeneous set of equations is, we discuss one of the simplest possible illustrations of *I-I*.

Example 13 Here is an illustration of how this method of proof works in the case of the following equation.

$$\downarrow\textbf{True}(\textbf{this}) \rightleftharpoons \downarrow\textbf{True}(\textbf{True}(\textbf{this}))$$

To find a homogeneous set S of equations containing this equation, we apply the Normal Form Lemma to obtain normal form equations. Then whenever we find that we have committed ourselves to an equation $\textbf{True}(\varphi) \rightleftharpoons \textbf{True}(\psi)$ being in S, we add $\varphi \rightleftharpoons \psi$ to S. If we were ever to find, say, an equation of the form $\textbf{True}(\varphi) \rightleftharpoons \psi$ where ψ was in normal form but not of the form $\textbf{True}(\psi_0)$, then we would run afoul of homogeneity: we would have uncovered a structural difference that will be reflected in the propositions these sentences express. However, in this example we do not encounter such problems. The process rapidly closes off, showing that the sentences do express the same proposition.

We now turn to a precise statement of the rule *I-I*. To aid in the statement of the following definition, let us define the extension E_S of a set S of equations to be the set of all sentences φ such that, for some ψ, $\varphi \rightleftharpoons \psi$ is in S. If φ and ψ are in normal form, we say that the equation $\varphi \rightleftharpoons \psi$ is *at least plausible* if one of the following holds:

- both φ and ψ are conjunctions, or both are disjunctions;

- both φ and ψ are atomic sentences involving the predicate **True**, or both are negated atomic, involving $\neg\textbf{True}$;

- both φ and ψ are atomic sentences of the form **a Has c** and they are equal;

- both φ and ψ are negated atomic sentences of the form $\neg(\textbf{a Has c})$ and they are equal;

- both φ and ψ are atomic sentences of the forms (**a Believes** φ_0) and (**a Believes** ψ_0), respectively, with the same individual constant **a**; or

- both φ and ψ are atomic sentences of the forms $\neg(\mathbf{a\ Believes}\ \varphi_0)$ and $\neg(\mathbf{a\ Believes}\ \psi_0)$, respectively, with the same individual constant $\mathbf{a}$.

Definition 12 Let S be a set of equations of $\mathcal{L}$. We say that S is *homogeneous* provided the following conditions hold.

- If $\varphi \in E_S$ then there is a patently obvious equation $\varphi \rightleftharpoons \psi$ in S such that ψ is in normal form.

- S is closed under the rules of symmetry and transitivity.

- If $\varphi \rightleftharpoons \psi$ is in S, where both φ and ψ are in normal form, then $\varphi \rightleftharpoons \psi$ is at least plausible.

- If $\varphi_1 \wedge \varphi_2 \rightleftharpoons \psi_1 \wedge \psi_2$ is in S, then so are either both $\varphi_1 \rightleftharpoons \psi_1$ and $\varphi_2 \rightleftharpoons \psi_2$, or both $\varphi_1 \rightleftharpoons \psi_2$ and $\varphi_2 \rightleftharpoons \psi_1$.

- If $\varphi_1 \vee \varphi_2 \rightleftharpoons \psi_1 \vee \psi_2$ is in S, then so are either both $\varphi_1 \rightleftharpoons \psi_1$ and $\varphi_2 \rightleftharpoons \psi_2$, or both $\varphi_1 \rightleftharpoons \psi_2$ and $\varphi_2 \rightleftharpoons \psi_1$.

- If $\theta(\mathbf{this})$ is an atomic or negated atomic sentence and $\theta(\mathbf{this}/\varphi) \rightleftharpoons \theta(\mathbf{this}/\psi)$ is in S, then $\varphi \rightleftharpoons \psi$ is also in S.

Oddly enough, the soundness of this rule, and hence of the proof theory, is less obvious than its completeness. To motivate the proof of soundness, we present the following exercise.

Exercise 50 Consider the sentence $\varphi =$

$$\downarrow((\mathbf{a\ Has\ c}) \wedge \mathbf{True(this)})$$

and the sentence $\psi =$

$$\downarrow(\mathbf{True(True(this)} \wedge (\mathbf{a\ Has\ c})) \wedge (\mathbf{a\ Has\ c})).$$

1. Show that both φ and ψ express the proposition p given by the equation

$$p = [a\ H\ c] \wedge [Tr\ p].$$

2. Find a homogeneous set of equations containing $\varphi \rightleftharpoons \psi$.

3. Show that $\rightleftharpoons$ defines an equivalence relation on the set of sentences in S, with three equivalence classes, S_1, S_2, and S_3, where the sentences in S_1 express $[a\ H\ c]$, those in S_2 express p and those in S_3 express $[Tr\ p]$.

Lemma 21 *If S is a homogeneous set of equations and $\varphi \rightleftharpoons \psi$ is in S, then $Exp(\varphi) = Exp(\psi)$.*

Proof: The proof is simply a generalization of Exercise 50. Since S is closed under the rules of symmetry and transitivity, the following defines an equivalence relation $\equiv$ on E_S:

$$\varphi \equiv \psi \text{ iff } (\varphi \rightleftharpoons \psi) \in S.$$

We let $e, e', \ldots$ range over equivalence classes $[\varphi]$, for $\varphi \in E_S$. For each such equivalence class e, introduce a propositional indeterminate $\mathbf{p}_e$. We want to find a system $\mathcal{E}$ of equations in these indeterminates, say,

$$\mathbf{p}_e = a_e(\mathbf{p}_e, \mathbf{p}_{e'}, \ldots),$$

where a_e reflects the set-theoretic structure of the proposition expressed by sentences in e. We will read this structure off the normal form sentences in e. Let us consider a couple of cases.

Suppose we find a normal form sentence φ in e of the form (**a Believes** φ_0). Then every normal form sentence ψ in e is of the form (**a Believes** ψ_0), and furthermore, $\varphi_0 \equiv \psi_0$. Let $e_0 = [\varphi_0]$. Then the equation we want is:

$$\mathbf{p}_e = [a \ Bel \ \mathbf{p}_{e_0}].$$

(Note that it is possible that $e = e_0$, so this might be an equation of the form $\mathbf{p}_e = [a \ Bel \ \mathbf{p}_e]$.)

Now consider an equivalence class e where some, hence all, normal form sentences $\varphi \in e$ are of the form $(\varphi_0 \wedge \varphi_1)$. Let $e_0 = [\varphi_0], e_1 = [\varphi_1]$ and let the equation for $\mathbf{p}_e$ be

$$\mathbf{p}_e = \bigwedge \{\mathbf{p}_{e_0}, \mathbf{p}_{e_1}\}.$$

The clause for $\wedge$ in the definition of homogeneous insures that this is well defined.

Now let F be any assignment to these indeterminates satisfying

$$F(\mathbf{p}_e) = Exp(\varphi) \text{ for some } \varphi \in e.$$

It is clear that F satisfies all these equations. However, by the Solution Lemma, each system of equations has a unique solution. Consequently, there is only one such assignment, that is,

$$F(\mathbf{p}_e) = Exp(\varphi) \text{ for } all \ \varphi \in e.$$

In other words, if $(\varphi \rightleftharpoons \psi) \in S$, then $Exp(\varphi) = Exp(\psi)$. $\square$

With this lemma, we can now prove the following:

Theorem 22 (Russellian Soundness Theorem) *For any two sentences φ, ψ of $\mathcal{L}$, if the equation $\varphi \rightleftharpoons \psi$ is provable, then $Exp(\varphi) = Exp(\psi)$.*

Proof: This is proven by induction on the length of the derivation. The only nontrivial step is the rule *I-I*, which is taken care of by the previous lemma. $\square$

We now turn to the converse, the question of completeness. Again, we begin with an exercise.

Exercise 51 Let S be the set of all equations of the form $\varphi \rightleftharpoons \psi$ where φ and ψ are normal form sentences and $Exp(\varphi) = Exp(\psi)$, or else where $\varphi \rightleftharpoons \psi$ is patently obvious. Show that S is homogeneous.

Theorem 23 (Russellian Completeness Theorem) *For any two sentences φ, ψ of $\mathcal{L}$, if $Exp(\varphi) = Exp(\psi)$ then the equation $\varphi \rightleftharpoons \psi$ is provable.*

Proof: Assume $Exp(\varphi) = Exp(\psi)$. By Lemma 20, we can also assume that φ and ψ are in normal form. We want to show that there is a finite homogeneous set S of equations with $(\varphi \rightleftharpoons \psi) \in S$. Given the above exercise, the only problem comes in the finiteness.

Let A be a finite set of sentences containing φ and ψ, and closed under the following:

1. If $(\varphi \wedge \psi) \in A$ then $\varphi, \psi \in A$.

2. If $(\varphi \vee \psi) \in A$ then $\varphi, \psi \in A$.

3. If $\theta(\textbf{this})$ is atomic or negated atomic and $\theta(\textbf{this}/\varphi) \in A$ then $\varphi \in A$.

4. If $\varphi \in A$ then there is a normal form φ' such that $(\varphi \rightleftharpoons \varphi')$ is patently obvious, and $\varphi' \in A$.

To see that there must be such a finite set, note that the closure conditions all involve direct decomposition, with the exception of condition (4). But this condition will only be invoked when we have a sentence $\varphi \in A$ which is not in normal form. Since we started with normal form sentences, this can only happen if $\theta(\mathbf{this}/\varphi) \in A$ and $\varphi = \downarrow\psi$, where ψ is in normal form. But then $\downarrow\psi \rightleftharpoons \psi(\mathbf{this}/\downarrow\psi)$ is patently obvious, and $\psi(\mathbf{this}/\downarrow\psi)$ is in normal form. In decomposing this, we will come back to $\downarrow\psi$ in a finite number of steps, thus closing off the process.

Now simply let S be the set of all equations of the form $(\varphi_0 \rightleftharpoons \psi_0)$ such that $\varphi_0, \psi_0 \in A$, and $Exp(\varphi_0) = Exp(\psi_0)$. Then S is a finite homogeneous set and $(\varphi \rightleftharpoons \psi) \in S$. $\square$

Corollary 24 *The relation on $\mathcal{L}$ sentences of expressing the same proposition is a decidable relation.*

Proof: This can be seen by examining the proof of the Completeness Theorem, where it is seen that one can delimit in advance the set of possible equations that are relevant to a proof: the set must be some subset of $A \times A$. $\square$

Exercise 52 Carry out the details of the proof of Example 13, page 111.

Open Problem 1 Extend the Completeness Theorem given here to characterize, for arbitrary open formulas, the relation $Val(\varphi) = Val(\psi)$.

Paradoxical sentences

In this section we continue to ignore sentences with the demonstratives $\mathbf{that}_i$ in them, so that each sentence φ under consideration expresses, on the Russellian conception, a unique proposition $Exp(\varphi)$. In this way we can transfer properties and relations that hold of propositions to properties and relations holding of the sentences that express them. For example, we could say that a sentence φ is false in a model $\mathfrak{M}$, or is classical, or is intrinsically paradoxical, just in case the proposition $Exp(\varphi)$ expressed by φ is false in $\mathfrak{M}$, or classical, or intrinsically paradoxical. Our aim in this section is to characterize some of these properties of sentences.

The characterizations are not particularly pretty, but they do give us the tools we need. Our real objective is to compare and contrast the Russellian and Austinian accounts, and what they say about truth, paradox, and the world. The notions introduced below will allow us to carry out this comparison in Part III.

Definition 13

1. A *syntactic witnessing function* w is a partial function from normal form sentences of $\mathcal{L}$ to sets of atomic sentences satisfying the following conditions.

   - If $\varphi = (\textbf{True } \psi) \in dom(w)$ then there is a normal form sentence $\psi' \in dom(w)$ such that $\psi \rightleftharpoons \psi'$ is patently obvious and $w(\psi') \cup \{\varphi\} \subseteq w(\varphi)$.

   - If $\varphi = \neg(\textbf{True } \psi) \in dom(w)$ then there is a normal form sentence $\psi' \in dom(w)$ such that $\neg\psi \rightleftharpoons \psi'$ is patently obvious and $w(\psi') \cup \{\varphi\} \subseteq w(\varphi)$.

   - If φ is an atomic or negated atomic sentence not covered by the above and $\varphi \in dom(w)$, then $\varphi \in w(\varphi)$

   - If $\varphi = (\psi_1 \wedge \psi_2) \in dom(w)$ then $\psi_1, \psi_2 \in dom(w)$ and $w(\psi_1) \cup w(\psi_2) \subseteq w(\varphi)$.

   - If $\varphi = (\psi_1 \vee \psi_2) \in dom(w)$ then either $\psi_1 \in dom(w)$ and $w(\psi_1) \subseteq w(\varphi)$, or $\psi_2 \in dom(w)$ and $w(\psi_2) \subseteq w(\varphi)$.

2. A set of sentences Φ of $\mathcal{L}$ is *superficially consistent* if there are no sentences $\varphi, \psi \in \Phi$ such that the equation $\neg\varphi \rightleftharpoons \psi$ is valid, i.e., if no proposition and its negation are both expressed by sentences of Φ.

3. A syntactic witnessing function w is *consistent* if the set $\Phi = \bigcup\{w(\varphi) \mid \varphi \in dom(w)\}$ is superficially consistent.

4. A set Φ of normal form sentences is *consistent* if $\Phi \subseteq dom(w)$ for some consistent syntactic witnessing function w. An arbitrary set Φ of sentences is *consistent* if there is a consistent set Φ' of closed normal form sentences such that every expression $\varphi \in \Phi$ expresses the same proposition as some $\varphi' \in \Phi'$.

Theorem 25 (Sentential Model Existence Theorem) *A set Φ of normal form sentences is consistent iff there is a model $\mathfrak{M}$ such that for each $\varphi \in \Phi$, $\mathfrak{M} \models Exp(\varphi)$.*

Proof: Assume that Φ is consistent, and so is a subset of $dom(w)$, where w is a consistent syntactic witnessing function. We transform w into a witnessing function w' for the set of propositions

$P = \{Exp(\varphi) \mid \varphi \in \Phi\}$ in an obvious way. Namely, each atomic or negated atomic sentence φ is associated with the natural soa σ_φ needed to guarantee the truth of φ. For example, if $\varphi =$ (**a Believes** ψ) then $\sigma_\varphi = \langle Bel, a, Exp(\psi); 1 \rangle$. Using these, we can define

$$w'(\psi) = \{\sigma_\varphi \mid \varphi \in w(\psi)\}$$

for each $\psi \in dom(w)$. It is now routine to verify that w' is a witnessing function. It is coherent since w is consistent. Thus the result follows from the Extended Model Existence Theorem, stated in Exercise 39, page 92. The converse direction is straightforward. □

Corollary 26 *A sentence φ expresses an intrinsically paradoxical Russellian proposition iff every syntactic witnessing function w with $(\varphi \vee \neg\varphi) \in dom(w)$ is inconsistent.*

We want to extend the theorem to give us a test for when a set of sentences has a model $\mathfrak{M}$ extending some given model $\mathfrak{M}_0$. We do this as follows, using the association of soa σ_φ with sentence φ used in the previous proof. First, we say that a set Φ of atomic sentences is *superficially consistent* with $\mathfrak{M}_0$ if $\mathfrak{M}_0 \cup \{\sigma_\varphi \mid \varphi \in \Phi\}$ is coherent. Note that in general this condition does not guarantee that this collection is even a weak model. Next, we say that a syntactic witnessing function is *consistent* with $\mathfrak{M}_0$ if the union of its range is superficially consistent with $\mathfrak{M}_0$. Finally, we say that a set Φ of normal form sentences is *consistent* with $\mathfrak{M}_0$ if $\Phi \subseteq dom(w)$ for some syntactic witnessing function consistent with $\mathfrak{M}_0$. Extending the proof of the above in the obvious way, we have:

Theorem 27 (Extended Sentential Model Existence Theorem) *A set Φ of normal form sentences is consistent with $\mathfrak{M}_0$ iff there is a model $\mathfrak{M} \supseteq \mathfrak{M}_0$ such that for each $\varphi \in \Phi$, $True_{\mathfrak{M}}(Exp(\varphi))$.*

Exercise 53   Use the Sentential Model Existence Theorem to prove a version of the Compactness Theorem for our language $\mathcal{L}$:

Theorem 28 (Compactness Theorem) *Let Φ be a set of sentences such that every finite subset has a model (extending some model $\mathfrak{M}_0$). Then Φ itself has such a model.*

(*Hint:* Enumerate the closed normal form sentences of $\mathcal{L}$ in an ω-sequence $\theta_1, \theta_2, \theta_3, \ldots$, and build the domain of a consistent syntactic witnessing function in stages. Make sure that as you define stage w_n, $d = dom(w_n)$ has the following property †: For each finite subset Φ_0 of Φ there is a consistent syntactic witnessing function w with $\Phi \cup d \subseteq dom(w)$. The crucial step is the one for disjunctions. Given a disjunction $\theta_n = (\psi_1 \vee \psi_2)$ such that $dom(w_n) \cup \{\theta_n\}$ has †, there is an $i = 1, 2$ such that $dom(w_n) \cup \{\theta_n, \psi_i\}$ has †. One then throws ψ_i into $dom(w_{n+1})$.)

Part III

Austinian Propositions and the Liar

8

Modeling Austinian Propositions

According to the Russellian view of language, when we use a sentence like

(Claire Has 3♣)

containing no explicit contextually sensitive elements, the proposition is uniquely determined by the sentence used.[1] But on the Austinian view, this is never the case; there is always, in effect, at least one contextually sensitive feature of the utterance, namely, the situation the proposition is about. Thus, according to Austin, the sentence **(Claire Has 3♣)** can be used to express different propositions, propositions that diverge in the situation they are about.

Even in the case of such a simple sentence, there is a significant difference between these two accounts. We might imagine, for example, that there are two card games going on, one across town from the other: Max is playing cards with Emily and Sophie, and Claire is playing cards with Dana. Suppose someone watching the former game mistakes Emily for Claire, and claims that Claire has the three of clubs. She would be wrong, on the Austinian account, even if Claire had the three of clubs across town. On the Russellian account, though, the claim would be true.

---

[1] Of course, this presupposes that the terms **Claire** and **3♣** refer to unique individuals, independent of use. But we are setting aside this element of context sensitivity.

The added degree of freedom offered by the Austinian conception of language becomes increasingly significant when we consider linguistic mechanisms that bring in "nonpersistence," mechanisms like denial, universal quantification, and definite descriptions. Suppose that we were to claim, about the first of the above card games, that everyone has at least three of a kind. It is clear that the intent of our assertion is to describe a limited part of the world. In particular, we are not claiming anything about Claire or Dana's hands. In terms of the Austinian account, our assertion is true about the situation we are talking about, but might be false about other situations. We will say that the sentence is nonpersistent, in this case because it can express a true proposition about one situation, but express a false proposition about an extension of that situation.

Once we adopt the Austinian perspective, we see that there are many different ways a sentence can be nonpersistent. An important kind of nonpersistence arises with sentences containing definite descriptions like "the dealer." If we say that the dealer has sticky fingers, our statement will only successfully express a proposition if the situation it is about contains a unique dealer; otherwise it simply misfires. In this case, the sentence is nonpersistent since it can express a true proposition about one situation, but might not even express a proposition if used about a larger situation. Russell's view of propositions forced him to forgo this simple account of definite descriptions. He construed sentences containing definite descriptions as expressing uniqueness claims about the entire world.

We will see that issues concerning changes in the situation a proposition is about, and so of persistence and nonpersistence, are crucial to understanding the behavior of the Liar on the Austinian account. But before we can discuss this in any detail, we need to develop some basic machinery for modeling Austinian propositions in a precise way.

Basic definitions

We remind the reader that an Austinian proposition is determined by two constituents: a situation determined by "demonstrative conventions," and a type determined by "descriptive conventions." The proposition p is true if the situation the proposition is about,

About(*p*), is of the constituent type, *Type*(*p*). To model such propositions, and the attendant account of the relation between language and the world, we will need four classes: states of affairs (*SOA*), situations (*SIT*), types (*TYPE*), and propositions (*PROP*). They must be defined simultaneously, since, for example, situations are constituents of propositions and vice versa. Later we will introduce the notion of a model of the world. The notions of fact and actual situation will be relative to a given model of the world.

Before giving the definition, we remind the reader of the two versions of the definition of the class *PROP* in Part II, one that detoured through the larger class *PrePROP*, the other that employed an inductive operator (see Exercise 28, page 68) and thereby avoided the detour. This time around, we will not bother with the detour, but will take the direct approach. So in the following definition, the closure $\Gamma(X)$ of X is again the smallest collection containing X and closed under:

- If $Y \subseteq \Gamma(X)$ is a set, then $[\bigwedge Y]$ and $[\bigvee Y]$ are in $\Gamma(X)$.

In the following definition we define the class *AtTYPE* of *atomic types*. We take the class *TYPE* of all types to be its closure $\Gamma(AtTYPE)$. This procedure allows us to avoid, in the Austinian model, problems analogous to those caused by the nonsubstantive Russellian prepropositions.

Definition 1 Let *SOA, SIT, AtTYPE, PROP* be the largest classes satisfying:

- Every $\sigma \in SOA$ is either of the form:
    - $\langle H, a, c; i \rangle$, or
    - $\langle Tr, p; i \rangle$, or
    - $\langle Bel, a, p; i \rangle$;

  where H, Tr, and Bel, are distinct atoms, a is Claire or Max, c is one of the standard cards; i is either 0 or 1; $p \in PROP$.

- Every $s \in SIT$ is a subset (with stress on *set*) of *SOA*.

- Every $p \in PROP$ is of the form $\{s; T\}$, where $s \in SIT$ and $T \in \Gamma(AtTYPE)$.

- Every $T \in AtTYPE$ is of the form $[\sigma]$, where $\sigma \in SOA$.

As in the Russellian case, there are some comments that should be made. We are again assuming some standard technique for systematically representing distinct objects by distinct sets. For example, we aren't concerned with exactly how elements of *PROP* are distinguished from elements of *TYPE*, except that they should be so distinguished. Thus, we use $\{s; T\}$ for that set-theoretic object which represents a proposition completely determined by the situation s and type T, and we use $[\sigma]$ for a type completely determined by the state of affairs σ.[2] Just how these are represented by sets will not really matter. If $p = \{s; T\}$, we will use $About(p)$ for the situation s that the proposition is about, and $Type(p)$ for the constituent type T. So for any proposition p, $p = \{About(p); Type(p)\}$.

We need to define various properties and relations that hold among these things, like the relation on $SIT \times TYPE$ of a situation's being of a type, and the property of a proposition's being true. But before doing this, let's run through a few examples of the new objects at our disposal, and describe the intuitions our definition is meant to capture.

Example 1 Let $p = \{s; [H, \text{Claire}, 3\clubsuit; 1]\}$.[3] We want to define the relations mentioned so that this faithfully models the Austinian proposition *about s*, that claims that s is of the type in which Claire has the three of clubs. Given that we are modeling situations as sets of states of affairs, this proposition should in turn be true just in case $\langle H, \text{Claire}, 3\clubsuit; 1 \rangle \in s$.

Example 2 (Austinian Liars) For any situation s and proposition p, there is a proposition which claims that p is false in s, that is, that its falsity is a fact of s. This is the proposition:

$$F(s, p) = \{s; [Tr, p; 0]\}.$$

Using AFA, we obtain a fixed point, f_s, which is the unique proposition $p = F(s, p)$. That is, we obtain, for each s, the liar proposition:

$$f_s = \{s; [Tr, f_s; 0]\}.$$

---

[2] One might in fact want to identify the state of affairs σ with the type $[\sigma]$. While we do not make this identification, we will adopt an abbreviation when describing atomic types that allows us to leave out the angle brackets. Thus, for example, instead of writing $[\langle H, \text{Claire}, 3\clubsuit; 1 \rangle]$, we will simply write $[H, \text{Claire}, 3\clubsuit; 1]$. This convention increases legibility.

[3] Recall from footnote 2 that this is shorthand for $\{s; [\langle H, \text{Claire}, 3\clubsuit; 1 \rangle]\}$.

The proposition f_s claims that the falsity of f_s is a fact about s.

Example 3 (Austinian Truth-tellers) There is, for any s, a Truth-teller proposition:

$$t_s = \{s; [Tr, t_s; 1]\}.$$

Example 4 (Liar cycle) Consider the Liar cycle, say of length two. Imagine two people, say a_1 and a_2, and suppose each expresses a proposition, p_1 and p_2, respectively, where p_1 claims that p_2 is true, while p_2 claims that p_1 is false. On the Austinian account, these propositions must be about situations, say s_1 and s_2. They might be the same situation, or they might not. Thus in the general case, we have the following propositions.

$$p_1 = \{s_1; [Tr, p_2; 1]\}$$

$$p_2 = \{s_2; [Tr, p_1; 0]\}$$

Example 5 Next consider the case where two people each use the sentence "This proposition is true but that proposition is false" to make contradictory claims about one another. To model this, we can consider two situations u_1 and u_2, and the propositions:

$$p_1 = \{u_1; [[Tr, p_1; 1] \wedge [Tr, p_2; 0]]\}$$

$$p_2 = \{u_2; [[Tr, p_2; 1] \wedge [Tr, p_1; 0]]\}.$$

Each of these claims that its own truth and the other's falsity are facts of the situation it is about.

Example 6 Let p be the proposition defined in Example 1, and let q be the proposition $\{s; [Bel, \text{Max}, p; 1]\}$. This is a proposition that is about the same situation p is about. It claims that s is the type of situation in which Max believes Claire has (then and there) the three of clubs.

Example 7 For a more sophisticated example, consider the proposition b_s, about s, with the following type.[4]

$$[[H, \text{Claire}, 3\clubsuit; 1] \wedge [Bel, \text{Max}, b_s; 1] \wedge [Bel, \text{Claire}, b_s; 1]]$$

---

[4]Note that we are using an obvious abbreviation for the conjunctive type in question.

This proposition claims that s is a situation in which Claire has the three of clubs, and in which this is *mutually* believed by Claire and Max. Under idealized conditions, this proposition implies that Claire believes that Max believes that she has the three of clubs, as well as further iterations (though the conditions become less plausible with further iterations).[5] The fact that we can model such a proposition depends, of course, on AFA.

Example 8 For any proposition p (and situation s), consider the proposition that claims (about s) that Max believes p, but that p is false.

$$\{s; [[Bel, \text{Max}, p; 1] \wedge [Tr, p; 0]]\}$$

Again, by AFA, we can obtain a fixed point.

$$q = \{s; [[Bel, \text{Max}, q; 1] \wedge [Tr, q; 0]]\}$$

This proposition is Liar-like in character. It will be true only if Max has a belief that that very belief is false.

Truth of Austinian propositions

With these examples to guide and motivate us, let's turn to the definition of the class of true propositions. To define what it means for an Austinian proposition to be true, we must first define what it means for a situation to be of a type. We do this by defining, coinductively, the class OF of pairs $\langle s, T \rangle$ such that s is of type T.

Definition 2 Let OF be the unique subclass of $SIT \times TYPE$ satisfying the following conditions.

- $\langle s, [\sigma] \rangle \in OF$ iff $\sigma \in s$.
- $\langle s, [\bigwedge X] \rangle \in OF$ iff $\langle s, T \rangle \in OF$, for all $T \in X$.
- $\langle s, [\bigvee X] \rangle \in OF$ iff $\langle s, T \rangle \in OF$, for some $T \in X$.

It is important to note that, for example, saying a situation s is not of type $[H, \text{Claire}, 3\clubsuit; 1]$ is not equivalent to saying s is of the dual type $[H, \text{Claire}, 3\clubsuit; 0]$. We take this as capturing an important intuition about the partiality of Austinian situations: there is a difference between situations in which Claire fails to have

---

[5]See, e.g., Harman (1977) or Barwise (1985).

the three of clubs, and situations which simply don't determine whether Claire has that card (perhaps because Claire is not even around).

The following lemma, though extremely simple, is important for modeling the Austinian notion of truth.

Proposition 1 *For any s and T:*

1. *Situation s is either of type T or it isn't, and not both.*

2. *Situation s is of type $[\sigma]$ if and only if $\sigma \in s$.*

3. *Situation s is of type $[\bigwedge X]$ if and only if s is of type T for each $T \in X$.*

4. *Situation s is of type $[\bigvee X]$ if and only if s is of type T for some $T \in X$.*

Proof: (1) is immediate from the law of excluded middle, and parts (2)–(4) all follow from general facts about coinductive definitions. For example, to prove (2) we need to show that $\langle s, [\sigma] \rangle \in OF$ if and only if $\sigma \in s$. The "only if" part follows from the requirement that OF be a class satisfying the clauses in its definition. The "if" part follows from the requirement that OF be the largest such class. That is, if $\sigma \in s$ then $OF \cup \{\langle s, [\sigma] \rangle\}$ satisfies all the clauses, so is equal to OF. □

We will define the class *TRUE* to be the class of those $p \in PROP$ such that $p = \{s; T\}$ where s is of type T. We call any proposition in this class *true*, and all others *false*. This definition has the following expected and desirable properties:

Proposition 2

1. *Every proposition is either true or false, and not both.*

2. *The proposition $\{s; [\sigma]\}$ is true if and only if $\sigma \in s$.*

3. *The proposition $\{s; [\bigwedge X]\}$ is true if and only if $\{s; T\}$ is true for each $T \in X$.*

4. *The proposition $\{s; [\bigvee X]\}$ is true if and only if $\{s; T\}$ is true for some $T \in X$.*

5. *Some propositions are true, some are false.*

Proof: Parts (1)–(4) are immediate from the corresponding parts of Proposition 1. To prove (5) consider the type $T = [\sigma]$ where $\sigma = \langle H, \text{Claire}, 3\clubsuit; 1 \rangle$. Let s_0 be any subset of SOA not containing σ, s_1 any subset of SOA containing σ. Then $\{s_1; T\}$ is true and $\{s_0; T\}$ false; both by (2). □

Notice once again that, although every proposition is either true or false, it might be the case that both of the following propositions are false.

$$\{s; [H, \text{Claire}, 3\diamondsuit; 1]\}$$
$$\{s; [H, \text{Claire}, 3\diamondsuit; 0]\}$$

Again, this will happen if s is a situation where Claire simply isn't present, and so neither *has* the three of clubs in s nor *fails* to have it in s. In other words, the situation s would then be of neither of the types it is claimed to be in these propositions.

9

Austinian Propositions and the World

Accessible Austinian propositions

At first sight, there is something startling about the simple results of the last chapter, especially Proposition 2. This proposition seems to indicate that Austinian propositions, at least as we've construed them, are true or false independent of the way the world actually happens to be. After all, we have defined the notions of proposition and truth without bringing in the world at all. There are two ways to think about this, ways that are formally indistinguishable in our modeling, but which still raise philosophically interesting issues.

One line that could be taken is that this result is just an artifact of our use of sets to model situations. Real Austinian propositions are about real situations, not about their set-theoretic counterparts. Where the world comes in (on this line) is in determining what the facts are in a given real situation, and so what its appropriate set-theoretic counterpart is. In other words, if the world were different, the same situation would be modeled by a different set-theoretic object, a different member of *SIT*. This is analogous to what happens when we model properties with sets: the same set could not have had different members, though the same property could well have applied to different things. But all this means is that, had the world been different, the same property would have had a different set-theoretic counterpart, not that the modeling technique is thereby faulty, or that properties hold of their objects necessarily. As an artifact, it signifies nothing.

A different line would be to say that the individuation of real situations is itself determined by the facts that hold in them, so that situations, like sets, could not have had different "constituents." In which case, whether or not a situation is of a given type really is independent of the world. What the world determines is simply which situations are real or actual; it has nothing to say about what facts hold in a given situation. On this line, the move from a situation to its set-theoretic counterpart is entirely independent of the world, though the question of whether a given member of *SIT* corresponds to a real situation still requires that we consult the world.

For our purposes there is no need to take a stand on this issue. The issue concerns the metaphysics of real ("historical") situations, and the question of whether the same situation could have had different facts as constituents. Either way we look at it, though, we have available a superfluity of "propositions" in *PROP,* namely all those that are about sets that aren't counterparts of real situations. Or, to put it more gently, the propositions are really divided into two classes, those that are about real situations and those that are about nonreal situations. Only those that are about real situations can actually be expressed, on Austin's account. We will say that all other propositions are *inaccessible* in the actual world.

Notice, though, that to restrict attention to propositions that are about real situations is not to restrict attention to true propositions. There are still false propositions about real situations, just as there are true propositions about unreal situations.

The distinction between propositions that are accessible and those that are not is important to understanding the Austinian Liar. To this end, we will turn in the next section to the task of modeling the world. This will enable us to distinguish accessible propositions from those that are not. But first we note the following proposition.

Proposition 3 *There are true Liars and false Liars.*

Proof: There are obviously situations s such that the Liar f_s about s is false. For example, any situation that only contains states of affairs of the form $\langle H, a, c; i \rangle$ will be such a situation, by part (2) of Proposition 2. Further, we can extend any situation s to one whose Liar is true by using AFA to obtain an $s' = s \cup \{\langle Tr, f_{s'}; 0\rangle\}$. Again apply (2) from the previous result. $\square$

The proof of this proposition actually gives us the following, which will be useful.

Proposition 4 *Given any situation s, there is a situation $s' \supseteq s$ such that the Liar proposition $f_{s'}$ about s' is true.*

Exercise 54 Show that for any situation s, there is a situation $s' \supseteq s$ such that the Liar proposition $f_{s'}$ about s' is false. (Hint: The notion of a protected situation, introduced in the next chapter, is useful here.)

Modeling the Austinian world

To depict the role the actual world plays in the Austinian framework, we need to bring in models of the world and introduce the notion of a proposition being accessible relative to a given model $\mathfrak{A}$ of the world. As in the Russellian case, we also bring in coherence conditions to rule out various sorts of logical incoherence in these models. The coherence conditions are a bit simpler, though, since the truth of a proposition p need not be relativized to the model $\mathfrak{A}$.

Definition 3

1. A *partial model $\mathfrak{A}$ of the world* is a collection of *SOA*'s satisfying the following conditions.

   - No soa and its dual[1] are in $\mathfrak{A}$.
   - If $\langle Tr, p; 1\rangle \in \mathfrak{A}$ then p is true.
   - If $\langle Tr, p; 0\rangle \in \mathfrak{A}$ then p is false.

2. A situation s is *actual* in model $\mathfrak{A}$ if $s \subseteq \mathfrak{A}$; it is *possible* if it is actual in some model $\mathfrak{A}$.

3. A proposition p is *accessible* in a model $\mathfrak{A}$ if $About(p)$ is actual in $\mathfrak{A}$.

4. A model $\mathfrak{A}$ is *total* if it is not properly contained in any other partial model.

---

[1] By the *dual* of an soa σ we mean, of course, the soa $\bar{\sigma}$ just like σ but with the opposite polarity.

Our definition of a total model is parallel to that of a Russellian maximal model. But in the Russellian case, maximal models are not really total, in the obvious sense that they cannot contain every state of affairs or its dual, thanks to Liar-like phenomena. In contrast, the following shows that we are justified in calling maximal models total in the Austinian case.

Proposition 5 *Let $\mathfrak{A}$ be a total model. Then for any soa σ, exactly one of σ and its dual are in $\mathfrak{A}$. In particular:*

- *For $a \in \{Claire,\ Max\}$ and c any card, either $\langle H, a, c; 1 \rangle$ or $\langle H, a, c; 0 \rangle$ is in $\mathfrak{A}$, and not both.*
- *For $a \in \{Claire,\ Max\}$ and p any proposition, either $\langle Bel, a, p; 1 \rangle$ or $\langle Bel, a, p; 0 \rangle$ is in $\mathfrak{A}$, and not both.*
- $\langle Tr, p; 1 \rangle \in \mathfrak{A}$ *iff p is true.*
- $\langle Tr, p; 0 \rangle \in \mathfrak{A}$ *iff p is false.*

Proof: Consider the last item, since it is the surprising one. Suppose $\mathfrak{A}$ is a total model and p is false. Then $\mathfrak{A} \cup \langle Tr, p; 0 \rangle$ is also a model, and so must be equal to $\mathfrak{A}$. $\square$

Trivial as this proposition may be, it indicates that something strikingly different is happening on this view of propositions. Let us now return to the Liar. Recall that any given proposition is either true or false, and not both.

Theorem 6 *Let s be an actual situation in some model. Then the Liar proposition about s, f_s, is false. In other words, any Liar proposition accessible in a model is simply false.*

Proof: If f_s is true, then $\langle Tr, f_s; 0 \rangle \in s$. But s is actual in some $\mathfrak{A}$, and so f_s must be false by the definition of a model of the world. $\square$

The falsity of any Liar f_s accessible from a total model $\mathfrak{A}$ should not surprise us, in view of our experience in the Russellian case. What is striking here, however, is that Proposition 5 assures us that the corresponding fact, $\langle Tr, f_s; 0 \rangle$, will be a part of $\mathfrak{A}$, even though it diagonalizes out of s. This would seem to leave us perilously close to paradox. For after all, if f_s is false, doesn't that make it true? Obviously not, since all we've done so far is construct a model within a demonstrably consistent set theory. But this alone does not provide the kind of diagnosis we are after. In subsequent sections we will see that there are actually at least three different things going on here; none of them paradoxical, though all easily overlooked.

Let's now turn to the Truth-teller. The intuition we wanted to capture here is that its truth value is up for grabs. The Austinian approach captures this intuition in the following way. The sentence that expresses the Truth-teller can be used to make statements about various actual situations. Some of the resulting propositions are true, while others turn out to be false. All, though, are accessible, their constituent situations being actual. It should be emphasized that this is quite different from the Liar propositions, since all the accessible Liars are false.

Theorem 7 *Let $\mathfrak{A}$ be any total model of the world. For some actual situations s, the Truth-teller:*

$$t_s = \{s; [Tr, t_s; 1]\}$$

is true, for other actual situations it is false.

Proof: Obviously t_s is false for any situation that contains no semantical facts. To show that there are actual situations whose Truth-tellers are true, we start with any actual situation s and consider $t_{s'}$, where s' is the situation $s \cup \{\langle Tr, t_{s'}; 1 \rangle\}$. Since $t_{s'}$ is true, the state of affairs $\langle Tr, t_{s'}; 1 \rangle$ must be in $\mathfrak{A}$, and so s' is actual. $\square$

Recall that just as there are true Truth-tellers and false Truth-tellers, there are true Liars and false Liars. The difference is that none of the true Liars can be about actual situations.

Exercise 55 Show that for any actual situation s (in some total model $\mathfrak{A}$), there is an actual $s' \supseteq s$ for which $t_{s'}$ is true, and another actual $s'' \supseteq s$ for which $t_{s''}$ is false.

The T-schema in the Austinian world

What happens to the intuitions that make the Liar and related propositions paradoxical on this account? That is, once we see that a Liar f_s is false, why don't we discover that it is true, and so paradoxical? We know this is not so, by the first part of Proposition 2, but why? To answer this we introduce the notions of T-closed and F-closed model and situation.

In our treatment of Russellian propositions, we learned that we had to give up one basic intuition. We could keep the Russellian version of the T-schema, but we had to give up the intuition embodied in the F-schema, the intuition that if a proposition is made false by the world, its being false is itself a fact of the world. We now turn to the Austinian versions of the schemata, to see how they fare here. What moral does the Liar now hold?

Let us say that a model $\mathfrak{A}$ is *T-closed* if, for any true proposition p, $\langle Tr, p; 1 \rangle \in \mathfrak{A}$; $\mathfrak{A}$ is *F-closed* if, for any false p, $\langle Tr, p; 0 \rangle \in \mathfrak{A}$. Say that a model is *semantically closed* if it is both T-closed and F-closed. The following is an immediate consequence of Proposition 5.

Proposition 8 *Every total model is semantically closed.*

For the remainder of this section, let us fix some total model $\mathfrak{A}$ of the world, and treat all notions (like accessible proposition and actual situation) as relative to this model. Proposition 8 shows that on the Austinian account, we do not need to abandon the intuition behind the T- and F-schema at all, at least not for the world at large. But what about for situations, the parts of the world that, on the Austinian view, we actually talk about? Can actual situations be T-closed and F-closed?

The answer is "no," but for somewhat artifactual reasons. That is, situations are sets, but the collections of true and false propositions are both proper classes, so no situation can contain enough facts to be either T-closed or F-closed. However, this reason is not very compelling. It seems that we ought to have a local, restricted notion of T- and F-closure that would not permit the unsatisfying answer forced on us by the set/class distinction.

The first thing one might think of is this. For any set P of propositions, say that a situation s is *T-closed with respect to P* if, for any true proposition $p \in P$, $\langle Tr, p; 1 \rangle \in s$: while s is *F-closed with respect to P* if, for any false $p \in P$, $\langle Tr, p; 0 \rangle \in s$. The following result shows that for any fixed set P of propositions, we can always assume we are dealing with a situation that is both T- and F-closed with respect to P.

Proposition 9 *For any actual s and set P of propositions, there is an actual* $s' \supseteq s$ *that is both T- and F-closed with respect to P.*

Proof: The set containing $\langle Tr, p; 1 \rangle$ for all true $p \in P$, plus $\langle Tr, p; 0 \rangle$ for all false $p \in P$, is a subset of $\mathfrak{A}$. Hence so is the union of this set and s. □

This result might seem a bit surprising at first. After all, what about the Liar? Our experience in the Russellian case would suggest that the Liar should prevent some kind of F-closure. Indeed there are a number of ways of seeing that the above notions of T- and F-closure do not adequately capture the intuitions behind the T- and F-schemas. Consider, for example, the following simple observation.

Proposition 10 *Let P be any set of propositions and let s be any actual situation which is F-closed with respect to P. Then the Liar proposition* f_s *about s is not in P.*

Proof: f_s is, by Theorem 6, false. But if $\langle Tr, f_s; 0 \rangle \in s$ then f_s would be true. □

Proposition 10 brings out the deceptiveness of Proposition 9. It is true that, given any previously chosen set P of propositions, we can find an actual situation s which contains the semantic facts about those propositions. But then the Liar proposition f_s for the F-closed situation s cannot have been in the original set P of propositions. In other words, we can look at the Liar as providing us with a propositional function from situations s to propositions f_s, one that can be used to diagonalize out of any set P of propositions.

In the next chapter we will introduce new notions of T- and F-closure which, in effect, replace the arbitrary set P of propositions with the set of all propositional functions expressible in our language. For now, though, let us pause to take a closer look at what is happening with the propositional function f_s given to us by the Liar. Once we have defined the Austinian semantics for our language $\mathcal{L}$, we will see that this function is the one naturally associated with the Liar sentence, λ. When λ is used to make a statement about any actual situation s_1, it expresses something false (f_{s_1}), but the fact of that proposition's being false ($\langle Tr, f_{s_1}; 0 \rangle$), while it is in the model $\mathfrak{A}$, cannot be in the situation s_1 itself. If we

Table I

Situation				Actual	Liar?
s_1				assumed	f_{s_1} is false
s_2	$=$	s_1 $\cup$	$\{\langle Tr, f_{s_1}; 0\rangle\}$	yes	f_{s_2} is false
s_3	$=$	s_2 $\cup$	$\{\langle Tr, f_{s_2}; 0\rangle\}$	yes	f_{s_3} is false
s_4	$=$	s_3 $\cup$	$\{\langle Tr, f_{s_3}; 0\rangle\}$	yes	f_{s_4} is false
		$\vdots$		$\vdots$	$\vdots$
s^*	$=$	s_1 $\cup$	$\{\langle Tr, f_{s^*}; 0\rangle\}$	no	f_{s^*} is true

add this fact to s_1, we get a different actual situation s_2. The Liar proposition f_{s_2} about s_2 is also false, but it is simply a different proposition. And so on.

There is, though, an importantly different tack we could take, one that could easily be confused with the procedure we've just described. If we start with the same actual situation s_1, but instead of forming s_2 as above, we apply Proposition 4 from page 131, then we obtain a situation s^* containing s_1 as a subset, but whose Liar, f_{s^*}, is true. It follows, of course, that s^* is not actual or, for that matter, even possible. We summarize these observations in Table I.

When we think about the Liar on an intuitive level, there is an inclination to claim that the truth value "flips back and forth." First we see that it is false, then that it is true, then that it is false, and so forth. At first this flip flop does not seem to be captured in our picture: the truth value of all of the f_{s_i}'s is simply false. However, there is another sequence of propositions that we

Table II

Proposition			Truth value
f_{s_1}	$=$	$\{s_1; [Tr, f_{s_1}; 0]\}$	False
p_{s_1}	$=$	$\{s_2; [Tr, f_{s_1}; 0]\}$	True
f_{s_2}	$=$	$\{s_2; [Tr, f_{s_2}; 0]\}$	False
p_{s_2}	$=$	$\{s_3; [Tr, f_{s_2}; 0]\}$	True
f_{s_3}	$=$	$\{s_3; [Tr, f_{s_3}; 0]\}$	False
p_{s_3}	$=$	$\{s_4; [Tr, f_{s_3}; 0]\}$	True
$\vdots$			$\vdots$

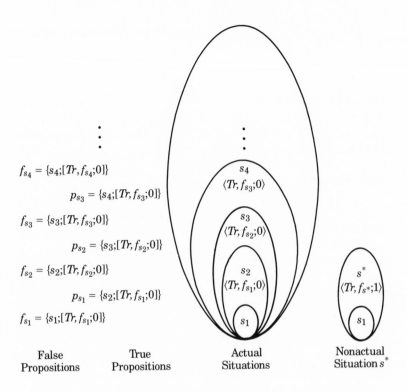

$$f_{s_4} = \{s_4; [Tr, f_{s_4}; 0]\}$$

$$p_{s_3} = \{s_4; [Tr, f_{s_3}; 0]\}$$

$$f_{s_3} = \{s_3; [Tr, f_{s_3}; 0]\}$$

$$p_{s_2} = \{s_3; [Tr, f_{s_2}; 0]\}$$

$$f_{s_2} = \{s_2; [Tr, f_{s_2}; 0]\}$$

$$p_{s_1} = \{s_2; [Tr, f_{s_1}; 0]\}$$

$$f_{s_1} = \{s_1; [Tr, f_{s_1}; 0]\}$$

| False Propositions | True Propositions | Actual Situations | Nonactual Situation s^* |

Figure 16

have not yet considered. Given s_1, the proposition p_{s_1} defined by $\{s_2; [Tr, f_{s_1}; 0]\}$ is *true*: this is the proposition that says, *about the expanded s_2*, that the Liar f_{s_1} is false. Similarly, with the proposition p_{s_2} that claims, about s_3, that f_{s_2} is false. This sequence of propositions, interlaced with the previous hierarchy, exhibits the intuited behavior. (See Table II.)

The information in the preceeding two tables is depicted in Figure 16.

Once we've given an Austinian semantics for $\mathcal{L}$, it will turn out that the hierarchy of Liar propositions f_{s_i} displayed in the right-hand column of the first table are all expressed by the Liar sentence,

$$\neg\textbf{True(this).}$$

Where the difference in the propositions comes is entirely in the situations they are about. In contrast, the propositions p_{s_i} appearing in the second table will be expressed by the slightly different sentence:

$$\neg\mathbf{True}(\mathbf{that}_1)$$

where $\mathbf{that}_1$ is used to refer to the Liar proposition f_{s_i}. In other words, the true propositions p_{s_i} are exactly the propositions needed for a resolution of the Strengthened Liar. They allow our logician to step back, recognize the falsity of f_{s_1}, consider that new fact, and use it to say, about the extended situation s_2, that f_{s_1} is not true. The proposition has the same type as the Liar, but differs in the situation it is about. In this way we respect both the intuition that λ_1 and λ_2 express closely related propositions, and the intuition that the latter proposition is true, not false.

Notice that if the Austinian treatment is correct, we have uncovered two separate ambiguities that cannot be accounted for either in the Russellian treatment, or in any treatment that assigns truth to sentences rather than propositions. Let's distinguish between the meaning of a sentence and the propositional content of a statement made with it. Intuitively, the former should be a propositional function, something that gives us a proposition when supplied with the situation the proposition is about, while the latter would be such a proposition. Thus a sentence can be ambiguous in terms of propositional content without having two separate meanings, without expressing two distinct propositional functions. This is the kind of ambiguity captured in the first of the above tables.

The second ambiguity concerns the way the expression "this proposition" functions in English. The English pronoun "this" has both a reflexive use, corresponding to our **this**, but also a demonstrative use, corresponding to our **that**$_1$. That means that the sentence "This proposition is not true" can be used to make a statement about any salient proposition, including the Liar f_{s_1}. Since the situation under discussion is almost always implicit, the Liar sentence in English could be used to express the true proposition p_{s_1} as well as the false f_{s_1}.

As if two ambiguities were not enough, in Chapter 12 we will discuss what may well be the most insidious ambiguity involved in the Liar paradox, the ambiguity between negation and denial.

An Austinian Semantics

The Austinian semantics for $\mathcal{L}$

We will now show how Austinian propositions, including circular propositions, can be the semantical values of the sentences of our language $\mathcal{L}$. This time the basic intuition we must capture is this: given any sentence $\varphi(\mathbf{this}, \mathbf{that}_1, \ldots, \mathbf{that}_n)$, and any assignment $q_1, \ldots, q_n$ of propositions to the propositional demonstratives $\mathbf{that}_1, \ldots, \mathbf{that}_n$, and any actual situation s, one can use φ to express a proposition p about s while at the same time using the demonstrative $\mathbf{this}$ to refer to that very same proposition.

Toward this end, define an Austinian *assignment* to be any function c defined on some set of propositional demonstratives and taking Austinian propositions as values. By an Austinian *context* c_s for a sentence φ, we mean a pair $\langle s, c \rangle$ of a situation s and an assignment c defined on all of the propositional demonstratives of φ except for the demonstrative $\mathbf{this}$. When φ contains no demonstratives except $\mathbf{this}$, we will simply write s for any context of the form c_s. By a *statement* Φ we mean a sentence φ paired with a context c_s for φ. A *legitimate statement* Φ is one where the situation s is actual.

We define the proposition expressed by a statement Φ, $Exp(\Phi)$, in two steps, closely paralleling the definition in the Russellian case. First we assign to each formula $\varphi(\mathbf{this}, \mathbf{that}_1, \ldots, \mathbf{that}_n)$ a parametric proposition (or propositional function) $Val(\varphi)$ in the propositional indeterminates $\mathbf{p}, \mathbf{q}_1, \ldots$, and the single situation indeterminate $\mathbf{s}$. When φ is a sentence, the indeterminate $\mathbf{p}$ will not occur in $Val(\varphi)$, and so we can define $Exp(\Phi)$ to be the proposition that results from the propositional function $Val(\varphi)$ by plugging in for the indeterminates $\mathbf{q}_i$ and $\mathbf{s}$ the values specified by the context c_s.

The formal definition is entirely analogous to its Russellian counterpart, though slightly more complex due to the richer structure of the new, Austinian propositions. First we introduce propositional indeterminates $\mathbf{p}, \mathbf{q}_1, \ldots, \mathbf{q}_n, \ldots$, but also a situation indeterminate $\mathbf{s}$. We define the classes of parametric states of affairs, situations, types, and propositions, $ParSOA$, $ParSIT$, $ParTYPE$, and $ParPROP$, in a way parallel to Definition 1, except that we also allow $\mathbf{s} \in ParSIT$ and $\mathbf{p}, \mathbf{q}_1, \ldots \in ParPROP$. In giving our definition of Val, we write $\overline{T}$ for the *dual* of the parametric type T, that is:

- $\overline{[\sigma]} = [\sigma']$, where σ' is the dual of σ,

- $\overline{\bigwedge\{T, U, ...\}} = \bigvee\{\overline{T}, \overline{U}, ...\}$,

- $\overline{\bigvee\{T, U, ...\}} = \bigwedge\{\overline{T}, \overline{U}, ...\}$.

A simple application of the Solution Lemma shows this definition to be welldefined.

Definition 4 We define a function $Val(\varphi)$ from sentences to parametric propositions as follows:

1. If φ is (**a Has c**), then $Val(\varphi) = \{\mathbf{s}; [H, a, c; 1]\}$.

2. If φ is (**a Believes that$_i$**), then $Val(\varphi) = \{\mathbf{s}; [Bel, a, \mathbf{q}_i; 1]\}$.

3. If φ is (**a Believes this**), then $Val(\varphi) = \{\mathbf{s}; [Bel, a, \mathbf{p}; 1]\}$.

4. If φ is (**a Believes** ψ) and $Val(\psi) = q$, then $Val(\varphi) = \{\mathbf{s}; [Bel, a, q; 1]\}$.

5. If φ is (**True that$_i$**), then $Val(\varphi) = \{\mathbf{s}; [Tr, \mathbf{q}_i; 1]\}$.

6. If φ is (**True this**), then $Val(\varphi) = \{\mathbf{s}; [Tr, \mathbf{p}; 1]\}$.

7. If φ is (**True** ψ) and $Val(\psi) = q$, then $Val(\varphi) = \{\mathbf{s}; [Tr, q; 1]\}$.

8. If φ is $(\psi_1 \wedge \psi_2)$ and $Type(Val(\psi_i)) = T_i$, then $Val(\varphi)$ is $\{\mathbf{s}; \bigwedge\{T_1, T_2\}\}$. If φ is $(\psi_1 \vee \psi_2)$ and $Type(Val(\psi_i)) = T_i$, then $Val(\varphi)$ is $\{\mathbf{s}; \bigvee\{T_1, T_2\}\}$.

9. If φ is $\neg\psi$ and $Type(Val(\psi)) = T$ then $Val(\varphi) = \{\mathbf{s}; \overline{T}\}$.

10. If φ is $\downarrow\psi$ then $Val(\varphi) =$ the unique solution $p \in ParPROP$ to the equation

$$\mathbf{p} = Val(\psi)(\mathbf{p}, \mathbf{q}_1, \ldots).$$

Once again, by a simple induction on formulas, applying the Solution Lemma for clause (10), we have the following:

Lemma 11 $Val(\varphi)$ *is a parametric proposition containing the parameters* **s** *and* $\mathbf{q}_i$, *for each* **that**$_i$ *occurring in* φ, *and containing the additional parameter* **p** *if* **this** *is loose in* φ.

Next, we define the proposition expressed by φ in context c_s in the obvious way:

$$Exp(\varphi, c_s) = Val(\varphi)(s, c)$$

where the right hand side indicates the assignment of s to **s**, and $c(\mathbf{that}_i)$ to $\mathbf{q}_i$. The following is an immediate consequence of Lemma 11 and the definition of *PROP*.

Theorem 12 *For any sentence* φ *and context* c_s *for* φ, *there is a unique proposition* $Exp(\varphi, c_s)$ *in PROP.*

For any statement Φ consisting of a sentence φ and a context c_s, we define $Exp(\Phi) = Exp(\varphi, c_s)$. We note that if Φ is a legitimate statement, then $Exp(\Phi)$ is an accessible proposition.

At this point, let's see how our definitions capture the basic Austinian picture of how language works. Recall that according to Austin, the act of making a statement consists of the utterance of a sentence in a context, part of which includes reference to some actual (or "historical") situation. This is what justifies our representation of statements by means of sentence/context pairs. According to Austin, the statement is true if the situation determined by the context is of a particular type, namely, the type determined by the semantic (or "descriptive") conventions of the language.

Definition 4 attempts to spell out for our simple, artificial language just what these descriptive conventions come to. Theorem 12 tells us that these descriptive conventions always allow us to use the word **this** to refer to the proposition being expressed. Let's look at some examples to see how this works out in practice.

Example 9 Suppose Φ is the statement $\langle \varphi, s \rangle$ where φ is $\neg(\mathbf{Max}$ $\mathbf{Has}\ 5\Diamond)$. This represents an utterance where the speaker claims, about a particular situation s, that it is one in which Max does not have the five of diamonds. According to Definition 4, $Exp(\Phi) = \{s; [H, \mathrm{Max}, 5\Diamond; 0]\}$. This proposition is true just in case $\langle H, \mathrm{Max}, 5\Diamond; 0\rangle$ is in s.

Example 10 Recall the Truth-teller sentence τ: $\downarrow$**True(this)**. A legitimate context for this sentence simply requires an actual situation for the statement to be about. Thus any statement of the form $\langle \tau, s\rangle$, for arbitrary actual situations s, is legitimate. The definition of Val tells us that $Val(\textbf{True(this)}) = \{s; [Tr, \mathbf{p}; 1]\}$, and so $Val(\tau)$ is the unique member p of $ParPROP$ satisfying

$$p = \{s; [Tr, p; 1]\}.$$

Replacing the indeterminate $\mathbf{s}$ with s, this simply gives us the equation used in defining the Truth-teller proposition t_s about s. Thus $Exp(\tau, s) = t_s$, as expected. An earlier theorem shows that some legitimate statements of the form $\langle \tau, s\rangle$ express true propositions, while some express false propositions.

Example 11 Recall that the Liar sentence λ is the sentence $\downarrow \neg$**True(this)**. Thus a legitimate Liar statement consists of a pair $\langle \lambda, s\rangle$, where s is actual. According to the above definition, this statement expresses the unique proposition $p = \{s; [Tr, p; 0]\}$. This is the Liar proposition f_s used above. Since the statement is assumed to be legitimate, s is actual and hence f_s is false.

In the last chapter, we discussed viewing the Liar sentence as giving us a propositional function from situations to propositions. We can now identify this with the parametric proposition $Val(\lambda)$. More generally, for any sentence φ not containing **that**$_1$, **that**$_2$, ..., $Val(\varphi)$ is a parametric proposition $p(\mathbf{s})$ in the single parameter $\mathbf{s}$.

Exercise 56 Given an actual situation s, let s' be the situation

$$s \cup \{\langle Tr, f_s; 0\rangle\},$$

and let $c_{s'}$ be a context which assigns f_s to **that**$_1$. Identify the proposition $Exp(\neg\textbf{True(that}_1), c_{s'})$, and determine its truth value.

Exercise 57 In giving the Russellian semantics for $\mathcal{L}$, we explicitly showed how to extend the semantics from single sentences to

sequences of sentences in such a way that the demonstrative **that**$_i$
automatically referred to the ith proposition expressed by the sequence. We leave the analogous extension of the above definitions
as an exercise for the reader.

T-closure for expressible propositions

Let's now return to the issue of T- and F-closure discussed at the
end of Chapter 9. There, we had a simple, contrasting pair of results concerning situations that were closed with respect to a set P
of propositions. Specifically, we saw that if we start with a fixed P
and s, we can always expand s to a situation s' that is both T- and
F-closed with respect to P. Indeed this is possible even if P contains the Liar proposition f_s. However, P necessarily won't contain
the Liar proposition $f_{s'}$ about the newly constructed situation.

These results suggest that our formulation of T- and F-closure
is missing something crucial. If we restrict our attention to propositions that are expressible, the latter result indicates that no actual
situation s can be F-closed with respect to the set of expressible
propositions about s. This raises the question of whether we can
attain T-closure with respect to all expressible propositions, that
is, whether there are actual situations s that are T-closed for all
expressible propositions about that very s.

To answer this in the affirmative, and so to draw a strong contrast between T- and F-closure, we introduce the new notions of T-
and F-closure for expressible propositions. For simplicity, we will
assume that our sentences do not contain any demonstratives of
the form **that**$_i$. We will say that a proposition p about s is *expressible* if $p = Exp(\varphi, s)$ for some sentence φ. A situation s is *T-closed
for expressible propositions* (*F-closed for expressible propositions*)
if s is T-closed (F-closed) with respect to the set of all expressible
propositions about s.

As we indicated in Example 11, our Austinian semantics gives
us a natural way of associating with each sentence φ a parametric
proposition $p_\varphi(\mathbf{s})$. We can think of the new closure properties as
parametric versions of the old ones, where the set P is in effect
replaced by a set of propositional functions in the indeterminate $\mathbf{s}$.
So, for example, a situation s is T-closed for expressible propositions just in case for each propositional function of the form p_φ, if
$p_\varphi(s)$ is true, then that fact is in s.

As before, assume we are working with some fixed total model
$\mathfrak{A}$. Then we have the following result.

Theorem 13

- *Let s_0 be an actual situation. Then there is an actual situation s such that $s_0 \subseteq s$ and s is T-closed for expressible
  propositions.*

- *No actual situation is F-closed for expressible propositions.*

The second of these results follows from the earlier observation
about the Liar sentence λ. Its parametric proposition diagonalizes
out of any possible situation. The proof of the first result is more
involved, and proceeds roughly as follows. Starting with a situation
s_0, we form a set T of sentences that either express truths about
s_0 or would express truths if s_0 were T-closed. Using this set,
and AFA, we then form an expanded situation s in which the
proposition $Exp(\varphi, s)$ is true, for each $\varphi \in T$. But there is a
hitch. In certain cases, we cannot be sure that a sentence φ that
expresses a truth about s_0 will express a truth about the resulting
s. For example, consider the sentence $\neg$**True(Claire Has 3♣)**.
This will express a truth about s_0 if $\langle Tr, p_{s_0}; 0 \rangle \in s_0$, where $p_{s_0} =
\{s_0; [H, \text{Claire}, 3♣; 1]\}$. Notice, though, that there is nothing to
prevent s_0 from also containing facts of the form $\langle Tr, p_s; 1 \rangle$, where
$p_s = \{s; [H, \text{Claire}, 3♣; 1]\}$, for various situations $s \supseteq s_0$. Indeed,
Claire may have the three of clubs in the larger situation, and so
$\neg$**True(Claire Has 3♣)** could not express a true proposition about
it, even though this same sentence expressed a true proposition
about the original situation s_0.

To prove our theorem, then, we need to find a way of guarantee-
ing that the s we ultimately construct is one that s_0 says nothing
about. To do this we introduce the notion of protection. Call
a situation s *protected* if for every proposition p in the transitive
closure[1] of s, $s \not\subseteq About(p)$. If we start with a protected situation
s_0, then we don't have to worry about any sentence expressing
a true proposition about s_0 and a false proposition about some
expanded situation $s \supseteq s_0$. The following lemma shows that in

---

[1]Recall from Exercise 12 (page 43) that a set B is transitive if $x \in y \in B$
implies $x \in B$. The transitive closure of a set is the smallest transitive set
containing it.

carrying out the above construction we can assume we are dealing with a protected situation.

Lemma 14 *Every actual situation s_0 is contained in a protected actual situation s.*

Proof: We can assume that s_0 contains some card fact σ; if not just throw one in. The fact σ generates a proper class of distinct types using only conjunction of types. Choose one of these types, say T, not in the transitive closure of s_0. Then the proposition $p = \{s_0; T\}$ is true, and not in the transitive closure of s_0. Let $s = s_0 \cup \{\langle Tr, p; 1\rangle\}$, and note that s is a proper extension of s_0. Assume that s is not protected. Then there must be a proposition q in the transitive closure of s such that $s \subseteq About(q)$. But q must either be p or be in the transitive closure of s_0. However, it is easy to see that either assumption leads to a contradiction. $\square$

To prove Theorem 13 we will need one other lemma. The lemma uses the notion of provability introduced in Chapter 7.

Lemma 15 *Let ψ and ψ' be sentences of $\mathcal{L}$. The following are equivalent.*

1. *There is a situation s such that $Exp(\psi, s) = Exp(\psi', s)$.*

2. *For any situation s, $Exp(\psi, s) = Exp(\psi', s)$.*

3. *$\psi \rightleftharpoons \psi'$ is provable.*

We will simply assume this lemma now; it is the main result of the next section on our Austinian proof theory. Using these lemmas, we can now proceed to prove the theorem. We present the proof in some detail, since the ideas will be used in the proof of one of our main results, the Reflection Theorem in Chapter 11.

Assume s_0 is protected. Let T be the set of normal form sentences defined by:

1. if φ is **(a Has c)** or $\neg$**(a Has c)**, then $\varphi \in T$ iff $Exp(\varphi, s_0)$ is true;

2. if φ is an atomic or negated atomic belief sentence, or a sentence of the form $(\neg$**True** $\psi)$, then $\varphi \notin T$;

3. if φ is of the form $($**True** $\psi)$, then $\varphi \in T$ iff there is a normal form sentence $\psi' \in T$ such that $\psi \rightleftharpoons \psi'$ is provable;

4. if $\varphi = \psi_1 \wedge \psi_2$, then $\varphi \in T$ iff $\psi_1 \in T$ and $\psi_2 \in T$;

5. if $\varphi = \psi_1 \vee \psi_2$, then $\varphi \in T$ iff $\psi_1 \in T$ or $\psi_2 \in T$.

Given T, we define s as follows, using the Solution Lemma.

$$s = s_0 \cup \{\langle Tr, Exp(\varphi, s); 1\rangle \mid \varphi \in T\}$$

Our claim is that for any normal form sentence φ,

$$\varphi \in T \text{ iff } Exp(\varphi, s) \text{ is true.}$$

Let's assume this claim for a moment and finish the proof of the theorem. First, it follows immediately from this that all the facts $\langle Tr, p; 1\rangle \in (s - s_0)$ are facts of the model $\mathfrak{A}$, so s is actual. We can now see that s is T-closed for expressible propositions. For let p be a true, expressible proposition about s. Since any expressible proposition is expressible by a normal form sentence, it follows that $p = Exp(\varphi, s)$ is also true, for some $\varphi \in T$. Thus $\langle Tr, p; 1\rangle \in s$, as desired.

To finish the proof, we need only establish the above claim about closed, normal form sentences. This is proved by induction on φ. The cases follow the above definition by cases of T. Case 1 follows immediately from the definition. Case 2 uses the assumption that s is protected, which insures that no sentences of these forms can express true propositions about s. Case 3, where φ is of the form (**True** ψ), is the main case. First assume $Exp(\varphi, s)$ is true. Since ψ is also a sentence, it must be the case that $Exp(\psi, s) = Exp(\psi', s)$ for some $\psi' \in T$. But then, by the result of the next section, $\psi \rightleftharpoons \psi'$ is provable. But then $\varphi \in T$. The converse is easier. Cases 4 and 5 are also routine, and are left to the reader.

This concludes the proof of the theorem. $\square$

Open Problem 2 The proof of this theorem is a little unsatisfactory, in that we have to move first to a protected situation. What makes this unsatisfactory is that the problem solved by protection results from an expressive limitation of our formal language $\mathcal{L}$, or rather, of the simplified Austinian semantics we have given it. Consider a sentence φ contained in some larger sentence ψ, like (**True** φ) or (**a Believes** φ). Our current semantics only allows for the case where both the embedded and embedding sentences are used to describe the very same situation. We have made this assumption in order to simplify things, and to facilitate comparison with the Russellian case. However, from the Austinian perspective, this is an unnatural restriction. A speaker should be able to report, about one situation, that Max has a belief whose propositional content is about some *other* situation. There should be a fuller account that would increase the expressive power of $\mathcal{L}$ in the way just suggested. Such an account would presumably allow us to prove a version of Theorem 13 that does not require the detour through a protected situation.

Further examples reanalyzed

With Theorem 13 at our disposal, we can now turn to a reexamination of the various examples presented in Chapter 1, to see how they fare on the Austinian account. We have already discussed the Liar in some detail, though we will have more to say about it in Chapter 12. We have also briefly characterized the behavior of the Truth-teller in Theorem 7. But a few remarks should be made about the difference between the two treatments of the Truth-teller. In the Russellian treatment, there is only one proposition expressible by the sentence

(τ) **True(this).**

The proposition so expressed was classical, but indeterminate. This meant that it came out true in some maximal models and false in others. But whether it was true or false could not be determined from the nonsemantical facts of the model.

In the Austinian treatment, τ can be used to express many different propositions, propositions that differ in the situation they are about. We have already noted that in our model of the Austinian account, the truth or falsity of a proposition is independent of the model $\mathfrak{A}$ of the world. Where the model comes in is in determining which of the propositions are accessible: here we have for simplicity assumed that propositions are accessible if and only if they're about actual situations. From this point of view, whether or not we can really use the English version of τ to express a true proposition hinges on whether there is a real situation modeled by such "actual" situations as the one constructed in Theorem 7. But on certain views about truth, including those of a verificationist or procedural bent, there may not be any real situation corresponding to, for example, the following:

$$s = \{\langle Tr, t_s; 1 \rangle\}.$$

Our account need take no stand on such issues: it would be perfectly consistent with the abstract account to say that, as a matter of fact, all *genuinely* accessible Truth-tellers are false, or even that they are all true. Of course, we'd have to give independent justification for thinking that no real situation s involves the fact $\langle Tr, t_s; 1 \rangle$, or for thinking that they all do.

The situation here is analogous to one in set theory. What Russell's paradox shows us is that the collection of all sets that are not members of themselves cannot itself be a set, and so must be a proper class. But what about the collection of sets that *are* members of themselves? No set-theoretic paradox provides us with an answer. On the Zermelo conception, this is indeed a set, namely, the empty set. On the other hand, on Aczel's conception it is a proper class. Just as logic alone is neutral when it comes to the size of this collection, so too, logic alone does not tell us whether we can use the Truth-teller sentence to express a true proposition.

Let's next consider the shortest *Liar cycle*. Thus we have two sentences, $\alpha = \textbf{True}(\textbf{that}_2)$ and $\beta = \neg\textbf{True}(\textbf{that}_1)$. For simplicity, suppose that the speakers are talking about the same actual situation s, though this assumption won't play any role in the analysis.

Proposition 16

1. *For any actual situation s, the proposition $Exp(\alpha,s)$ is false.*

2. *There are actual situations s for which $Exp(\beta, s)$ is true.*

3. *However, if s is T-closed for expressible propositions, then $Exp(\beta, s)$ is false.*

Proof: (1) Let p and q be the propositions about s expressed by α and β, respectively. To see that p is false, assume it were true. Then $\langle Tr, q; 1 \rangle \in s$. But then since s is actual, q is true. But q asserts that the falsity of p is a fact of s. So p is false.

(2) Consider a situation $s = \{\langle Tr, Exp(\alpha, s); 0 \rangle\}$. Let p and q be the propositions about s expressed by α and β, respectively.

Then obviously q is true and p is false. The latter fact makes s actual.

(3) This is a routine extension of the argument for (1), except for one detail. We need to make sure that the propositions expressed by α and β are expressible without the demonstratives **that**$_1$, **that**$_2$. To see this, consider the propositions about s expressed by **True**($\neg$**True**(**this**)) and $\neg$**True**(**True**(**this**)). It is easy to see that these are the desired propositions. $\square$

Proposition 16 shows that on the Austinian account, there is a slight asymmetry between the two participants in the shortest Liar cycle. The person who asserts α is just wrong: what he says must be false. However, the person asserting β could be talking about a very restricted situation, in which case what he said might be true, but true in a way that does not make the first claim true. The third part of Proposition 16, though, shows that if we restrict attention to those actual situations that are T-closed for expressible propositions, then this cannot happen.

Exercise 58 Show that for any actual situation s_0 there is an actual situation $s \supseteq s_0$ for which the proposition about s expressed by β is true.

Exercise 59 Proposition 16 raises the question as to whether all the α_i in a Liar cycle $\alpha_1, \ldots, \alpha_n, \beta$ act the same, or whether there is something special about one of them, maybe the first or last. To answer this question consider, for any situation s, the Liar cycle $p_1(s), p_2(s), q(s) \ (= Exp(\alpha_1, \alpha_2, \beta; s))$.

1. Show that if s is actual, then the proposition $p_1(s)$ is false.

2. Find an actual situation s for which $p_2(s)$ and $q(s)$ are true.

3. Show that, by contrast, if s is T-closed for expressible propositions, then $p_2(s)$ and $q(s)$ are also false.

Next we turn to the case of two people each claiming that their own claim is true, while the other's is false. Thus we are interested in the sentences (**True**(**this**) $\wedge \neg$**True**(**that**$_2$)) and (**True**(**this**) $\wedge \neg$**True**(**that**$_1$)). To ease the notation, let us define, for any two situations s_1, s_2, the propositions $p(s_1, s_2)$ and $q(s_1, s_2)$ by the following equations.

$$p = \{s_1; [Tr, p; 1] \wedge [Tr, q; 0]\}$$
$$q = \{s_2; [Tr, q; 1] \wedge [Tr, p; 0]\}.$$

Proposition 17

1. *For any actual situations s_1, s_2, at most one of the propositions $p(s_1, s_2)$ and $q(s_1, s_2)$ is true.*

2. *There are actual situations s_1, s_2 for which $p(s_1, s_2)$ is true while $q(s_1, s_2)$ is false. Similarly the other way around.*

3. *There are actual situations s_1, s_2 for which neither $p(s_1, s_2)$ nor $q(s_1, s_2)$ is true.*

We leave the proof of this as an exercise. Note, though, that if both speakers are expressing propositions about the same actual situation, then for the same (artifactual) reasons as in the Russellian case, they have actually expressed the same proposition. In this case they have both expressed something that is contradictory, and so false. Consequently, the only interesting case is where they are talking about different situations. Thus the reader should also verify that the third part of Proposition 17 is true even if we restrict attention to distinct situations.

Next we turn to a couple of sentences which, on the Russellian semantics, expressed *Contingent Liars*.

$$\textbf{(Max Has 3\clubsuit)} \vee \neg\textbf{True(this)}$$
$$\textbf{(Max Has 3\clubsuit)} \wedge \neg\textbf{True(this)}$$

It's easy to see that if these sentences are used to express propositions about an actual situation s which does not contain the fact of Max having the three of clubs, then they are both false. On the other hand, if they are used to express propositions about an actual situation s in which Max does have the three of clubs, then the first must be true, the second false.

Exercise 60 Give an Austinian analysis of the Contingent Liar Cycle in the case where Max does not have the three of clubs.

Let's now turn to the *Gupta Puzzle*. We will see that we don't yet have at our disposal all the tools we need for a fully adequate treatment of this puzzle on the Austinian account. Assume, for simplicity, that both speakers are expressing propositions about the same actual situation s, one that contains the soa's

$\langle H, \text{Claire}, A\clubsuit; 1 \rangle$ and $\langle H, \text{Max}, A\clubsuit; 0 \rangle$. Here are the propositions about s expressed by each speaker.

R's claims:

$$r_1(s) = \{s; [H, \text{Max}, A\clubsuit; 1]\}$$
$$r_2(s) = \{s; [Tr, p_1(s); 1] \wedge [Tr, p_2(s); 1]\}$$
$$r_3(s) = \{s; [Tr, p_1(s); 0] \vee [Tr, p_2(s); 0]\}$$

P's claims:

$$p_1(s) = \{s; [H, \text{Claire}, A\clubsuit; 1]\}$$
$$p_2(s) = \{s; [[Tr, r_1(s); 0] \wedge [Tr, r_2(s); 0]] \vee$$
$$[[Tr, r_1(s); 0] \wedge [Tr, r_3(s); 0]]\}$$

First, it is clear that $p_1(s)$ is true, while $r_1(s)$ is false. Second, it is clear that one of $r_2(s)$ and $r_3(s)$ is false. However, that does not, in this context, guarantee that $p_2(s)$ is true. The relevant fact just might be missing from s. If $p_2(s)$ is true, and if s is T-closed for expressible propositions, then we could conclude that $r_2(s)$ is true and $r_3(s)$ false. In general, though, there is nothing to guarantee that $p_2(s)$ is true. However, by what is now a standard construction, we can show that every actual situation s_0 is part of an actual situation s where things turn out as desired. For the moment, this is the best we can do.

There are two ways to look at what is going on here. One is that we need an instance of F-closure to obtain the truth of p_2, and we don't yet have it. In the next chapter, though, we will prove the existence of arbitrarily large situations that behave like maximal Russellian models, and so have enough F-closure to get us past this step. Another way to look at it has to do with the difference between negation and denial. It might make more sense to treat P's second statement as expressing something weaker than $p_2(s)$, something that would be true in the above circumstances. We will return to this suggestion in the penultimate chapter.

The final example in our budget of paradoxes was the *Strengthened Liar*, as expressed by the pair of sentences λ_1 and λ_2. But we've already discussed these at the end of the previous chapter. There we noted that λ_1 expresses the Liar f_{s_1} while λ_2 can be used to express the true proposition p_{s_1}. The latter is the proposition that f_{s_1} is false, not about s_1, but about the larger situation $s_1 \cup \{\langle Tr, f_{s_1}; 0\rangle\}$. Thus in sharp contrast to the Russellian account, an Austinian logician can recognize the falsity of the Liar f_{s_1}, step back, and express that fact with the sentence λ_2.

Exercise 61 Show that the propositions $r_1(s), r_2(s), r_3(s), p_1(s)$, and $p_2(s)$ can each be expressed using individual sentences, that is, without using propositional demonstratives other than **this**. This result will be appealed to when we return to the Gupta Puzzle in the next chapter.

Exercise 62 Show that for every actual situation s_0 there is an actual situation $s \supseteq s_0$ such that $p_2(s)$ and $r_2(s)$ are true.

The Austinian Completeness Theorem

This section presupposes the material presented in Chapter 7. In that chapter we developed a proof theory for analyzing the relation that holds between sentences when they express the same Russellian proposition. In this section, we show that the very same proof theory used there also analyzes the relation of expressing the same Austinian proposition, in a very strong sense.

Theorem 18 (Austinian Soundness and Completeness Theorem) *For any two sentences φ, ψ of $\mathcal{L}$, the following are equivalent:*

1. *$\varphi \rightleftharpoons \psi$ is derivable using the axioms and rules of Chapter 7.*
2. *For some situation s, $Exp(\varphi,s) = Exp(\psi,s)$.*
3. *For every situation s, $Exp(\varphi,s) = Exp(\psi,s)$.*

This result has two useful corollaries. The first is that sentences express the same Russellian proposition just in case they express the same Austinian proposition about some situation s. Second, we see that if two sentences express the same proposition about one situation s_1, they also express the same proposition about any other situation s_2. Thus the relation of expressing the same proposition is independent of which account we are interested in, and in the Austinian case, also transfers from one situation to another. This result was assumed in the proof of Theorem 13 and will also be needed to prove the Reflection Theorem of the next chapter.[2] Indeed, the need for these results was the original motivation for developing our proof theory.

---

[2] What we will need, in particular, is that, given a sentence φ, there is a normal form sentence ψ such that $\varphi \rightleftharpoons \psi$ is provable, so that ψ expresses the same proposition, in all these senses, as the original φ.

The proofs of the two nontrivial parts of the Soundness and Completeness Theorem are basically just parameterized versions of the proofs of the corresponding Russellian results, and so can be described very briefly, given the earlier proofs.

Proof of (1) ⇒ (3): This proof is entirely analogous to the proof of the Soundness Theorem in Chapter 7, page 114. The only point of divergence is that the assignment functions F must satisfy: $F(\mathbf{p}_e) = Exp(\varphi, s)$ for some $\varphi \in e$ and some s. We leave it to the reader to satisfy himself that this is the case. □

Proof of (2) ⇒ (1): This proof is entirely analogous to the Completeness Theorem in Chapter 7, page 114. Fix a particular situation s. Define A as in that proof and consider the set S as described there, except that we want $\varphi_0 \rightleftharpoons \psi_0$ in S iff $Exp(\varphi_0, s) = Exp(\psi_0, s)$. Again it is obvious that S is homogeneous. □

11

Relating the Russellian and Austinian Accounts

The Liar as a diagonal argument

In our Russellian development, we were confronted with an unintuitive partiality of the world. Liar-like propositions generated a host of second-class "facts" concerning their truth values which could not actually be incorporated into the world, on pain of paradox. This partiality does not infect the Austinian world: the truth value of every proposition is a first-class fact, a genuine constituent of the world. Yet there remains an essential partiality. The partiality is not a property of the world itself, but of those parts of the world that propositions can be about. Or if we think of it in terms of language, we see that while the world is as total as one could want, we cannot, in general, make statements about the world as a whole.

This conclusion, implicit in much of the Austinian development, can be made explicit and removed from our particular model of propositions. Assume that there are propositions of the sort modeled in this part of the book, and that they are about portions of the real world, portions we will call "actual situations." We begin with the general observation that facts about certain propositions automatically diagonalize out of the actual situations those propositions are about. Thus for any actual situation s, the falsehood of its Liar f_s simply cannot be a fact of s. This is analogous to the general observation that for any set a (wellfounded or not), the

Russell set $z_a = \{x \in a \mid x \notin x\}$ cannot be a member of a. From either of these observations we may draw a more specific conclusion. From the latter, we can conclude that no set is universal, that no set contains all sets as members: any candidate for the universal set u will at least omit the set z_u, and hence fail to be universal. Just so, from the former observation we can conclude that no actual situation is universal, that no actual situation can contain all the facts of the world. For no matter how comprehensive we take an actual situation w to be, it must at least omit the first-class fact that f_w is false. Thus, just as the Russell construction shows us that there cannot be a universal set, the Liar construction shows that the situations propositions can be about fall short of universality.

The reader will have noted that both of our accounts presuppose the set/class distinction, though not too much has been made of it. In both accounts the (maximal/total) models of the world were proper classes, while situations were sets. But in the Russellian case, this feature was simply an artifact of the model. There, we could easily have limited ourselves to finite or countable propositions, and then our models of the world would also have been sets. Had we done this, there would have been no need to limit the size of the set of facts, the situation, that plays the key role in the definition of $\mathfrak{M} \models p$.

This contrasts sharply with the Austinian construction. For the diagonal argument given above shows that something like the set/class distinction is forced on us in modeling the Austinian conception. To be sure, we could have guaranteed that total models were sets by restricting both situations and propositions to be smaller than some fixed cardinality. But then the Liar construction would show that our models of the world, though sets, are too big to be situations. Thus it is unavoidable that Austinian models of the world should outstrip their constituent situations, if not due to the set/class distinction, then for other reasons. This is simply an upshot of our embedding the Liar construction into our set-theoretic model.

Taken together, the above considerations suggest that we think of the Austinian conception of language and its relation to the world as a kind of completion of the simpler, Russellian conception. That is, we can think of the Russellian's world as simply *part* of the real total world, a part that a proposition can be about. Of course it cannot encompass everything there is, and so there remain facts that the Austinian can both grasp and express, but which lie beyond the scope of the Russellian. Thus what initially appears to be an expressive limitation of Austinian propositions is actually a reflection of their greater expressive power, their ability to reach beyond the fixed boundaries imposed by the Russellian conception. In the next section, we take this intuitive idea and give it more rigorous expression in the "Reflection" Theorem.

The Reflection Theorem

The basic idea behind the Reflection Theorem is that, at least as far as expressible propositions go, any Russellian model $\mathfrak{M}$ can be mirrored by an Austinian situation m. By this, we mean roughly that if a sentence φ expresses a Russellian proposition p that is true (or false) *in* $\mathfrak{M}$, then φ can be used to express an Austinian proposition p_m about m, one with the same truth value in m. Thus, a Russellian can always think of himself as expressing a proposition about the whole world, but an Austinian will view it as being about some large actual situation, but not the whole world, which is total. The advantage is obvious, since it allows the world itself to be total in just the way one wants, and so we save the intuition that, if the Liar is false, its falsity must be part of the world.

Let us say that a possible situation m *mirrors* a maximal Russellian model $\mathfrak{M}$ if for each sentence φ of $\mathcal{L}$ the following holds:

$$\mathfrak{M} \models Exp(\varphi) \text{ iff } Exp(\varphi, m) \text{ is true.}$$

Notice that if a situation m mirrors a Russellian model $\mathfrak{M}$, then m will reflect the conditions imposed on such models in the definition of almost semantically closed. Before showing that mirrors exist, we spell out this fact and some of its simple consequences in the form of a proposition.

Proposition 19 *Let m be a mirror of some maximal Russellian model. Then for any sentence φ of $\mathcal{L}$,*

1. *$\langle Tr, Exp(\varphi, m); 1 \rangle \in m$ iff $Exp(\varphi, m)$ is true.*
2. *$\langle Tr, Exp(\varphi, m); 0 \rangle \in m$ iff $Exp(\neg\varphi, m)$ is true.*
3. *$Exp((\textbf{True } \varphi), m)$ is true iff $Exp(\varphi, m)$ is true.*
4. *$Exp(\neg(\textbf{True } \varphi), m)$ is true iff $Exp(\neg\varphi, m)$ is true.*

5. $Exp((\mathbf{True}\ \varphi \wedge \psi), m)$ *is true iff* $Exp((\mathbf{True}\ \varphi), m)$ *is true and* $Exp((\mathbf{True}\ \psi), m)$ *is true.*

6. $Exp(\neg(\mathbf{True}\ \varphi \wedge \psi), m)$ *is true iff* $Exp(\neg(\mathbf{True}\ \varphi), m)$ *is true or*
$Exp(\neg(\mathbf{True}\ \psi), m)$ *is true.*

Proof: Items (1) and (2) follow from the definition of a mirror and the fact that maximal Russellian models are almost semantically closed. The remainder just play out a few consequences of these items. □

Note that, in particular, mirrors are T-closed. The strength of these closure properties shows that there is going to be some work involved in proving that mirrors exist, since the fact that there are almost semantically closed Russellian models was not immediately obvious. Also, note that AFA will be crucial to the proof, since mirrors are necessarily circular. We turn to that task now.

Theorem 20 (Reflection Theorem) *Every maximal Russellian model of the world is mirrored by some possible situation. Indeed, given any maximal Russellian model $\mathfrak{M}$ and any possible situation s compatible with the basic "card facts" of $\mathfrak{M}$, there is a possible situation $m \supseteq s$ such that m mirrors $\mathfrak{M}$.*

Proof: The proof of this result is similar to the proof that every actual situation is contained in an actual, T-closed situation and uses the same lemmas. The intuitive idea is that a Russellian model $\mathfrak{M}$ provides us with enough coherence to construct a possible situation m mirroring $\mathfrak{M}$.

Assume that s is protected. Let At be the set of those atomic sentences φ such that $Exp(\varphi)$ is not paradoxical in $\mathfrak{M}$. By maximality, this is equivalent to saying that $\mathfrak{M} \models Exp(\varphi \vee \neg \varphi)$. Let At_1 be the set of those members of At that express true propositions in $\mathfrak{M}$, At_0 those that express false propositions in $\mathfrak{M}$. For each $\varphi \in At$, we define a parametric soa as follows:

- If φ is $(\mathbf{True}\ \psi)$, then $\sigma_\varphi(\mathbf{s}) = \langle Tr, Val(\psi); i \rangle$, where $\varphi \in At_i$;

- If φ is $(\mathbf{a\ Has\ c})$, then $\sigma_\varphi(\mathbf{s}) = \langle H, a, c; i \rangle$, where $\varphi \in At_i$.

- If φ is $(\mathbf{a\ Believes}\ \psi)$, then $\sigma_\varphi(\mathbf{s}) = \langle Bel, a, Val(\psi); i \rangle$, where again, $\varphi \in At_i$.

The reason these are *parametric* soa's stems from the fact that we are using the parametric propositions of the form $Val(\psi)$ in the first and third lines. These have a single parameter ranging over situations.

We are now ready to define the desired mirror:

$$m = s \cup \{\sigma_\varphi(m) \mid \varphi \in At\}.$$

Such a situation exists by the Solution Lemma. We will first show that (1) if $\mathfrak{M} \models Exp(\varphi)$ then $Exp(\varphi, m)$ is true. It suffices to prove this for normal form sentences (by the theorem of the previous section). For atomic and negated atomic sentences, this follows immediately from the definition of m. The inductive step is standard.

Using (1), we prove that (2) m is a possible situation. We first observe that m is coherent, by the fact that s is protected. It follows from this that there is no expressible type T such that m is of type T and also of type $\overline{T}$. It remains to show that (3) if $\langle Tr, Exp(\psi, m); 1 \rangle \in m$, then $Exp(\psi, m)$ is true, and (4) if $\langle Tr, Exp(\psi, m); 0 \rangle \in m$, then $Exp(\psi, m)$ is false. These two results are parallel, so we will show (4).

Assume $\langle Tr, Exp(\psi, m); 0 \rangle \in m$. Then there is a $\varphi \in At_0$ such that $\sigma_\varphi(m) = \langle Tr, Exp(\psi, m); 0 \rangle$. In order for this equality to hold, φ must be of the form (**True** ψ'), where $Exp(\psi, m) = Exp(\psi', m)$. Since $\varphi \in At_0$, $\mathfrak{M} \models Exp(\neg(\textbf{True } \psi'))$, and since $\mathfrak{M}$ is almost semantically closed, $\mathfrak{M} \models Exp(\neg\psi')$. By (1) above, the Austinian proposition $Exp(\neg\psi', m)$ is true. Consequently, by the above remark about types and their duals, $Exp(\psi', m)$ is false. But this just is the proposition $Exp(\psi, m)$.

To conclude the proof, we need to show that (5) if $Exp(\varphi, m)$ is true then $\mathfrak{M} \models Exp(\varphi)$. We use the Sentential Model Existence Theorem from page 116. Thus, by the maximality of $\mathfrak{M}$, it suffices to show that φ is consistent with $\mathfrak{M}$, that is, that there is a syntactic witnessing function w with φ in its domain such that w is consistent with $\mathfrak{M}$. We can take the domain of w to be all the normal form sentences ψ for which $Exp(\psi, m)$ is true. For any such ψ we let $w(\psi)$ be the set of all atomic and negated atomic sentences which express true propositions about m. It is easy to see that w is a syntactic witnessing function, and that it is consistent with $\mathfrak{M}$, since m is coherent. $\square$

The intuitive importance of the Reflection Theorem is obvious. The move from the Russellian perspective to the Austinian involves giving up the belief that we can use any sentence to express propositions about the whole world. At first glance, this may seem to involve a considerable limitation in our expressive power. What the Reflection Theorem shows is that this limitation is illusory. For we can express propositions about situations that, in effect, encompass everything contained in a Russellian world. And even this is not an upper bound: for whenever we have a situation m that mirrors a Russellian world, we can go on to express Austinian propositions about even more encompassing situations, including $m \cup \{\langle Tr, f_m; 0 \rangle\}$. Thus we can talk about situations which in a sense reach beyond the boundaries of any coherent Russellian model. Far from being a limitation, the Austinian treatment in a clear sense increases our expressive power.

Throughout our treatment, we have assumed that absolutely any set of facts, any subset of the total model $\mathfrak{A}$, constitutes a situation. Furthermore, we have assumed that one can make a legitimate statement about any such situation. With this liberal interpretation of a situation, there will be legitimate statements expressing some very unnatural propositions. For example, if

$$s = \{\langle H, \text{Max}, 3\clubsuit; 1 \rangle\}$$

then the proposition about s expressed by

(Max Has 3♣) ∧ (True(Max Has 3♣))

will be false. But this seems to violate the intuition that, in general, semantic facts are parasitic on the brute facts that underlie them.

These intuitions suggest that speakers automatically rely on some kind of semantic closure in the situations they talk about. Of course the Liar shows us that we cannot have full closure, since the falsity of the Liar proposition f_s automatically diagonalizes out of any actual situation s. We could introduce the notion of an almost semantically closed situation, parallel to the notion employed in the Russellian treatment, and restrict our attention to propositions about such situations. The Reflection Theorem shows us that there would be a rich collection of these situations. If we did this, the truth of the assertion **(Max Has 3♣)** about a situation s would guarantee the truth of the assertion **(True(Max Has 3♣))** about that same s.

These considerations raise two important issues about the relationship between our model-theoretic account and real language used in the real world. One is the question of which of the set-theoretic situations we dubbed "actual" genuinely represent real situations. The other is the question of which real situations the conventions of language allow us to talk about. Nothing in our account commits us to the claim that every set of soa's in a model corresponds to a real situation: real situations clearly satisfy additional constraints that we have not built into our model. Neither does anything in our account commit us to the claim that one can make a statement about an arbitrary real situation. For example, it may be that we can only make claims about situations that meet certain closure conditions.

Earlier, we did introduce the notion of a T-closed situation, and relied on that in our discussion of various examples like the Liar cycles. There was, however, one example which did not immediately fall out the way our intuitions suggest it should, namely the Gupta Puzzle. There, we could not rely on any sort of maximality for the situation referred to, and hence we could not conclude that $p_2(s)$ was true. But situations that mirror maximal models provide precisely the missing completeness needed to carry out the intuitive reasoning involved in this case.

Exercise 63 Let m be a mirror of a maximal model, and consider the propositions $r_1(m), r_2(m), r_3(m), p_1(m), p_2(m)$ about m as generated by the Gupta Puzzle. Show that they have the desired truth values.

What is crucial to Gupta's Puzzle is that we reason about specifically semantical facts concerning the various propositions. In the intuitive reasoning we have free access to all the relevant semantical facts about the propositions involved. In the Russellian case, we saw that maximal models automatically provided us with such access. Once we move to the Austinian view that propositions are about specific situations, we see that the reasoning won't be valid unless the situation in question gives us similar access to all the relevant semantical facts. T-closed situations do not suffice here, but mirrors of maximal models do.

Exercise 64 The Reflection Theorem is a kind of Löwenheim-Skolem Theorem, but one that makes essential use of AFA, since every mirror is nonwellfounded with a vengeance. Whereas a maximal Russellian model $\mathfrak{M}$ is always a proper class, a mirror m of it must always be a set. Calculate the cardinality of the mirror constructed in the proof of the Reflection Theorem.

Open Problem 3 Our definition of an Austinian mirror depends on the notion of a maximal Russellian model. It seems that one should be able to characterize this notion directly, in purely Austinian terms.

Open Problem 4 David Kueker has shown that there are interesting converses to the usual Löwenheim-Skolem Theorem.[1] In particular, he defines a notion of "almost every countable model" and shows, for various languages, that a sentence holds in an uncountable model if and only if it holds in almost every countable submodel. Looking at the Reflection Theorem as a Löwenheim-Skolem Theorem suggests looking for a similar sort of converse. Can one make sense of the idea of a sentence φ expressing a true proposition $Exp(\varphi, s)$ about "almost every" actual situation? The aim would be to show that for any total Austinian model $\mathfrak{A}$ there is a maximal Russellian model $\mathfrak{M}_{\mathfrak{A}}$ such that for any sentence φ, $\mathfrak{M} \models Exp(\varphi)$ iff for almost every actual situation of $\mathfrak{A}$, the proposition $Exp(\varphi, s)$ is true. Our conjecture is that if one could come up with such a notion, and prove this result, one would also show that almost every actual situation of $\mathfrak{A}$ was a mirror of $\mathfrak{M}_{\mathfrak{A}}$.

Characterizing paradoxical sentences

We've presented two competing accounts of the relationship between sentences, propositions and truth. By and large, the second, Austinian account seems to respect more of our pretheoretic semantic intuitions: every proposition is either true or not, the world is semantically closed, and no distinction between internal and external falsity arises. So far, however, there is one fact that remains unexplained on this account, namely, the simple fact that Liar-like sentences do strike us as intuitively problematic. At first glance, it may seem that the Austinian account is too clean, in that it fails to distinguish these problematic sentences from other, more run-of-the-mill sentences. In this section, we will use earlier results, in particular the Reflection Theorem, to show that the

---

[1] See Kueker (1977), for example.

Austinian account does provide a natural characterization of these
intuitively problematic sentences.

Definition 5 A sentence φ of $\mathcal{L}$ is *intrinsically paradoxical* (relative to the Russellian semantics) if $Exp(\varphi)$ is intrinsically paradoxical. On the other hand, a sentence is *necessarily false* (relative
to the Austinian semantics) if for every possible situation s, the
proposition $Exp(\varphi, s)$ is false.

There are many necessarily false sentences, sentences that cannot hold of any possible situation. However, usually the negation
of such a sentence will hold of some situation. This is the case
for run-of-the-mill contradictions, and their tautological negations.
Similarly, the sentence

$$((\mathbf{True}\ \varphi) \wedge \neg\varphi)$$

is necessarily false, but its negation is not.

The Liar sentence λ is different, though. Neither it nor its negation can be used to express a true proposition about any possible
situation. And it turns out that this is a general characterization
of the sentences that are intrinsically paradoxical relative to the
Russellian semantics.

Theorem 21 *A sentence φ is intrinsically paradoxical in the Russellian semantics just in case both φ and $\neg\varphi$ are necessarily false
in the Austinian semantics.*

Proof: Half of this follows directly from the Reflection Theorem,
which shows that if a sentence expresses a proposition which is
true (or false) in some Russellian model, then there is a possible
situation s such that the Austinian proposition expressed about s
has the same value. On the other hand, it is easy to show that if
either φ or $\neg\varphi$ express a true proposition about some possible situation, then there is a consistent syntactic witnessing function for
the respective sentence, just as in the final step in the proof of the
Reflection Theorem. Thus the result follows from the Sentential
Model Existence Theorem. $\square$

Another way to put this is that a closed sentence φ is intrinsically paradoxical just in case $\varphi \vee \neg\varphi$ is necessarily false. This
looks like we are giving up classical logic, but this appearance is

largely syntactic. Up to now we have been treating all uses of $\neg\varphi$ as assertions. But when we recall the distinction between assertions and denials, we realize that an assertion of $\neg\varphi$ is not the same as a denial of the proposition expressed by φ. If the proposition expressed by φ is false, then clearly its denial is true. But in the Austinian framework, as so far developed, this denial simply cannot be expressed. In the next chapter we extend our account to encompass denials.

Exercise 65 Extend the above theorem to give an Austinian characterization of those sentences that express contingently paradoxical propositions.

Exercise 66 Characterize, using the Austinian framework, those sentences that express classical propositions in the Russellian framework.

Exercise 67 Give an Austinian characterization of those sentences that express grounded and determinate Russellian propositions.

12

Negation and Denial

In certain respects, the Austinian treatment of the Liar seems almost too good to be true. Simply by making explicit the situation a proposition is about, we seem to have salvaged virtually all our pretheoretic intuitions about truth and falsity. Every proposition is true or false, and nothing prevents any such fact from being part of the world. In particular, we do not need to distinguish semantic facts that are internal to the world from those external to it, as we did in the Russellian case.

Confronted with this solution to the paradox, people frequently react with the charge that the Austinian account simply sidesteps the paradox by avoiding genuine negation. To be sure, for propositions we take falsity simply to be the failure of truth. But still, all of our Austinian propositions have a positive character, including those expressed using sentences that involve negation. We can say of a situation that it is of the type in which Max doesn't have the three of clubs, but not that it is *not* of the type in which Max *has* the three of clubs. Since situations are partial, there is a big difference between the two.

Likewise with the Liar. With the mechanisms introduced so far, we can assert that a situation s is of a negative type, that it is one in which the Liar is not true. But we cannot deny the positive claim that s is of the type where the Liar *is* true. Does the success of the Austinian account depend crucially on this expressive limitation? Is it because Austinian assertions are always essentially positive that we've escaped with our other intuitions unscathed?

Austin himself argues that there is a crucial distinction to be made between the assertion of a negative sentence and a genuine denial. In this section, we will briefly explore what happens when our class of Austinian propositions is expanded to include denials, as well as positive assertions. To this end, let us add propositions of the form $\overline{\{s;T\}}$, which will be true just in case situation s is *not* of type T. Of course, adding these new propositions will also generate new states of affairs, new situations and new types. Our definition exactly parallels the original definition, with *TYPE* being the closure $\Gamma(AtTYPE)$ of the atomic types under conjunction and disjunction.

Definition 6 Let *SOA, SIT, AtTYPE, PROP* be the largest classes satisfying:

- Every *PROP* is either of the form:
    ○ $\{s;T\}$, or
    ○ $\overline{\{s;T\}}$,
    where $s \in SIT$ and $T \in \Gamma(AtTYPE)$.
- Every *SOA* is either of the form:
    ○ $\langle H, a, c; i\rangle$, or
    ○ $\langle Tr, p; i\rangle$, or
    ○ $\langle Bel, a, p; i\rangle$,
    where H, Tr, and Bel, are distinct atoms, a is Claire or Max, c is one of the standard cards; i is either 0 or 1; $p \in PROP$.
- Every *SIT* is a subset (with stress on *set*) of *SOA*.
- Every *AtTYPE* is of the form $[\sigma]$, where $\sigma \in SOA$.

Our definition of the relation *OF* remains unchanged, though of course the relation itself expands to accommodate the new situations and types. The definition of truth now needs an additional clause, however:

Definition 7 Let *TRUE* be the class of those $p \in PROP$ such that either:

- $p = \{s;T\}$ and s is of type T, or
- $p = \overline{\{s;T\}}$ and s is not of type T.

No changes need to be made to our definitions of partial and total models of the world, nor to the related notions of actual situation and accessible proposition. We repeat the definitions simply for the reader's convenience.

Definition 8

1. A *partial model* $\mathfrak{A}$ *of the world* is a set or class of *SOA*'s satisfying:

   - No soa and its dual are in $\mathfrak{A}$.
   - If $\langle Tr, p; 1 \rangle \in \mathfrak{A}$ then p is true.
   - If $\langle Tr, p; 0 \rangle \in \mathfrak{A}$ then p is false.

2. A situation s is *actual* in model $\mathfrak{A}$ if $s \subseteq \mathfrak{A}$.

3. A proposition p is *accessible* in model $\mathfrak{A}$ if *About(p)* is actual in $\mathfrak{A}$.

4. A model $\mathfrak{A}$ is *total* if it is not properly contained in any other partial model.

Let us turn now to some examples.

Example 12 Let

$$p = \{s; [H, \text{Max}, 3\clubsuit; 0]\},$$
$$q = \overline{\{s; [H, \text{Max}, 3\clubsuit; 1]\}}.$$

The proposition p is true if $\langle H, \text{Max}, 3\clubsuit; 0 \rangle \in s$, while q is true if $\langle H, \text{Max}, 3\clubsuit; 1 \rangle \notin s$.

Example 13 (Denial Liar) For any situation s and proposition p, there is a proposition which denies that p is true in s, i.e., denies that its truth is a fact of s. This is the proposition:

$$D(s, p) = \overline{\{s; [Tr, p; 1]\}}.$$

Again, using AFA we obtain a fixed point, d_s, which is the unique proposition $p = D(s, p)$. That is, we obtain, for each s, a new Liar proposition:

$$d_s = \overline{\{s; [Tr, d_s; 1]\}}.$$

The proposition d_s denies that the truth of d_s is a fact of s. If we interpret someone's saying "this proposition is not true" not as an assertion but as a denial, then it will express the proposition d_s, as opposed to the earlier "Assertive" Liar f_s.

Superficially, these Denial Liars look and act much like the Assertive Liars. In particular, some of them will be true and others false. However:

Theorem 22 *If s is actual, then the Denial Liar about s, d_s, is true, whereas the Assertive Liar, f_s, is false.*

Proof: Assume d_s is not true. Then s is of type $[Tr, d_s; 1]$. But then, by our coherence conditions on models, d_s must be true. $\square$

The point of giving this simple proof is to contrast it with the proof of the corresponding theorem about the Assertive Liar, and to compare them both with the intuitive reasoning about the Liar given in Chapter 1, page 20. The reader is encouraged to consult steps (3) and (4) in that reasoning. Note that while the proof of Theorem 6 uses the reasoning of step (3), the proof of the above theorem uses the reasoning of step (4). This suggests that the intuitive reasoning that gives rise to the paradox plays on yet another ambiguity, one that does not involve a shift in situation, but rather conflating the assertion of a negative claim (the Assertive Liar) with the denial of a positive one (the Denial Liar).

Here we see associated with the Liar a new "flip-flop," one quite different from that described at the end of Chapter 9. There we noted that as we expanded our situation s to include the falsity of the Liar f_s, the proposition p_s, which said of the newly expanded situation that f_s is false, was true. But then the Liar proposition about the new situation again turned out to be false, and so on. This hierarchy of propositions with alternating truth values depended on the hierarchy of ever-expanding situations, each encompassing more semantic facts. The existence of this infinite hierarchy of propositions associated with a single pair of sentences trades on the ambiguity of the situation the propositions so expressed are about.

The new "flip-flop" does not involve shifting situations. For, even with a fixed situation s, the Assertive Liar f_s is false, while the Denial Liar d_s is true. Thus a failure to distinguish clearly between denial and negation causes us to conflate a true proposition with a false one. What makes this conflation even harder to avoid is the fact that the denial of the *Assertive* Liar about s (the proposition $\overline{\{s; [Tr, f_s; 0]\}}$), like the Denial Liar about s, is true. (This follows from Theorem 6.) This should be contrasted with the assertion that the Assertive Liar is false, which is just the Assertive Liar itself.

Exercise 68 Show that there is an actual situation s such that the denial of f_s is true, while q is false, where

$$q = \{s; [Tr, d_s; 1]\}.$$

Exercise 69 It is frequently argued that denials presuppose the proposition to be denied. This would seem to preclude propositions that are their own denials. Show that in the present framework, no proposition is its own denial. We leave as an open question whether there is any natural extension which admits such a proposition, noting that such a move would seem to require the introduction of nonsubstantive propositions.

There are two principles which, if we ignore the partiality of situations, would seem plausible, but would get us into trouble. Let us examine them in turn.

The first principle is one that Austin himself may well have assumed. To be accurate, Austin distinguished between negation and falsity, not between negation and denial, though his examples are examples of our distinction. Thus he seemed to be assuming that one could identify the denial of a proposition with the assertion that the proposition was false. Such a conflation would presuppose the principle that if the denial of a proposition p is true, then the proposition that p is false must be true. In the current framework, this is made precise by:

If $\overline{\{s; T\}}$ is true, then $\{s; [Tr, \{s; T\}; 0]\}$ is true.

The second principle is that if the denial q of a proposition p is true, then the proposition that q is true is also true:

If $\overline{\{s; T\}}$ is true, then $\{s; [Tr, \overline{\{s; T\}}; 1]\}$ is true.

The informal English renditions of these principles seem plausible. However when we make explicit the hidden parameter that appears in the Austinian version, we see that their plausibility depends on our thinking of s as encompassing everything that is the case. And indeed neither principle can be held in full generality in the face of Liar-like phenomena. In particular, the first principle runs afoul of the Assertive Liar, the second of the Denial Liar.

Notice that, although both of these principles must be rejected, there are closely related principles that are true. In particular, if a denial $\overline{\{s; T\}}$ is true, then we know that there will always be a situation $s' \supseteq s$ for which both $\{s'; [Tr, \{s; T\}; 0]\}$ and $\{s'; [Tr, \overline{\{s; T\}}; 1]\}$ are true. And indeed, for ordinary, nonproblematic propositions, we may well have $s' = s$.

We have made no attempt to use denial propositions as semantic values for our language $\mathcal{L}$. To do so would involve us in untangling one of the most basic conflations in the logical literature, the conflation of negation and denial. To do justice to these phenomena, we would have to expand our language to include an additional negation operator, or some other device for indicating denial. Many decisions would have to be made in order to carry out this modification, decisions that would take us far from the topic of this book. There would, however, be at least one important advantage to the treatment that would result. Closing the class of propositions under conjunction, disjunction, and denial would result in a notion of proposition whose logic is entirely classical. Such propositions would admit of circularity, would contain both assertions and denials, but would also provide interpretations for all the standard laws of propositional logic, without exception. In this way, it would become transparent that nothing in the Austinian view of language drives one away from standard logic, in spite of superficial appearances to the contrary in results like Theorem 21. We would then see that such apparent violations of classical logic all involve internal negation, while the sort of negation involved in denial behaves as logicians have come to expect.

As a way of driving home the claim that one source of difficulty with the Liar has to do with the ambiguity between negation and denial, let's restate our characterization of the intrinsically paradoxical sentences solely in terms of negation and denial. Say that a sentence φ is *intrinsically deniable* if for every possible situation s, the denial of $Exp(\varphi, s)$ is true. With the Liar sentence, we have an example of a sentence which is intrinsically deniable, but whose negation is necessarily false. The following corollary is simply a reformulation of Theorem 21.

Corollary 23 *A sentence φ is intrinsically paradoxical in the Russellian semantics just in case φ is intrinsically deniable, while $\neg\varphi$ is necessarily false.*

The difference between denial and negation, once pointed out, is easy enough to acknowledge, but even easier to forget. This is especially true in logic, where the emphasis is placed on truth as a property of sentences, and denials are relegated to the pragmatic wastebasket. And in general, ignoring this distinction does little serious harm, any more than ignoring relativistic effects causes problems in trips to the supermarket. But at speeds approaching that of light, ignoring relativistic effects gives paradoxical results. Similarly, in the realm of semantics. Corollary 23 points out that, when approaching sentences like the Liar, we risk paradox if we ignore the difference between negation and denial.

13

Conclusions

We have followed a long and somewhat technical path, in our attempts to understand the semantical mechanisms that seem to give rise to the paradoxes. Let us step off the path, at its end, and summarize what we have learned, and put it in some sort of perspective.

The proper treatment of a paradox

Paradoxes in any domain are important: they force us to make explicit assumptions usually left implicit, and to test those assumptions in limiting cases. What's more, a common thread runs through the solution of many of the well-known paradoxes, namely, the uncovering of some hidden parameter, a parameter whose value shifts during the reasoning that leads to the paradox.

Whenever one encounters an apparent incoherence in the world, a natural thing to look for is some implicit parameter that is changing values. Consider a couple of trivial examples, examples so simple that they would never earn the title of paradoxes. Suppose we are talking on the phone and I know it is 4 PM while you insist it is 7 PM. Can we both be right? Of course: if I am in Palo Alto and you are in Boston. Times are generally treated like properties of an instant, and this assumption works fine for our more parochial activities. But in long-distance communication and travel, we are forced to pay attention to the additional parameter at work in our system of assigning times: our location on the Earth. We might put it this way. The assigned time is not a simple property of an instant, but a relation between the instant and the location; our baby "paradox" forces us to make the added parameter explicit.

Take another example. Suppose we are looking at two people, and I say A is to the left of B, while you say B is to the left of A. Can we both be right? Of course, since we can have different perspectives on A and B. Here, what is generally expressed as a two-place relation is really a three- (or more) place relation, with one argument fixed by the location of the speaker. Examples of this sort abound, and some are not nearly so easy to see through. For instance, the so-called paradoxes of relativity are not really paradoxes, but show that what seems like a two-place relation—that of two events being simultaneous—is actually a three-place relation: that of two events being simultaneous *relative to an observer*. It is our difficulty taking this third parameter into account that leads us into error when considering velocities approaching the speed of light.

Moving closer to the traditional paradoxes, consider Russell's famous barber. Can the sentence "there is a man who shaves all and only the men who don't shave themselves" be used to express a true proposition? Certainly not if the barber himself falls in the range of the quantifier phrase "all the men," for then the barber would have to shave himself if and only if he doesn't. But this sentence could express a truth if the context implicitly restricts the quantifier, say to all the men who live in Oxford. What then follows is only that the barber cannot himself live in Oxford. Here the implicit parameter provides us with some limited collection, Oxford men, and the barber simply "diagonalizes out" of that collection. No man from Oxford could shave every man from Oxford who doesn't shave himself. But a woman could, or a man from Kidlington.

Even the paradoxes of naive set theory work this way, though they're rarely presented from quite this perspective. Recall that Russell's paradox involved a set defined in the following way:

$$z = \{x \mid x \notin x\}.$$

The familiar chain of reasoning shows that this alleged set must both *be* and *not be* a member of itself, and so we are threatened with paradox. The solution to the paradox is to introduce a new parameter in the operation of defining or "comprehending" sets.

What the new comprehension principle gives us is a parameterized version of Russell's definition, one that characterizes a set z_a for each set a:

$$z_a = \{x \in a \mid x \notin x\}.$$

Now notice that once this parameter is made explicit, the reasoning that earlier seemed to lead to paradox no longer does. This, even if we admit nonwellfounded sets into our universe of sets. If a is wellfounded, then $z_a = a$, while if $a = \{Max, \Omega, a\}$, then $z_a = \{Max\}$. What the erstwhile paradox now shows, whether we are dealing with wellfounded sets or not, is simply that z_a can never be a member of a. And from this we can conclude that there is no "universal" set. For if there were a universal set u, then z_u would have to be in it, by u's universality, but at the same time could not be in it, by our general conclusion about the sets z_a. In other words, since z_u diagonalizes out of u, like the barber out of Oxford, u could not have been the universal set in the first place. Thus, what appeared a paradox when we ignored the comprehension parameter becomes a lesson—striking, but nonetheless palatable—once the parameter is exposed.

Our Austinian solution to the Liar paradox follows in this same tradition. There is a hidden parameter in the Russellian account which the Austinian diagnosis makes explicit: the portion of the world that the proposition is about. The Russellian assumes that this "portion" encompasses the world in its entirety. But just as the set-theoretic paradox shows that we cannot in general comprehend relative to the universe of all sets, so too the Liar paradox shows that we cannot in general make statements about the universe of all facts. If we held on to the Russellian view of propositions, the Liar would then force us to acknowledge an essential partiality in the world: there are propositions which aren't true, but whose falsehood somehow lies outside the universe of facts, outside the "world."

The Austinian solution provides a new conception of propositions by making explicit the parameter the Russellian leaves implicit and tries to fill with the world as a whole. Once this move is made, both the coherence and the totality of the world is preserved. Every proposition is either true or false, and what's more, nothing prevents that truth or falsity from being a fact in the world, a fact that can in turn be characterized by propositions. The Liar now issues in a lesson, not a paradox: the falsity of a Liar proposition, though a perfectly respectable feature of the world at large, cannot be a feature of the specific situation the proposition is about. Here, the Liar's falsity simply diagonalizes out of the limited situation it is about, where before, in the Russellian treatment, it seemed to diagonalize out of the entire world. It was that, plus our intuition that the world should encompass everything that is the case, that made the paradox seem so puzzling from the Russellian perspective.

What we give up on the Russellian view is the totality of the world. On the Austinian account, we need give up no such deeply held metaphysical view. But something has to go, and what goes is the belief that propositions can, in general, be about the world as a whole. Just how much do we give up when we give up that? Arguably, not much. For the lesson of the Reflection Theorem is that Austinian propositions can be about extremely comprehensive situations, situations that effectively encompass everything contained in a Russellian world. Furthermore, we can then, in an unproblematic fashion, step outside such a situation and describe the behavior of its Liar. Thus in an odd sense, what first strikes one as a limitation in expressive power actually clears the way for greater expressibility. In particular, we are no longer in the peculiar position of recognizing the Liar's falsity, but not being able to express it. This is the moral of the contrasting consequences of the two accounts when confronted with the sentence that expresses the Strengthened Liar.

Lessons for the skeptic

The whole framework we used in both the Russellian and Austinian treatments presupposes a rich ontology that includes properties, relations, propositions, and situations. This framework may run counter to the nominalist tendencies of some readers. We do not share these tendencies, and indeed, think the attractive solution that emerges on the Austinian account argues against the overly austere, nominalist stance. Nevertheless, we believe there are lessons to be extracted from this work and incorporated into sparser accounts of language and the world.

Consider, for example, how we have characterized the source of the paradox on the Russellian model. We said that the problem arose from the tension between, on the one hand, the perfectly correct reasoning that led to the conclusion that the Liar proposition can't be true, and on the other, our insistence that the world be the totality of facts. This latter intuition leads us to throw the fact of the Liar's falsity into the world, or rather, to suppose it was there all the time. But once this move is made, we land in paradox.

While this characterization is full of talk of propositions, facts, and the world, the basic insight is one about language use, and is independent of the ontology used to express it. However described, the reasoning that makes the Liar look paradoxical has three distinctive stages. We first engage in a piece of metalevel argumentation which shows that the Liar cannot be true. Second, we objectify this conclusion and assume it to be a feature of the world, a feature that can influence truth and falsity. There is a clear move here from the realm of semantic facts to the typically nonsemantic domain that our statements describe. The third step involves using this newly discovered feature of the domain of discourse as premise for a further piece of metalevel reasoning, reasoning that shows the Liar to be true. Whence the paradox.

One recourse open to the nominalist is to parallel the Russellian account, and so argue that the second step in the above reasoning simply cannot be taken. Another recourse, though, would be to mimic the Austinian treatment. Even the most nominalistic tradition in semantics, that pursuing the Davidsonian program, admits that a theory of truth for natural language must incorporate parameters that are set by the context of a sentence's use. Such parameters are of course needed for the treatment of standard indexicals, but also for fixing more global features of an utterance like the intended domain of quantification. The nominalist might take the lesson of the Austinian account to be that there is yet another contextual parameter, one corresponding to Austin's described situation, a parameter whose value necessarily changes with the utterance of, or reasoning about, a sentence like the Liar.

Another form of skepticism about the Austinian account may stem from the discrepancy between the vagueness of the ordinary notion of a situation and the precise, set-theoretic representatives used in our model. It might seem that our account is crucially dependent on being able to distinguish the exact facts that hold in a situation from those that don't, whereas with real situations, such boundaries are never quite so clear. But this is to misunderstand the relationship between the model and the semantic mechanisms modeled.

Whenever one thing is used to model another, various features of the first are significant to the representation, while others are not. Only certain properties of the representation represent properties of the thing represented; others are simply artifacts of the model. For example, the actual size of a balsa model of an airplane is an artifact, but the proportions of the model represent proportions in the plane modeled. Similarly, many features of our set-theoretic model must not be taken as representative of corresponding features of the domain modeled. For example, real propositions are not sets, nor need they display characteristics corresponding to such features as the cardinality of the sets used to represent them. Likewise, real situations are not sets, and the precise boundaries of the set-theoretic model need not represent precise boundaries in the situation modeled. This is similar to the use of real numbers to represent temperature, velocity, or position in physics: the precision of the model is a mere idealization of the phenomena so represented.

On the Austinian view, whenever we make a claim, it is a claim about some situation or other. But obviously, even Austin himself would admit that it is seldom clear exactly what situation a person is referring to. And indeed, the exact boundaries of the situation usually don't matter. Boundaries of some sort do matter, though, if one is expressing what we earlier called a nonpersistent proposition, say the claim that everyone has a full house, or that the dealer has two of a kind. Similarly, they matter in the case of the Liar. But nothing hangs on those boundaries being as precise as those in our set-theoretic models.

The fact that the boundaries of real situations are unclear only makes it that much easier to fall into the trap of ignoring them altogether. And once we do that, it's easy to think, upon expressing the Liar proposition, that the fact of its falsehood may well have been part of the situation referred to in the first place. Yet that can never be, and not because we were somehow careful to leave it out. On the contrary, no matter what real situation we refer to, careful or not, the falsehood of its Liar is necessarily excluded, just as the Russell set z_a is excluded from s. Our unclarity about the boundaries does not alter this fact, though it may well have made it harder to see.

If our Austinian account is correct, the ambiguity this vagueness injects into the everyday use of language is one of the factors that has made the Liar seem so intractable a problem. But it is by no means the only one. Another factor has to do with the ambiguity between negation and denial, between the act of asserting a negative claim and denying a positive one. As logicians, we are used to restricting attention to sentences taken as assertions, thereby ignoring all the other things we do with language. This is a complaint frequently registered by speech act theorists, but largely ignored by the practicing logician. Again, the Austinian account suggests that assertions and denials interact in complicated ways, and that a full resolution of the Liar paradox demands that attention be paid to both. Indeed, the speech act perspective, with its emphasis on the effect of language use itself on the world, seems quite compatible, perhaps not surprisingly, with the Austinian resolution of the Liar.

Yet a third source of ambiguity that gains significance in our analysis of the Liar revolves around the referent of the term "this," and the fact that in English it can be used either demonstratively or reflexively. In particular, in the Austinian analysis of the Strengthened Liar we saw that a reflexive use of "this proposition" in the Liar sentence forces us to say something false about any actual situation, whereas a demonstrative use of the same "this proposition," in the same sentence, made with reference to a Liar proposition, would allow us to say something true, namely that the Liar proposition referred to is not true.

From the Austinian perspective, the Liar sentence gives rise to no genuine paradox. Rather, it is a sentence that can be used in many different ways to say many different things. What once appeared as paradox now looks like pervasive ambiguity. There is one unfortunate feature of this otherwise elegant solution to the Liar. Logicians abhor ambiguity but love paradox.

Bibliography

Aczel, Peter. *Lectures on Nonwellfounded Sets.* CSLI Lecture Notes No. 9 (1987).

Austin, John L., "Truth." *Proceedings of the Aristotelian Society.* Supp. vol. xxiv (1950). Reprinted in *Philosophical Papers.* J. O. Urmson and G. J. Warnock, eds. Oxford: Oxford University Press (1961): 117–133.

Barwise, Jon. "Modeling Shared Understanding," Working paper, Center for the Study of Language and Information, Stanford University (1985).

Barwise, Jon. "The Situation in Logic—II: Conditionals and Conditional Information." Report No. CSLI–84–21. Center for the Study of Language and Information, Stanford University (1984). Also in Eds. E. C. Traugott, C. A. Ferguson, and J. S. Reilly, *On Conditionals.* Cambridge, England: Cambridge University Press (1986): 21–54

Barwise, Jon and John Perry. *Situations and Attitudes.* Cambridge, Mass.: Bradford Books/MIT Press, 1983.

Barwise, Jon and John Perry. "Shifting Situations and Shaken Attitudes." *Linguistics and Philosophy* 8 (1985): 105–161.

Boolos, George and Richard Jeffrey. *Computability and Logic.* 2d ed. Cambridge, England: Cambridge University Press, 1980.

Burge, Tyler, "Semantical Paradox." *The Journal of Philosophy* 76 (1979): 169–198. Reprinted in Martin (1984): 83–117.

Chihara, Charles. "The Semantic Paradoxes: a Diagnostic Investigation." *The Philosophical Review* 88 (1979): 590–618.

Etchemendy, John, "Tarski on Truth and Logical Consequence." *The Journal of Symbolic Logic* 52 (1987).

Gupta, Anil. "Truth and Paradox." *Journal of Philosophical Logic* 11 (1982): 1–60. Reprinted in Martin (1984): 175–236.

Harman, Gilbert. Review of *Linguistic Behavior*, by Jonathan Bennett. *Language* 53 (1977): 417–424.

Keisler, H. Jerome. *The Model Theory of Infinitary Logic*. Amsterdam: North Holland Studies in Logic, 1971.

Kripke, Saul. "Outline of a Theory of Truth." *The Journal of Philosophy* 72 (1975): 690–716. Reprinted in Martin (1984): 53–81.

Kueker, D. W. "Countable approximations and Löwenheim-Skolem theorems." *Annals of Mathematical Logic*, 11 (1977): 57–103.

Kunen, Kenneth. *Set Theory: An Introduction to Independence Proofs*. Amsterdam: North-Holland, 1980.

Martin, Robert L. *Recent Essays on Truth and the Liar Paradox*. New York: Oxford University Press, 1984.

Parsons, Charles. "The Liar Paradox." *Journal of Philosophical Logic* 3 (1974): 381–412. Reprinted with a postscript in Martin (1984): 9–46.

Parsons, Terry. "Assertion, Denial and the Liar Paradox." *Journal of Philosophical Logic* 13 (1984): 137-152.

Tarski, Alfred. "The Concept of Truth in Formalized Languages." *Logic, Semantics, Metamathematics*. Oxford: Clarendon Press, 1956: 152–277. This article is a translation of "Der Wahrheitsbegriff in den formalisierten Sprachen." *Studia Philosophica* 1 (1935): 261–405. This in turn is a translation of the Polish original *Pojęcie prawdy w językach nauk dedukcyjnych*. Prace Towarzystwa Naukowego Warszawskiego, Wydział III matematyczno-fizycznych, No. 34, Warsaw 1933.

Index

Kripke, Saul, *viii*, 6, 6n, 14, 22,
    24, 85ff, 87n, 92, 94n, 99,
    180
Kripke's least fixed point, 24,
    86
Kueker, David, 161, 161n, 180
Kunen, Kenneth, 41n, 180

$\mathcal{L}$, 30ff
    atomic formulas of, 31f
    Austinian semantics for,
        139ff
    formula of, 32
    Russellian semantics for,
        68ff
    sentence of, 33
Liar
    argument, 20, 79, 167, 175
    as a diagonal argument,
        154ff
    Austinian, 124, 130, 132,
        135ff
    Contingent, 22, 150
    Cycle, 22, 65, 97, 125, 148
        Contingent, 22, 99, 150
    Denial, 166f
    proposition, 12
    Russellian, 64, 79
    sentence, 12, 20, 135, 142
        of $\mathcal{L}$, 71
        ambiguity of, 138, 167,
            177
    Strengthened, 14, 24, 89,
        101, 138, 151, 174
loose occurrences of **this**, 32
Löb's Paradox, 23, 100
Löwenheim-Skolem Theorem,
    161

Martin, R. M., *viii*, 180

metalanguage, 5, 21, 88
mirror, 156ff
Model Existence Theorem, 91
    Extended, 92
    Extended Sentential, 117
    Sentential, 116
model
    almost semantically closed,
        81f, 84
    closable weak, 83f
    maximal vs. total, 132, 155
    maximal, 84
    of the world, 84, 131
    partial, 131
    semantically closed, 80,
        134
    total, 131f
    weak, 78
modeling
    facts, 30
    propositions, 27, 34, 42, 62,
        67, 124, 176
    situations, 129, 147, 160,
        175f
    the world, 30, 77, 131
monotone operator, 53, 53n
Mostowski's Collapsing
    Lemma, 41

N-closure, 81, 87ff
names, 15
negation, 16ff, 62f
    sentence, 17
    verb phrase, 17
    vs. denial, 164ff
nodes, 39
    children of, 39
nonpersistence, 122
normal form, 109f

Object language, 5, 21, 88

politicians who frequent the house, a refer-
...bt, to Pinochet's secret police, who disap-
...orters of the former socialist government
...nsidered to be threats to the regime.
...empt to expiate her morally degenerate
...nt Malva invites clergymen to the house so
... confess her sins. Her intention, which she
...tes, is to "cleanse" her lineage of any pos-
...ion." This vocabulary has not been chosen
...l Río is referring directly to the junta's pri-
...cal objective: to extirpate a growing "Marxist
...n the body politic.
...ochet regime, like other dictatorships,
... violence and state terror to subdue a citizenry
... challenge its authority. The homes of former
...pporters were frequently raided, and those
... be political dissidents taken prisoner. It is
... acknowledged that following the US-sup-
...itary coup of September 11, 1973, concentra-
... were established throughout Chile where
... the common method of destroying political
...and murder its frequent outcome. The punish-
... Malva inflicts on Carmen is analogous to the
...olence of Pinochet's secret police; Carmen's

TRANSLATOR'S FOREWORD

THIRTY years after the military coup that ousted Salvador Allende's democratically elected Socialist government, the literature written in Chile under the dictatorship of General Augusto Pinochet remains largely unknown to English-speaking audiences. American readers are familiar with the works of a number of Chilean exiles (Isabel Allende, Ariel Dorfman, and Antonio Skármeta are among the best known), but few books written inside Chile in the period 1973–90 have been translated into English. Notable are those works that offer a window into the politics and culture of Chile under Pinochet, and which contain covert challenges to the language and legitimacy of the dictatorship.

Ana María del Río's *Óxido de Carmen, Carmen's Rust*, published in Chile in 1986, is a powerful short novel that challenges the reader to read between the lines, to plumb its silences, and to decode its double meanings. Set during the second authoritarian government of General Carlos Ibáñez (1952–58)—a government plagued by inflation, unemployment, and discontent among the Chilean population—*Carmen's Rust* offers a political allegory built on the underpinnings of dictatorship: the decadence of the Chilean bourgeoisie, its economic hardships, and its rigidly traditionalist values. The mansion in which the story unfolds is a suffocating, violently authoritarian, hierarchical place. It reflects a world governed by appearances, where personal freedom and self-expression are greatly limited, where informants lurk around every corner, and where subversive or undesirable elements are simply disappeared from sight.

Those familiar with a number of works written during Pinochet's dictatorship will recognize these hermetic confines: large, labyrinthine mansions that serve as the backdrop for political allegory. In José Donoso's *A House in the Country* (1983), for example, a grandiose house serves as a microcosm of Chile—a space in which dictatorial characters determine the fates of those living within. What is impo[...] however, is not the po[...] the way in which it be[...] potential (although fr[...] tagonists.

Within the claustro[...] novel, a rebellious youn[...] overcome the prohibiti[...] matriarchs instill in her.[...] of resistance against the[...] codes her caretakers rep[...] symptom of the inevitab[...] the face of repression, fa[...] tive fear.

For both Aunt Malva[...] matriarchs interested onl[...] ating the bourgeois social[...] belong—the incestuous r[...] Carmen and her half-brot[...] be hidden and punished. [...] adolescent sexual antics, A[...] action to ensure that Carm[...] not continue. She sequeste[...] room far removed from vie[...]

the eminen[...] ence, no d[...] peared sup[...] who were[...]

In an a[...] behavior,[...] Carmen c[...] explicitly[...] sible "inf[...] casually. [...] mary pol[...] cancer" f[...]

The l[...] resorted[...] that wou[...] Allende[...] thought[...] now wid[...] ported[...] tion car[...] torture[...] resistan[...] ment A[...] extreme[...]

body thus serves as a symbol of both sexual repression and state domination.

For less daring members of society—like the narrator in *Carmen's Rust* who looks back longingly on his youthful, incestuous escapades—conformity is the only option. In the novel's epilogue we discover that he still lives in the old mansion, is unlucky in love, and earns a living working as an accountant (a detail which perhaps suggests a critique of Pinochet's neo-liberal economic policies).

With the passage of time, conformity is achieved at a considerable psychological cost. For the narrator, forced to carry inside the oxidized remnants of the past, memory is a source of both pleasure and pain. A deeper interpretation leads us to one of the most important questions still facing Chile thirteen years after the end of the dictatorship: the question of remembering and forgetting the past.

Would it be better for the narrator simply to forget Carmen ever existed, to live in perpetual silence (as Aunt Malva would have him), or is it better to remember her, to actualize her, to tell her story, to assimilate her ghost? Since the transition to democracy began in 1990, Chile has had great difficulty dealing with this issue. Is it preferable, as those who supported the military regime argue, to forget the pain and violence of the past and begin anew, or should Chile take the necessary steps to come to terms with its recent history, to account for those who disappeared, and to bring Pinochet to justice?

When I first read *Carmen's Rust*, I was bewitched by the novel's extraordinarily rich language and astonished by its many significant silences, and I also wondered why Del Río chose to invest the qualities of the Latin American dictator in female characters. Was it simply a literary trick to throw the censors off track? Or was there something subtler about her choice? I posed the question to her in an interview in 1998:

For me, dictatorships could never exist on a political level if they did not first exist on a familial level. Pinochet could never have come to power in Chile if first there weren't thousands and thousands of "table dictators" giving orders in every corner of the country. In the case of Carmen's Rust, it was very important to me that the dictator figures be women, because women are the ones who give the orders and provide stability within the family. The first orders that a child receives come from his mother. In my novel the father figure is intentionally absent. He has gone off to join the military. I include this detail (the absent father) in order to call particular attention to the rigid nature

of the female characters. I think women who choose to be rigid are
exceedingly more so than men. . . . Also, I am quite interested in the
private realm as opposed to the public because that is where power is
exercised. There is no one who supports the dictatorship who did not
come from this type of environment.

Apart from her covert allusions to Chile under
Pinochet, Ana María del Río makes her novel nostalgi-
cally Chilean by including a number of references to Santiago in the 1950s. Afternoon siestas, Gath and Chaves
department store, Kolynos toothpaste, the Alcázar Theater (where afternoons were spent watching double features), and the Plaza Brasil (a beautiful town square
where people in the city would go to see and be seen) all
conjure up images of bygone days.

One does not need to recognize these resonant cul-
tural references, however, to appreciate the universal
themes in the novel: transgression and repression; inno-
cence and guilt; freedom and imprisonment; reality and
appearance; life and death—all commingle within this
masterpiece. Its economy, its symbolic cohesion, and
especially its silences speak volumes to those not afraid
to listen.

Translating *Carmen's Rust* was not an easy task. The
Spanish text is full of slang, unusual syntax, and covert

meanings I have taken care to preserve. Such complexities, however, only add to the richness of Del Río's prose. Her literary lexicon demonstrates her creative, yet controlled, use of language in the face of censorship. It is a pleasure to introduce English-speaking readers to one of the most powerful and original voices in Chilean literature today.

MICHAEL J. LAZZARA

CARMEN'S RUST

ONE

Aunt Malva was furious when her husband, Don Pedro Bugeaut, a French physicist, distractedly spilled wine on the table as he was telling us about surface tension. She yanked off the tablecloth with everything on it and screamed at the top of her lungs about the martyrdom of living day-in and day-out with human sloth.

Uncle Pedro Bugeaut was charming. He didn't fix his tie or clear his throat like other mortals. He taught me how to make a praying mantis out of folded paper and how to make paper kites by the dozen. He would hide with us, all hunched up, under the arrangement of gigantic calla lilies and gladioluses in the umbrella room. He was as tall as a stevedore—at least that's what Aunt

Malva would say when she was angry, which she almost always was. He was so distractible he once left a hard-boiled egg in the pocket of his bathrobe. Aunt Malva spent lots of money on rat poison, soap for the maids, and household disinfectants before she finally discovered it.

We liked Uncle Pedro's hands. They were just about big enough to choke an evergreen oak, and his fingertips were like petals—thick petals.

It seemed to Carmen and me that Uncle Pedro constantly endured the torture of waking up next to Aunt Malva. She made a martyr of him with her paltry meals—lacking salt—and obliged him to be sure all the lights were out every night, no matter what. We're not about to waste electricity for the comfort of a stevedore, she'd say.

One day, Uncle Pedro Bugeaut went walking in Parque Forestal and never came back. Then, as punishment for our sins, Aunt Malva went to live in the upstairs of my grandmother's house under the main skylight.

It took her a week to move in. We watched as she penetrated the house like a fateful tempest of black trunks and brown paper packages tied up with strong rope—ropes that were like invisible nooses being slipped over our little heads. All of her boxes and wardrobes were dark, darker than her own eyebrows.

We also lived there. Dad had just separated from Mom, his second wife, after a series of vague episodes that filter through my nightmares but never materialize: screaming matches; people on their knees with open arms promising things; Dad covered with lather, brandishing his shaving brush like a dagger; stepped-on photographs all over the kitchen tiles; Mom saying that whoever offends her, even once, will lose their photos forever.

They sent Dad off to the Chena garrison because the army didn't think such an emotionally unstable person could survive in the capital.

I wasn't fully Carmen's brother, especially while her mother was alive. Her mother lived on the back patio in a glass room so she could be watched from afar as she sewed—because we weren't going to have her living with us for free, cloistered for life, Carmen said. Whenever Carmen spoke of her mother, her speech was full of ellipses. It was said she also had very dark hair, bad instincts, and could not pronounce the number eight correctly: *osssssho*, she'd say.

Carmen told me (or, better still, she confirmed for me) that her mother had been a dancer and a spy, and that those were two professions the elders could not tolerate in any setting other than in the movies. I managed only to see her mother's hair, which was as radiant as laughter—jet black—without even one red strand.

"And was she a good spy?" I asked Carmen. She responded in the affirmative, nodding her head, as if her mind had already strayed to other things.

On the other hand, as my grandmother confirmed, *my* mother was completely different: queen of the charity balls and whimsical beneficiary of the Lord Cochrane Sports Club and other important events and institutions in Punta Arenas. She possessed a tremendous knowledge of rouge and hair dyes that would have benefited any soul, and had inconceivable premonitions about the futures of her friends. She was frequently surrounded by dark-haired, passionate men (who were not difficult to find)—especially passionate eaters. She would arrive late to parties and was always impatiently awaited. Practically from birth she knew what kind and quantity of stemware was appropriate for society luncheons, and she knew who should sit with whom—even though she would sometimes break her own rules, giving a wink with one of her marvelous brown eyes.

My mother was elegant, strident. Her laughter had a glacial air that made it stand apart from all of the anguish. Her hands were as liberal and magical as her makeup was rigid, makeup that had to be imported and to which she dedicated three-quarters of her existence. She was always adorned with muffs made from authentic skins, accompanied by genuine porcelain, cut crystal, and by phrases like "nobody makes me wait" or "people are born, not made," which later I saw quoted in magazines that enjoy great popularity.

My mother was one of a kind. She turned my first Holy Communion into a festive parade full of photographs, with flashes like fleeting stars, and greenhouse flowers put to special use. I had never seen anything as unforgettable as the profusion of orchids bedecking the pews of the church in open, fleshy provocation amid the austere Punta Arenas wind. She showed me off to scores of her friends, who stroked the point of my chin without compassion, declaring that she and I looked exactly alike (she was already separated from my father). Some caressed my legs—still in green velvet shorts—a pathetic attempt to turn me into a pudgy, ten-year-old Tyrolean.

I cried when my mother left me at my grandmother's house with such a casual smile that I knew the separation would be forever: her petal-like mouth showering me with every kind of kiss, gesturing to me; and I, grievously ascending the marble staircase with my small suitcase and large *nécessaire* made of red leather, full of some absurd shaving implements, the brush I recognized with dread. . . .

(". . . and now, hurry up and shave that beard off for me, every night the same old story; I don't want to look like the wife of a terrorist, do you really think that Mr. Fuenzalida will give you an office with that beard, he'll keep you behind the counter forever; cut it off. I don't want to, I repeat, I'll never shave it off . . . period. But love, she interjects with her soapy voice, there is that marvelous set of antique shaving implements, they are probably made of fine silver, didn't they belong to your fath—?")

I cried when she turned to leave. She was fidgeting with two fingers that had nails like grapes, strangely unsettled by the personal victory that whisked her away to the station—forever.

I cried until I met Carmen, stretching and yawning in those rooms where horses were put out to pasture, sentenced for life to read Jackson Books and the Rivadeneira Collection of Spanish authors, with her savage black eyes, wending her way through the fissures of anything prohibited, with her long, exasperated thoughts as she sat among the branches of the trees, high above the poplars, twisting herself into the sewers, with a lettuce-like freshness for anything that pulsed with life.

I loved her wholeheartedly, without hesitation, because, at that time, to hesitate was cowardly.

I loved her without stopping to think of the horrible sin that it meant to them, as Aunt Malva would howl at me in the dining room with gestures of condemnation, pretending she was just passing me the salad.

Two

Around that time we got the piano. A truck arrived with MARGARITA FRIEDEMANN, MUSICAL INSTRUMENTS written on the side in Gothic letters. Eight sweaty gorillas climbed out, panting and holding filthy handkerchiefs. They carried the piano made of shiny varnished mahogany—a wooden miracle—hoisting it through the air toward the imperial staircase (which accommodated its dark color and its casters with plodding, monarchical anemia) and finally set it down in the great room. Aunt Malva's eyes sparkled. She combed the hair of her genius son, Carlitos, who would someday be President of the Republic, and sent him to swab his ears. She allowed herself to get a little nervous, and this nervousness became apparent as she repeatedly buttoned and unbuttoned the extremely long cuffs of her housecoat and walked through the hallways at varying speeds.

The piano from another world remained in the great room—the room with the lamp of ten thousand tears (and who knows how many had been broken by those Indian maids, Aunt Malva would say). The great room was opened only for my grandmother's birthdays and for celebrations that abounded with turkeys, truffles, wine, and senators.

This time, Meche had to wax the floor of the great room, groaning that it wasn't anyone's birthday; she had to dust all the silver knickknacks, inflecting her ejaculatory mutterings with furniture polish onto the end tables. "I don't know what has gotten into the *señora*, nor did she tell me that the German Symphony was invited." (Meche associates everything that is German with extreme quality, and she is not too far off the mark.)

Aunt Malva was beaming. She had bought a new suit for the President of the Republic that fit him loosely and creased in the appropriate places for musical study. But Carlitos woke up glum and walked around wrinkling up all the area rugs he could find. He wanted to be a physicist, not a concert pianist. Both things, you'll be both things, and that will be more than enough, replied Aunt Malva, smacking him upside the head. I think she had already purchased his law textbooks, her sights set on the fact that a President should be a legal virtuoso. The arts would be the perfect complement for such a special young man, she said.

One had to be careful to put on an attentive face when listening to her monologues about the congenial nature and aptitudes of the President, for they were as uncontrollable as the stars in heaven or the sand in the sea.

"Ever since he was a young boy—" Aunt Malva would begin, left alone because we knew an endless encomium on Carlitos' intellect was coming. He said "parallelepiped" before "papá." The two begin with "p," Grandmother replied. But Grandmother never allowed him to recite the list of biblical prophets or "El Monje," even though Carlitos knew them from memory. Her cutting hand established democracy at the table. We dined without exchanging personal niceties and were all equally obliged to eat the *charquicán*—an inconstant stew that varied depending on Meche's mood.

The next day the doorbell rang and my grandmother welcomed into the great room with the piano a man who could perfectly well have escaped from the cloak and dagger movies at the Alcázar Theater. He had a blonde lion's mane that clung to its most recent dye job and which shook constantly; a nose that if it wasn't fake, was unique; and a flowing cape that never got caught on the furniture like we thought it would. He carried a stack of yellow papers, which, although they seemed to shift around in beautiful disarray, I suspect were carefully numbered.

Instead of simply speaking to my grandmother, he seemed to be teaching her the choreography of a fencing match. It was quite difficult to follow what he was saying, because the man didn't speak normally. All of his sentences were epic, and he spoke them with the satisfaction of feeling them roll off his lips. I don't think he ever said anything banal like "pass the salt, please." His eyes spun around furiously as if he were in the heat of battle.

Aunt Malva pushed us into the hall. The President of the Republic waited there with freshly combed hair dripping with tonic that made his head look like the fringe of a stagecoach. Let's see your fingernails, *hijito*, your shoes, and your immaculate suit. Aunt Malva adjusted the label that read "Gath and Chaves" so it could be plainly seen.

"It's not from there," Carmen sighed, thoroughly amused. "She sewed it on herself."

Aunt Malva bent down in front of her son, buttoning his top button.

"First of all, say thank you to your grandmother, and then pay attention like you know how."

And in Aunt Malva's "you know how" there was something so threatening that even the President trembled.

Meanwhile, in the great room, the fluttering fencer went over to the piano and tapped the black wood a few times with his nut-like knuckles. Then he took the lid and propped it open with the bar. He moved toward the keyboard—an immense, placid lake—and contemplated it, closing his eyes.

Without opening them, he sat down on the stool that awaited him, nervous as an eighth note, and played a perfect ascending scale. Then, with his hands gliding along the rail with precision, another scale melded with the first, thick chords, fans of notes (Carmen later said they were called arpeggios). More scales. He looked approvingly at the piano.

"It's a Steinway," he declared.

Then my grandmother went to the door of the great room and brusquely opened it. She found us all in a clump, listening.

"Where is that girl Carmen?" she asked.

My sister stepped forward, trembling.

Grandmother muttered: "Your hair is always so unkempt. Starting today, you begin your piano lessons with Professor Liberdevsky, the composer. Do me a favor and pay attention to everything he says, because he is from the Conservatory, and he is the best there is. He will come every day for half the day."

She took her by the hand, guiding her among the carpets, the polished silver knickknacks, the sparkling tables, and the pompous curtains, guiding her along the path of the chosen to the center of the room.

"Professor, this is Carmen, my eldest granddaughter."

Professor Liberdevsky, with an immaculate twirl of his cape, took the tips of Carmen's fingers and placed them between his lips as if they were a napkin or a delicious piece of toast. From that moment forward I hated him and swore I would be someone in life, even if it were only for the express purpose of beating the shit out of him. Furious, I wanted to shove his cape into his mouth and make him choke on his own condescension.

(Carmen, on the other hand, seemed hypnotized by him. She sat down on the stool without uttering a word and later dedicated twenty pages of her diary to his fawning hands—pages I preferred to staple together without reading.)

I went up to the top floor of the house. Carmen's first piano lesson was accompanied by thick, deafening exclamations that fell toward the first floor like shingles on glass. I knew she would do something to us. She couldn't stand that I came to her house in the first place. And now she trashes me along with the daughter of that whore, whom she educates for naught because the raga-muffin in her will show through. It will show through! Fierce grimaces, eyebrows that come together in a single Promethean rage, step aside you animal. But, Mom! Don't "mom" me you imbecile, can't you see how you've humiliated us? If only it weren't for the fact that that dolt of a father of yours disappeared. I wish he were dead. But Mom! Shut up you idiot; I wish he were dead! It seems that here widows are the only ones who get any respect. Of course she—like it's nothing that she gets mixed up with her son's concubines—and he goes off and collects them like buttons. And she . . . her mother who ought to be keeping her out of the china closet permits piano lessons for orphans . . . as if such a thing . . . They always have to humiliate me. . . . Me . . . the one who keeps everything decent, clean as a whistle, who licks the furniture clean, if you will. . . . And Meche doesn't help me in the least. Bad manners, she has very bad manners with me. And I don't waste anything. And I bring honor upon our household with my father's last name (may he rest in peace). At least I didn't give birth to that stupid dimwit upstairs who studies flies.

Aunt Malva furiously cleaned all the glass in the upstairs gallery and still had enough rage left in her to clean the glass in her own room and in ours. It was she who had screamed about the lack of curtains and she who had been in charge of obtaining the matching cushions. Certainly everything was better, more orderly since her arrival.

I wanted Aunt Malva to clean the glass in the skylight, and I was sure that if she went up there we would see her from below, advancing like a giant spider.

I hid. If the President were to see me wandering around in the corridor, he would have pummeled me free of charge.

Then I remembered. I ascended one floor to the third, to the patio above the corridor, next to the skylight, where Uncle Ascanio lived—that stupid dimwit, as Aunt Malva would say.

Three

U NCLE ASCANIO lived in what he and Grandmother called his Bird Store. In reality, his room
had all of the trappings, as well as the smells, of a
primitive henhouse. Apparently Uncle Ascanio began by
collecting baby chicks in his room—future egg-layers—
with the intention of raising them to lay eggs for sale.
He was never able to convince them though; and later,
his mother, never one to give up, and praying upon the
family's coat-of-arms, bought him eggs arranged in a
multitude of purple cartons. But the capital quickly
turned rancid because Uncle Ascanio never sold anything.
He just filed his nails endlessly, staring straight ahead,
mesmerized by everything, as though an invisible door
were about to open.

My incorrigible grandmother kept on bringing him eggs—which just piled up—in the futile hope he would come down to earth and plant his feet firmly on the ground, that he would earn a living by working, just like any honorable man. That's the least we can ask, they would say. Evidently, Uncle Ascanio was not an honorable man.

Carmen and I loved him. He was virtually a transparent being—although he was anything but thin—with the most luminous smile I have ever seen and unbelievably smelly feet. This is the real test of our love, Carmen would say, laughing, as we went up to see him.

Uncle Ascanio's feet were huge and white. He always went without shoes despite the fact that Grandmother arranged house calls by specialists from Rodríguez Footwear who promised to outfit any foot perfectly, but who couldn't stand my uncle's welcoming toothy grin or the odor that assaulted them when they opened his door. The nail on his right big toe fascinated me: it was truly a violet-colored battleship. Smiling, without saying anything to us, he would let us touch it. He would let us do anything.

My grandmother's friends and people in general asked about the henhouse long after it was gone, even after stacks of egg cartons were left teetering on the street, forming two columns that were anything but stately.

Grandmother, happy to find a justification for the odor that filtered down the stairwells, insisted for years that the henhouse still existed.

Uncle Ascanio never went out again, not even down to the second floor. He stayed in his room so peacefully, un-whimsically, that we finally knew what it meant to be a saint. Aunt Malva swelled with repugnance, covering her nostrils. I don't know how mother puts up with it, it's uncultivated, it's savage. What would my father say? We'll all catch some terrible infection with that crazy man upstairs . . . puh!

But Uncle Ascanio's stinky feet were nothing compared to his sweet indifference. He was like a giant chicken hovering above the inanities of the human beings below. Aunt Malva, with her frenetic feather-dusters and fingers probing snail shells to clean out their insides, could never understand him. Whenever I wanted to touch the lining of heaven, I would go up to Uncle Ascanio's room. But I had a feeling Grandmother had sent him up to his sanctuary for a different reason. It was an honor to have him with us.

The disenchantment of the piano was also quite hard on Aunt Malva. For days she remained in her bedroom, hardened, like pasteboard, in front of a dry book, without moving, writhing from nostalgia for a life where people recognized her for what she was really worth. But suffering seemed to be the fare for traveling this route, and she always paid all of her debts.

"Uncle Ascanio is a good man, just like Uncle Pedro," I once said in the dining room, thinking it would please her.

"How can this child dare to compare? You don't seem normal!" Aunt Malva spit. "He grows a lot, he's quite tall, look mother. And as we know, tall boys always turn out to be stupid."

My grandmother made her shut up and said, "By the way, the President of the Republic is turning out a bit dwarfish."

Aunt Malva got up from the table, crying, not wanting to have dessert.

"This is the third one," she repeated.

"The third what?" my grandmother asked.

"The third humiliation in less than a month," she sobbed. "I simply can't take any more."

"Stop counting then," replied my grandmother, who, despite her rigidities, could be quite brilliant.

Four

I LOOKED at Carmen, and what we feared happened.
Aunt Malva focused on us the rage of her solitary
glands when she found out about the illegalities we
intended to commit. She was very intelligent. Don Pedro
Bugeaut must have been attracted to that; that's the only
reason we could think of for their having gotten
together. I will never forget how he looked at her when
Aunt Malva, face to face with him at the table, took for
granted his dejected presence—that of a lonely man who
for years had eaten every day in the same spot, always letting his food get cold.

To spice up our lives a little in that huge house, a few
games would be left sitting on top of Grandmother's
green tablecloth just after lunch, although by that time

we were already making overtures under the table—
rolling up napkins and playing footsie.

All our intentions became clear before my grandmother's eyes, miasmic intentions that filtered through
her ears; her simple veto power was enough to censure
anything forever.

We could no longer go upstairs to contemplate Uncle
Ascanio's contemplation, or steal eggs from him only to
poke them with a pin and suck them, and then watch his
wonderful perplexity when he'd take the eggs in his hands
and find that some weighed more than others.

We were also forbidden from going to the matinees
at the Alcázar with only one ticket. It was a system
Carmen had invented whereby she would pretend to
faint and would then come to, her body supported by
various ushers, drinking sugar water between her sighs,
which were different every time so no one would recognize her. (Carmen boasted of having three different
ways of opening her eyes.) In the confusion, I would
slip under the ropes for free, and shortly thereafter we
would meet in the darkness as the German newsreels
played. By doing this we got to see *Pickpockets on Board,*
The Daughter of Corsario Negro and *The Return of the
Deadman.*

During the racy scenes (that tended to feature two tormented people who inevitably would kiss each other after working hard not to give in to their temptations), I fixed my gaze on Carmen and disobeyed the social norms that held at school: take her hand firmly and be sure to put up with all of her hitting, pinching, and insults. *Hang on tight. If you let go you're not much of a man.*

Everything turned out the opposite of what I expected, because the one who had her gaze fixed on me during the scene where Corsario succumbs to the enchantments of the tanned Yáñez was Carmen.

She looked at me without wavering, making it quite clear that I was not Yáñez and that I would never be as tan or ever possess his package of muscles at any time in my life. I started to retreat like one who was defeated, but much to my surprise she grabbed my hand and held it in the hot dry oven of her own (I sweated so much I got her skirt wet).

We watched the movie six times and returned to the house on our tiptoes. We didn't remember, though, to slip in through the hallway that led to the maid's quarters. Aunt Malva and my grandmother were waiting for us in the large dining room. All the lights were on, and the two of them were staring at the grandfather clock. A bottle of wine from the day's meals—with my grand-mother's last name on the label—was all that was on the table. The level inside it had ebbed just a bit.

"Have you come to eat?" my grandmother asked. "If that's the case, I regret to inform you that the dinner hour ended two and a half hours ago."

"Your piano lessons, my dear," Aunt Malva said to Carmen, her voice projected at the wall, almost weak. "It would be a shame if you missed out on them, especially since you have this opportunity to study with such a famous teacher. . . . This is truly the chance of a lifetime."

Turning toward her mother, Aunt Malva started to explain herself: although she couldn't be sure, Aunt Malva had come to suspect that Carmencita's studies were already no longer what they once were . . . that . . .

"Starting tomorrow, following your studies, the two of you will watch over me during my siesta," my grand-mother dictated. She considered going to the movies to be stupid for two reasons: first, for that parade of vulgar scenes in which women with long necks and huge mouths acted the protagonist; and second, for the money it cost to get in.

Tending to Grandmother's siesta was truly a punishment. I thought about the wooden stools we would have to sit on, straight-backed, like on a trip in THIRD CLASS, when everything hurts, right down to the tick-tock of the waiting room clock, where the passing hours bury themselves deep in your buttocks and remain there stuck. It would be horrible. And we knew whose idea it was.

FIVE

AUNT MALVA lurked in the most unusual places. There was secrecy in how she walked and how she ate: she would work around her plate, picking cautiously at her food, only to end up in the pantry eating a bit of cheese—this despite the clacking of Meche's heels as she walked by with her wounded pride, carrying the uneaten *charquicán*. She would crumble bread in search of God knows what pathogen. She never wore heels, and moved about like a cat, suddenly, more than anything, suddenly.

She surprised us once while we were kissing during Grandmother's siesta, a time when you had to be quiet and sit up straight on stools with no backs, while reading abridged editions of *Don Quixote* for imbeciles and watching the arrhythmia that made Grandmother's diamond broach jump. It was a present from Grandfather. This was the only misfortune that afflicted my grandmother. As far as I know, she never even had a cold.

Aunt Malva came in like a black cat just as we had managed to push our stools together and kiss like monkeys on a tightrope, never failing to remain bolt upright without ungluing ourselves from our seats.

The word *aberration* emerged from among Aunt Malva's skirts, and she spoke it with the skill of a chess player. Rumors and hands covering mouths reached the kitchen, where we were reminded about Cain and Abel.

"But those brothers were just the opposite," Carmen tells me with closed lips from across the table.

We can't talk to each other or to anyone else from now on. She even surprised us by popping out of a basket. I don't understand any of it, and I don't care.

Carmen shrinks a bit in the face of the rumors. She shrinks a bit from all of it. Grandmother paces through the halls quite perturbed. So that, that is to say, "this" does not spread, she has forced her to study something realistic: commercial editing. But Carmen does not even look at her book that bears the picture of a woman wearing long skirts flying upon the wings of success.

The teacher who climbs the marble staircase to teach Carmen commercial editing is as different from Liberdevsky as a snail from an eagle: shy, she bears more of a resemblance to Juanita the seamstress, who took the measurements for my first suit with a tape-measure and a fan of pins in her mouth. Look how tall he is, my God.

The commercial editing teacher doesn't look anything at all like the holder of the Key to the Future, as the textbooks claim. Carmen stares at her fixedly, as if she is contemplating the adjoining room; she says no one is going to mess up her life with fourteen different types of price cards.

I get wet just thinking about Carmen in her room, the room with the rabid curtains, in her petticoat of wretched lace, lace that gets caught on your fingers. A secretary's petticoat, Carmen says, dying of laughter, and she solemnly swears beneath the skylight that she will never learn commercial editing.

"And the piano?" I ask her, spiteful, touching her nimbly, only to encounter her erect nipples. "Liberdevsky hardly even approaches you . . . that . . . that . . . *charqui*-head, and there you are sitting on the floor following his hands. Tell me, has he touched you?" I say suddenly. Ferociously, I corner her, forcing her up against the

railing of the staircase and grabbing her by the wrists
(she bends with a threatening elasticity). "Answer me!
Has he touched you, that old son-of-a-bitch . . .?"

"Piano, meee?" Carmen sings. "How silly you are!
Don't you understand that I only learned the fifth opus,
and that's the only one I can play, backward and forward,
forward and backward, so he'll stop pestering me with
those exercises? The old boy never really has known what
it is I'm playing. I finish and he nods his head a bunch of
times, so many times it seems as though he must have
swallowed Jell-O. Piano, meee? Can you really picture me
all dressed up in a curtain, playing waltzes? Anyway, that
guy Liberdevsky is so gross; he has those buttery eyes
and a wart on the side of his nose that sometimes grazes
me. I don't think I'll ever see the other side, the one
without the wart, that is." We throw ourselves onto the
floor, laughing hysterically and repeating *firulí, pichulí, con-
chalí* until we're right next to each other. Her breath is
boiling; it's a deep well of jasmine and rotten orchids;
more, more, I tell her, and she kisses me long and wet
until I lose my breath. . . .

Six

AROUND that time my father came to see us. His mount was the fieriest steed of the garrison. So fiery, in fact, he could not dismount and had to shower us with affection from above—affection that consisted of a package of candied papayas.

"Remember, you have to share them," he said as he disappeared amid a cloud of vague inquiries about our health.

Grandmother remained quite nervous after his visit, and her arrhythmia got worse. She stopped wearing her usual blouses with ruffles up to her neck, and she forgot to oversee lunch one or two times. On those occasions Meche turned into a triumphant dictator, with her unusual meat stews, original inventions "made with leftovers."

In those days Grandmother flitted around running
"errands." She'd get up at the crack of dawn and leave the
house to make "special deliveries," but in reality she'd go
in and out of the Bank of Chile innumerable times carrying different papers, envelopes, stamps, and embossed
documents ever more voluminous. (She would take us
with her and push us up to the tall mahogany teller win-
dows so we could see.)

"This is the last time I'll let that child get me
involved in such messes," she said. But Carmen and I
knew it was just one of many times, and that even if she
had to sell the Mercedes that was rusting in the garage,
or even her own soul for that matter, she would get her
little Alejandrito out of a jam.

I got depressed after my father's visit. I realized
summer vacation was quickly coming to an end and a
horrible school year awaited me—an entire year in that
prison of a boarding school, where cases of pneumonia
were called colds and where teachers were as strict and
harsh as new brooms. The punishment for disorderliness
and dirtiness was to stand up straight with your arms
spread wide, holding a brick in each hand until your eyes
began to well up with tears. I wouldn't have marbles or
tops to play with, since they fell under the category of

"unnecessary things." I wouldn't even have Uncle Ascanio's eggs. I would have to sweep the terrace outside my room as well as the adjoining hallway every morning, for life.

Carmen, on the other hand, turned her sadness into laziness.

"Look at grandmother running around like some highfalutin kite. What's the reason for her hurry now? Do you know?" Carmen said, looking at me, full of fever. "Do you know what I would like most in the world? To know if when he engendered me he was thinking about my mother or yours." She remained quiet for a moment and then let out such a mature cackle that it scared me.

"You're as bad as a witch," I said to her.

"I am at that," she assured me. "Like a witch, I want to destroy everything with my fingertips. Don't you feel like doing that sometimes?"

At times I felt I didn't know her. She ran to the great room and moved all the sheet music around, sheet music that had laurel-leaf decorative borders. She put other papers on the music stands and turned off all the lights. "You won't be able to see anything. Shut up, silly, don't make any noise."

Carmen sat at the piano with perfect posture and, imperceptibly, the notes of some song that *wasn't* the piano lesson poured forth from the keyboard like violet smoke. Her voice, deep and slow (*adagio vivo* that imbecile Liberdevsky would say), moved freely between groans and anticipated notes, creating music that played in all of the soda fountains in those days: "Blue Moon." But Carmen swallowed the notes, rolling them around in her throat and braiding them passionately with her fingers, her feet on the pedals, those little enraged feet, ever stronger. Carmen, they're going to hear you. They're coming.

"Bluuuue Moooon . . ."

Carmen, they're coming downstairs. Start playing your exercises. But there was no music on the music stand, nor did the piano even exist. The twilight and Carmen became one and the abysmal grittiness of the syllables swelled in her mouth. Every shade of her pain unfolded like the marvelous journey of a sailboat.

No one ever appeared in the great room. Not even Meche, who was in the kitchen, could hear her. She was humming her perpetual "*malhoombree*," a drone appropriate for watching over puddings and for drying cups to the point of exasperation.

After my father's visit, everything gradually returned to normal and Grandmother went back to being her usual old self: ordering the maids around by names she thought they should have, names like Rosa or María, and specifying the number of lumps of sugar we should put in our tea. We're living in difficult times, children. Even though there was inflation under González Videla, with this one, God help us. From that moment on there were no more special dinners, and certainly no more cheese.

Aunt Malva shifted in her seat. No sir. She had been employed as a stenographer in Congress and she knew how these things worked. So don't start talking to me now about inflation, with the strikes and meetings and all. . . .

"That's enough," my grandmother interrupted. "We will save where it is reasonable to do so: on toothpaste," she decided. "We should use it sparingly."

It was astounding what it cost in those days, and all because it was being shipped on American boats, just because the boats had the little stars on them, the boats that brought the chewing gum. . . .

"You know very well I buy my own toothpaste," Malva retorted. "And that I would never . . ."

"I was speaking to the children," Grandmother responded dryly.

"Fine, but Carlitos, he'll never . . ."

"All the children will comply," she cut in.

Then we heard Aunt Malva's undulating voice: "Of course, all outings to the movies will have to cease until sunnier days are upon us. Isn't that right, mother?"

I saw Carmen's black smile, plastered across her face on the inside.

Seven

The days go by. I burn for Carmen. It's like drinking a glass of liquid fire. Oh God, may no one ever come and take me away from my grandmother's house.

At lunch today I asked her to show me her breasts—on a scrap of paper I passed to her stuck in a piece of bread, in the purest style of Lagardére. She was about to swallow the bread and the paper whole when she literally began choking at the table. Aunt Malva pretended to help her, but she was just trying to get her hands on the note. I was so terrified I almost threw up my flan. But Carmen, quick as a sparrow, snatched it up and hid it under her skirt like a flash of lightning. She continued with her severe coughing spell, as was to be expected of a girl from the steppes (Aunt Malva would be the bison).

She didn't answer me in writing, but spoke to me plainly—crystal clear—right in the middle of the dining room, despite the fact we had been strictly forbidden to speak to each other.

"It is improper to ask such a thing, especially in writing on a scrap of paper," she told me. "It's something you just do. But we have to watch out for her," she added. "The whole house is full of her presence: eyes, ears, searching for whatever evil they can hear. She twists words around like wool on a loom. Her bitterness is quite poisonous, and it sticks you know."

Then she coaxed me to her and grabbed me by the hair. I was dizzy with pleasure. Her acidic smell, like freshly-brewed coffee, made me more nostalgic by the mouthful.

"I want to see you naked," she sighed. "And you?"

"Me? Oh, yes, much more than want . . ." I was burning up from the ears down. "I love you . . ." I whispered, but so quietly she didn't hear me. Anyway, it sounded so trite to say those words, like a mere caricature of my real feelings.

"I want to see you naked in a dangerous place," Carmen continued. "Somewhere really dangerous. Like in Aunt Malva's bathroom."

EIGHT

And so there we went on that afternoon of quiet siestas, an afternoon when pigeons were melting under the cornices and I was trembling like a flag, trying to erase from my mind Aunt Malva's face, which appeared and disappeared at the bathroom door, with her voice as soft as torn curtains, carrying a hot iron rod with which to burn our pudenda. (*Pudenda*? Does that mean powerful? How am I supposed to know? Boy, the things you come up with, Carmen said.) I didn't enjoy seeing Carmen's breasts one bit. She revealed them to me slowly, as though her clothes were delicate husks. My hands were like coal beside the whiteness of her full breasts. Then she sat down on the bidet in a pose that later, when I remembered it, drove me crazy.

At the moment, however, I only managed to see the door where Aunt Malva's bathrobe hung, imperious and baby blue.

A sleepy silence burned on the bathroom tiles.

No one came. But something much worse happened.

All of a sudden, Carmen was just staring at me with her wandering eyes: "You're so weird with all of this, and it's not even that big a deal," she said, revealing herself to me even more. After making a circle on the mirror with Aunt Malva's Kolynos toothpaste, she got dressed, rhythmically and vibrantly, like a hundred drums on a battlefield.

She went into the hallway without looking at me.

I cleaned the mirror as best I could, and quickly turned off the faucet on the bidet. I ran after her. I begged her to believe how much I burned for her. But she looked at me the same way she looked at the delivery boys who came to the house balancing packages on their bicycles: from head to toe, slowly peeling off their clothes with her eyes, as if they were bananas in gray uniforms, leaving them to wonder whether her look was scorn or interest. Many succumbed to that look and tried to approach us at the matinees. But Carmen only drew closer to me, holding them at bay with an expression like the horizon.

I took hold of her shoulders.

She was my love, my only love, my ever-deepening, hellish sadness. She was everything to me. But what if Aunt Malva caught us? What would she be capable of doing? And what if she decided to separate us?

"Separate us?" Carmen said as she embraced me, trembling strangely.

And then, burning with passion, I lifted up her sweater so I could see her and lick her breasts, her erect nipples. But at that very instant he jumped out from behind a garbage can, that little cockroach, the President of the Republic.

He said nothing as he left the room, dragging his feet in front of us and licking his lips. It was disgusting, as though he, too, had latched on to Carmen's breasts with his leach-like mouth, if only for a moment. Then he continued to walk away, closing doors behind him.

Carmen and I stayed there discussing what had happened.

"I pulled your sweater down before he came in."

"No. You pulled it down after he already saw us," she said. That little brat has antennas for anything that's dirty.

"But your breasts are wonderful, not dirty."

"My breasts may not be dirty, but his eyes sure are."

"They're like the breasts of the Queen of the Caribbean," I said, inspired. "When you can see them through her tunic. No. Yours are even more beautiful."

"It doesn't matter." Carmen shrugged her shoulders, smiling (just like the Queen). "Whatever happens, happens."

That young warrior had no idea of the cross she would have to bear. I pressed her to my chest. She smelled of restlessness, a kind of bitter force that welled from her underarms.

THAT afternoon we didn't see each other. Having agreed, we each stayed in our own room, desiring each other like crazy, remembering every flash, every thread. I was more than restless. I was afraid of something that inevitably hung over us, like the impending days on a calendar.

I spent countless hours walking the hallways, waiting for Carmen to come out. The stools were pushed so close together there was hardly a gap between them.

Then dinnertime came. Aunt Malva, looking at the ceiling, began talking about morality, respect, high prices, bread lines, consideration—vague words, but polished ones. I was about to slip into a coma, when suddenly she let out a long sob and pushed her dishes away, saying that with all that had been going on she had lost her will to eat (funny, she didn't say anything about hunger).

"The criminal will soon hang on the gallows," Carmen muttered. "So in case I never see you again, farewell. I've craved you like the devil, more than I ever craved any of those imbeciles on the street."

She placed her hand on my stomach, wending her way under my shirt in a wonderfully savage gesture. I was bathed in delicious horror.

NINE

AUNT MALVA spoke first (after sighing, of course) about the complete collection of *Faustos* she was surprised to find under Carmen's mattress. They were magazines we had traded our old clothes for at the dime store. The President was the first to devour them. I got right in his face, furious, but he just kept on eating like a little saint. I was quickly admonished to keep quiet.

"They even read them on Sundays," the President assured his mother with his mouth full.

Aunt Malva gestured to my grandmother.

"I spoke with Professor Liberdevsky the other day," Grandmother said. He is unhappy with you, Carmen. He told me he feels you are making a deliberate effort, despite your facility and talent, not to come prepared to your lessons. He also says you have a very good voice, although I don't know why he would say that, since they are, in fact, piano lessons. With the memory God gave you, you should be his star student."

Carmen contemplated her stew as it got cold on the plate.

"Finish eating," my grandmother decreed. "I want to see what you've really learned."

We all waited for her (it even seemed as though I were there to judge you, oh Carmen) while she took her sweet time cutting every bite of food into little pieces. My grandmother drummed her fingertips on the table.

We went into the great room. They made her play some exercises from the first few pages of *Young Virtuoso.*

"She'll never reach the octave," Aunt Malva commented, craning her neck to examine Carmen's small hands; her pinkie fluttered desperately, struggling to reach the key.

Carmen only knew the *Fifth Opus.* She played it tirelessly in every one of the ten ways she knew how.

Aunt Malva stepped forward: "Look mother, the magazines. They're perfectly cut to fit the music stand. See? They have cut off the tops of the pages."

Carmen remained still in a silence that trembled. Her amazing defiance, which I have never again seen in another human soul, was welling up inside her; a sense of urgency compelled her to risk all she had right up to the end. I quickly ran to the piano to stop her, but it was too late. She was working the pedals wildly, affirming herself with every chord. Her thick voice, that of a woman in pain plagued by the mundane, left Aunt Malva paralyzed for a moment.

"Bluuuue . . . Moooon . . ." she sang with her mouth wide open, a red tunnel from which sound gushed forth. The force of her exquisite diction unfolded like a gentle, giant panther penetrating the room in an untimely manner.

The song pulsated, and so did we. We were consumed by the ecstasy of tumescent sound, no longer a classical air, a song fertilized by something much more powerful. My grandmother was the first to react.

"Stop that racket!" she demanded. "It has neither tempo nor style. She plays like a piano man in a saloon."

"But . . ." I stood up.

Aunt Malva shot me a threatening look and I quickly sat down again.

"She doesn't know anything," my grandmother said with a frown.

"She has to dedicate herself to the piano. Make it her vocation!" Aunt Malva shrieked. "And with what that composer charges, we will need all your efforts as well, mother, especially if we are depriving ourselves of sugar in order to . . ."

"Now don't go throwing that in my face," my grandmother said with a snort. "He came highly recommended," she continued, "but it would appear he has a pole stuck up his rear end just like the rest of them."

The President looked at us, eating his dessert like a driveling idiot.

Then Aunt Malva stepped forward and placed a square-shaped package wrapped in blue paper on her mother's lap. Carmen turned pale.

"Fairy . . . traitor . . ." she muttered.

They were her secret diaries, those she kept far away from her "official" diaries, the ones that contained quotations from Latin American writers and boring promises about how she would change her behavior. She would conveniently plant the official diaries throughout her dresser drawers, in between her underwear and other feminine things, so they could be found easily upon a cursory inspection.

I don't know how Aunt Malva found the secret diaries, but I suspect the President of the Republic gave her quite a bit of help. He would walk the halls with a book of easy piano pieces, singing scales, his hair slicked back the way my dead uncle used to wear his. He'd do anything to secure himself a place of honor.

They locked Carmen away. Her diaries . . . an arsenal of indecencies . . . But how, I don't know how that girl . . . Ever since she was a child she dressed like us and ate the same food. . . . It's her blood, mother, it's a shame, but it's her blood. . . . Can't you see this behavior just comes out of her naturally?

Almost all the "indecencies" they spoke of referred to me lying down. My God . . . What would Alejandrito say? I can't believe they are from the same gene pool. He is so refined and she . . . There were also some digressions about Professor Liberdevsky (but you didn't hear any of that, did you, Carmen?), his ceremonious kisses deposited in deep concavities—kisses that lasted longer than the silence of a domestic servant.

"Old prostate!" my grandmother howled, so flustered she was tongue-tied. She fired him in the act, without paying him a red cent. The poor old bastard was so stunned he tripped on the Capo di Monti urn in the foyer as he left, stumbling and muttering threats. Grandmother followed him with her sparkling eyes from the second floor banister, assuring him from that moment forward he would be forever banned from the Society of Friends of Music and from all the other societies, except, of course, the society of stray dogs.

On the final pages of the third secret diary, they found, spelled out in excruciating detail, a litany of different ways to assassinate Aunt Malva as painfully as possible, "even if we were to leave fingerprints." Aunt Malva cried when they showed her the paragraphs.

"Let's see, let's see," my grandmother said, interested. And she quickly became engrossed in her reading.

"It seems logical," she said at last. "It's not insanity. It's logical. And you, Malva, don't get all hysterical! We have to try to save her soul. Don't you see the state of moral degradation to which this kind of thinking leads? She gets it from over there," she added, looking toward the third patio. "This is just what I feared, that this dirt could not be washed away with soap and water, just like that. You will be in charge of this matter."

Then Grandmother took Aunt Malva by the shoulders, as if she were a seven-year-old child.

"You'll be in charge of the girl, and you'll make sure the purification is internal, do you understand? We cannot harbor this sort of infection in a family such as ours. We have never had it, and there is no reason why it should begin to crop up in this century. And I do not wish to hear another word about this. I have already had more than I can bear with all that we have read today," she said, pointing to the diaries. "Get them out of here and tell Meche to come in here and clean," she ordered.

It was Meche who received the direct order to burn them "without reading them under any circumstances."

(". . . I RAN to the kitchen and clung desperately to her apron while she was preparing the logs for the fire. After a number of heartfelt sobs, I managed to convince her to give me one of the diaries. I took it and buried it in my pants. Back then, just as today, I was a terrible pack rat, so much so it's almost impossible to keep my apartment

clean. I'm always saving peels, leftovers, hems, buttons
from old clothes are like treasures, looks already given . . .
What the hell do your old girlfriends and trysts matter
to me? You're a mess, what have you got there? Why don't
you throw out those old books, those boxes . . . ?")

Ten

I DIDN'T see Carmen for weeks.

The scandal lingered. It was unbelievable. Aunt
Malva rampaged throughout the house, going up and
down staircases, flying through hallways dressed like an
angel (she was always wearing white around that time).
She holed herself up with my sister for countless hours.

"What are you talking about? Sister? Better you not
even mention her name," Meche groaned as she carried
food to the room on trays made of rotting wood.

We were no longer permitted to go out together or to
see each other at all. Not even to go and buy bread, each
holding on to one handle of the basket, each helping to
balance the load while we chanted *al lirón, lirón, lirero, sancho
pan* . . . Not in our wildest dreams.

One day Aunt Malva came into the house brandishing a little black book.

"What's that, Aunt Malva?"

"An examination of conscience, the Benedictine version, which is the best," she added. "We'll just see if that little girl abandons her sinful instincts now. The poor wretch," she hissed. "In the final assessment, is it really her fault?"

Her voice, like a fine whip, dissipated until it was almost inaudible and turned into a funnel cloud of powerful skirts, closing the door behind her.

Eleven

B AD instincts had taken hold of Carmen, and they refused to let her go. It was just like the Evil Hydra of the Swamp that drowns the smuggler's daughter so he'll stop smuggling; and then the smuggler, seeing his dead daughter, simply smuggles twice as much, wounded and enraged (he wasn't enraged—Carmen said—his pride was hurt). Around that time, I stole a notebook and a pen from Meche and tried to write about sins of the flesh, but none came to mind, not a single one (and I still can't think of any).

That year at Grandmother's birthday party, a real scene ensued (a scene that wasn't the least bit noble) for the benefit of the Theresas (of Avila, Grandmother pointed out, stroking the table with her slender fingers).

They found Carmen in the pantry, perfectly drunk. How had she managed to find out where the liquor was hidden? Meche was howling at the top of her lungs as she tried to clean up the green vomit that was sliding down her apron.

"Now what am I supposed to wear when I serve the hors d'oeuvres, *señora?* Tell me! Tell me! And if you only give me one new apron a year . . . bah! I've had it up to here with that girl. . . ."

Carmen, her body turned to the shelf where they kept the jam, confessed her impure thoughts at the top of her voice. "Bad thoughts wend their way through my hair, they creep quietly up the nape of my neck, and fly out of me, through my forehead. Evil gazes . . . intentional looks . . . I don't know which way to turn anymore," she cried, forlorn.

My grandmother shot her a glance. Then she closed the pantry door, double locking it, and returned to the dining room through the foyer, carrying the big steaming turkey herself. On her face was plastered the same dusty smile she had worn for years. She caused a ruckus with her exclamations. The senators placed their hands over their mouths, just like Professor Liberdevsky. It was insane!

Like every other year, she dominated the conversation, holding it tautly under control at the end of her kite string. She would grant or deny minor interventions, but always manage to have the last word somehow. My grandmother spoke about her son Alejandro. What an appropriate name for a military man, Madame. Well, as you know, he is not just any soldier. My grandmother puffed up like a soufflé as she brought forth words to describe the golden triumphs of her son; he was already the commanding general of some garrison or other, a South American and Inter-American fencing champion. My son has been a warrior ever since he was born. He would never put up with anything. If you only knew . . .

But it was getting late that year. Everyone was mesmerized by her wise, cutting hands, which flitted through the air near the magnificent silver fountain. My grandmother did not explain why everyone applauded her final piano piece more effervescently than the previous ones.

CARMEN was supposed to be confined to her room, but she escaped. They looked for her during the entire morning as well as that afternoon, pretending it was nothing more than a casual disappearance. Now where might she have gone, Meche? Did you send her to buy bread? No, *señora*. Don't get me involved in that creature's messes. I have enough trouble just trying to make do with the miserable sum you give me to buy food. I just can't stretch it anymore, not even if I . . . All right, Meche, hold your horses. No one is accusing you of anything.

"Has anyone seen that little girl?" they asked, looking for her as one would a handkerchief only momentarily lost. "You, Carlitos, have you seen her?" The President shrugged his shoulders.

At lunchtime, Aunt Malva staged a nauseating series of entrances and exits with saucers and saltshakers and jars, all to hide Carmen's absence from the table. Grandmother said nothing and emptied her wine glass just as she did every other day.

The following afternoon, the search turned into a frenzied scaling of the imperial staircases, sweeps through the servants' quarters, a look toward the skylight in search of inspiration, the turning of doorknobs, a complete search of the laundry room. You, look there. Casual interrogations of the people at the dime store. Don't let my mother find out.

Grandmother presided over the uneasy silence from the second-floor hallway, standing behind the banister, erect as ever, in a mocking pose. The thump of her arrhythmia was the only sound that could be heard.

"If that girl decided to run away, then there is nothing we can do about it," she thundered. "I am going to take my siesta. I bet she did not even take a hairbrush with her."

Then she locked herself in her room.

Twelve

THEY had been looking for Carmen for three days.
Aunt Malva moved around the corridors in a
frenzy, opening doors that had been closed for years, desperate to delay the impending police investigation that
would certainly delve into the embarrassing details of her
social status (the police are so uncouth). There is no
reason why I should have to give details about my personal life. "What a shameful girl, thoughtlessness incar-
nate," she howled as she searched broom closets,
cupboards full of dust rags, and coal bins. I believe she
got as far as Carmen's mother's door, which she opened
with two fingers.

I knew Carmen hadn't gone out wandering the streets.
A layer of frost was still covering Santiago at night that

year (is that because spring was just a little late in coming for us?), and Carmen was sensitive to the cold.

I thought Aunt Malva would bring private search dogs to the house, she was such a fanatic.

Then, in four leaps, I went up to Uncle Ascanio's room. He received me with his splendid, salty smile, seated in his wicker rocking chair that rocked forward on its own, and which moved like a cradle even when there was no one sitting in it. He was still preoccupied with the difference in weight between the hollow eggs and the other ones.

I didn't even greet him. I headed straight for the piles of purple egg cartons accumulating at the back of his room, forming a sort of compact wall through which sound could barely penetrate.

There was Carmen, sitting on the floor, with her gaze fixed on a page of the black book containing the examination of conscience.

Aunt Malva came in right behind me, shouting orders like a drill sergeant and carrying soaps. "Get away from that filth immediately! Don't talk back! Take a bath and get into bed! How could you even think to act this way? One would think you had . . ."

"Yes!" Carmen jumped up with her eyes shining. "Say it, Aunt Malva! That's it! One would think that you had . . . the devil in your body. But from here down, not from here up. You're just born that way, isn't that right? No one knows how the devil descends upon certain cradles (like those on the third patio) and not upon others. Oh yes, yes, yes!"

Meche and another house servant had to carry her in the air, so quiet and compact, just like the piano.

There was no amount of human energy that could have wrenched the little black book from her hands. They had to bathe her with it.

"What theatrics, mother," Aunt Malva said, relieved that the authorities' questions about her personal life and Uncle Pedro's disappearance had vaporized. Later, she considered it her duty to clarify some things.

"I think it is a bit much that she went to hide with poor Ascanio, although, in the end, I suppose he *is* a part of us. But she is only one-third by blood, which hardly . . ."

"Half," my grandmother corrected her without looking at her.

"Half," Aunt Malva repeated. "But realize it's not because the poor man can't defend himself. . . ."

Grandmother was convinced they had removed the seed from Uncle Ascanio's soul. She even went up to see him, accompanied by her noisy entourage of enormous skirts, with Meche bearing little cushions. She only stayed for a short time. The midday sun separated him from the world. Besides, there was nothing to talk to him about.

When she came down, she drank three cups of herbal tea. It was the first time I had ever seen her retire to her quarters without eating. Meche says Grandmother interrogated Ascanio for three hours with no result other than a perfect smile and his passing her heavy and light eggs, one after another. Meche says that after his silence my grandmother lost the composure she had kept for almost fifty years, and began kicking egg cartons until she became exhausted, destroying the capital and slipping, furious, on the egg whites that oozed out into the dust and other stuff my big-toothed uncle had accumulated in his remarkable solitude.

"Calm yourself, *señora*. You're going to make yourself ill," Meche said, perturbed, holding the damp towel she always carried, cleaning. "It would be best if we just went downstairs. There are nothing but cartons up here, *señora*, and Ascanito doesn't speak, you know that."

. . .

THEN they really locked Carmen away, in another room, on a patio by herself—a patio without a palm tree.

We were forbidden to mention her name at the dinner table.

The President of the Republic yawned in the corridors. Grandmother forbade him to play the piano, and sent for him to replace us in watching her during her siesta. Aunt Malva considered this a big step, and she left me alone for a brief period of time. Besides, she was very busy going to and from the patio where Carmen was being held captive, with her missionary-like face. She would leave the house at dawn, with her brown mantilla, to ask advice at El Salvador Church.

Thirteen

A<small>UNT</small> M<small>ALVA</small> took the matter of Carmen's soul very seriously. Even so, we were prohibited from speaking to her. She went to the patio where Carmen was being held and clandestinely entered her room. She carried the little black book and put on dresses that more and more resembled the ones my grandmother wore.

I can't imagine what she could have said to her. I only saw the President of the Republic rolling his eyes and rubbing his knees with pleasure, as he sat on his haunches in front of the window.

Later, when the summer fell upon us like an insufferable cat, a friar wearing sandals came to the house and went directly to Carmen's room, without stopping to chat with Grandmother or have the obligatory glass of wine.

Before, when priests would visit the house on a daily basis, Aunt Malva dressed up like a young girl to receive them. She altered her way of speaking so radically her words turned into incomprehensible babble. She even held Grandmother's hand and peered through her curls at the clergymen. The cackles she let out instilled more fear in us than her usual lemon-like way of speaking. Aunt Malva was a completely different woman, but my grand-mother pretended she couldn't sense any change, pre-senting her to her hoity-toity friends with intentionally vague phrases.

This time, none of that happened. The friar left Carmen's room quite quickly, holding a cross high in the air. With my mouth wide open, I crossed the front patio in a single bound, ready to shed tears and barking questions.

"Insolent boy! What a ruckus! Can't you see that they are confessing her!" Meche passed by, sweeping.

Fourteen

ONE day, despite the prohibitions and the punishments that were hanging over my head, I secretly snuck into the room where they were keeping Carmen.

Every vestige of the decorative curtains that adorned her other room had disappeared. Nor did any trace remain of her fluffy bed with the white polka-dot comforter where we would disappear for hours, tickling each other among the giant cushions.

Her cell had only a bare couch toward the back. The window glowed upon the wall, which didn't have a single painting on it. The musty smell of isolation lingered in the room like lamplight.

Carmen received me as if I were Sandokán, adorning me with a series of attributes such as bravery and beauty, which I have never since possessed. She was crying and praying at the same time. I had never seen her so weak. That beautiful neck of lustrous insolence had disappeared, and her vertebrae could be seen between her elbows. Her eyes . . . I didn't see her eyes. She covered them constantly because she didn't wish to give in to temptation, she explained. She didn't want to get near anyone or anything. She had become incredibly emaciated. Either she did not want to eat, or Aunt Malva was sending her a special diet—nothing strange.

Suddenly, she sat up straight, and for an instant she went back to being her old self. She made me laugh by making faces at me. She told me—and her impersonations had always been brilliant—all about the clergymen who were visiting her. Later, in complete silence, we played *kai-kai*, using an elastic chord to form figures like the cradle and the obelisk. The chord slid between Carmen's alabaster fingers.

Suddenly, she spoke: "Do you think," she asked, embracing me, "that this is a sin? I looked at myself in the mirror on Sunday and I touched one of my breasts while I was getting dressed. Is it? And they get bigger when I think about you. They're pretty big, don't you think?"

No. I didn't think so. She was more incoherent than ever, but I assured her yes, they were big, like two turtle-doves in flight. I know I must have gotten that from somewhere, but I didn't think Carmen would remember the old novels we had once read.

"This is all sinful," she sighed. "If I die tonight I won't be able to save myself, because I haven't confessed and no one has given me penance. You can't be forgiven without penance. I can't even pray. I have forgotten how to say the Hail Mary. I have forgotten! Your neck is so warm, without stress and without knots. Be my confessor," she asked. "You're a man. You can give me temporary absolution."

Her small face was full of torment. I had to confess her and invent a momentary absolution so she could fall asleep. Carmen fell to her knees. She was so pale she seemed like a mere memory of the girl she had once been.

I vowed next time I would take her away, no matter what happened. Even if we only got as far as the Plaza Brasil, or around the block, at least we would be able to make fun of the people in the dime store. I would bring money to buy her an ice cream cone. I would find it somewhere.

Everything filled her with remorse (Aunt Malva's little black book was powerful)—even everyday things like touching a piece of fruit or walking across a fluffy rug. I saw her scream and cry just for passing her hand across a plate of raspberries, and even more forcefully for remembering having done it. The aroma of freshly baked bread horrified her.

She spent hours washing her hands with soap and a scouring pad until they were raw.

"I can't stop thinking," she said. "I just can't!"

One afternoon she cut off her hair in big chunks (her sumptuously wavy hair, your vivid hair, Carmen)—cut it above the ear. Aunt Malva became conveniently mortified in front of Grandmother, pushing her plate aside and throwing her hands in the air (around that time, the President, armed with his comb, was unrolling his third curl which fell like a vertical sideburn despite all his efforts to maintain an attractive wave).

When I tried to convince Carmen that afternoon, desperate because she did not even want to play *kai-kai* with me and didn't even want to lay next to me on the dilapidated sofa, I pointed out that her strong flecks of hair were standing on end. She recoiled.

"It's just that when I comb my hair, I touch my neck, and it tickles me in a way I know is sinful," she said.

Then she tried to bathe with her clothes on so she wouldn't see her own nakedness. She no longer smiled when I crept into the bathroom.

"Be my confessor," she pleaded, constantly, repeatedly, each time more tenuously. Her anxiousness was like the pecking of a bird or the fluttering of an eyelid. She was so transformed even I hardly recognized her amid the greasy hair that sprouted submissively from her scalp. With a slight movement of her head, she turned down the idea to embark upon a clandestine excursion. She didn't even want to go see Uncle Ascanio to tell him stories. Remember, Carmen, how much he likes your stories.

"I forgot them," she said. And she was right.

All her muscles were tense from thinking about her sinful intentions. She tore apart all the bindings of the dime store comic books. What if the people from the dime store come to ask for them, Carmen? Remember, we borrowed them.

"Then send them to talk with Aunt Malva," she said. "Then they'll find out what's really worthwhile! These magazines are a bunch of filth!"

"Carmen," I moved her, "who's hypnotizing you?" But she was looking away.

"Come here," I invited. "Let's go out for a walk. We'll leave through the back door. We'll only go as far as the plaza—to watch the sunset."

Then she looked at me with other eyes. Hers were somewhere else entirely, although I don't know where, broken into a thousand pieces.

"Get away from me," she said as she closed the door.

I WAS startled. I think it was on a Saturday (I remember because there were visitors and there was honey for our tea) when we saw a stream of water flow into the first-floor hallway carrying the arms and legs of destroyed dolls, the rubber parts all waterlogged, the smiling porcelain heads just floating there. I ran upstairs.

Carmen was quiet. She still had pieces of cloth in her hands and threads between her teeth.

"She told you to do this, didn't she?" I shook her. "No," I added, "she's too intelligent for that. She must have insinuated it in passing, right?"

She didn't answer.

FIFTEEN

I DIDN'T even have time to explain to anyone my love for Carmen—that it wasn't like the love you see in the movies, sticky and static. Nor could I tell anyone they kept her incommunicado—that they prohibited her from speaking even to Meche—and that Carmen was getting thinner by the day because she was flushing her food down the toilet. She wouldn't even eat the apples or the *alfajores* I saved for her. She just waited for an opportunity to slip out the window so she could change into a good girl, hoping no one would see her.

I didn't have much faith in that method of liberation, mainly because Aunt Malva would most certainly find out about it just as it was about to happen. But Carmen grabbed both my hands, stubborn, pale, with her eyes like caverns carved into her tearful face.

"It won't be much longer," she said.

She was always watching for some secret obscenity, looking over her shoulder as though she had seen black ravens. She hardly had enough strength to smooth out her dress, which just hung there, full of wrinkles that didn't used to exist.

"I'm almost not a sinner anymore," she assured me, half smiling. "Now I really have to *try* to think bad thoughts."

Sixteen

ONE afternoon, one accursed afternoon when I happened to be out of the house at the dime store, goofing off with the President, buying new magazines, we heard Aunt Malva's shriek pass by us like an electric lasso, surround my grandmother's house and hang there, stiff, filling the eardrums of all the churches.

We ran for it, leaving behind money and magazines.

"It's your fault if we get in trouble," the President said, running behind me, panting.

"Shut up, imbecile," I replied without looking at him.

I ENTERED the house barking, separating the flesh of old women from the old flesh of sour women who were hunched over the thinnest, most beautiful body of a threadlike girl, a body that rose in a spiral toward the lamp of ten-thousand tears, not one tear broken, crystalline-Carmen.

Never—not in the kitchen nor during our after-dinner conversations did they wish to tell me how it happened.

"Why stir up the pain, my child? Let what is in the ground rest peacefully," Meche said with a swipe of her dust rag.

But I don't want them to brainwash me. I'm positive Carmen had tried something, a final leap when she ripped off the scab that tormented her, some kind of acrobatics of the soul. She couldn't have just left, her bags in hand, like a deserter, as they would have me believe. Pray that God might forgive her, my child.

CARMEN seemed to float in that Snow White coffin my grandmother bought for her, among lace, iridescent crystals, and tons of flowers—surrounded by black busts. Each passerby asking himself: but how could this have happened; she's so beautiful. My father, his back turned, paced interminably around the patios. . . .

. . .

"WHAT a scare you gave us," I told her when I saw her come into the house, wrinkling my nose. "That's right, nothing is as clean as a whistle any more, like when Grandmother was alive. We had to sell the lamp. Shhh-hhhh. Don't startle Aunt Malva. She has an arrhythmia.

Epilogue

("... Sometimes the days have trouble advancing and they plunge headlong with the marigolds in the entranceway into a sea of sadness that goes against the grain. Days like those when Meche gets out the wax and the buffer, although she won't use the electric buffer—the devil's instrument as she calls it—and starts waxing just as I finally decide to make a decision, like a man, to let myself love the woman luck placed in my path, and to make something of the relationship, because it's not right to always keep putting things off. But today of all days, Meche has covered all of the furniture and has forbidden me to uncover it until she finishes waxing the floor, which won't happen for three, maybe even ten more days, since she waxes the house in sections, alleging that the

house is so filthy not even Ascanio, by God . . . Aren't
you a little old to be walking around in such a slovenly
state? Look at that collar! She takes off my shirt right
there and starts scrubbing it. Meche, don't worry about
it. I . . . I mean . . . if you . . . nothing. You may look
professional, but you shouldn't be left alone. . . . God
knows what might happen . . . and there is a shortage of
fine upstanding young women these days. She takes out
my catalogs and puts them in order all by herself, by
color, without letting me explain to her my methodology
or my code. I stand there horrified and just let her mess
up everything. To this day I have not been able to convince Meche to prepare food for two people and leave it
chilling in the refrigerator. Instead, she stands there
waiting for me in the kitchen, stirring the pots of food,
bundled up in her hot pink robe, her eyebrows raised,
asserting that the later I arrive the more gas she wastes.

'You never even stopped to consider that my bones
are aching from all this standing. It's not as if I were
made in Germany,' she adds. I ask her forgiveness. I
receive her ironic mm . . . mm . . . mm, and clean my
plate.

Then I go up to see Uncle Ascanio. Every time it gets
harder to find him because he is as limpid as a perfectly

formed drop. His brown jacket hangs there with no one inside it. The smell of stale hot air, or eggs, is no longer unbearable. Nor is the room as confining. Really, it's a beautiful sunroom where they keep Uncle Ascanio.

No one has keys to the doors anymore.

You're a real ladies man, my friends at the office tell me. And it's a big lie, because we have been going on dates to the movies for months. And she tells her friends: he behaves himself so well in the dark . . . so well, in fact, it's almost as though he actually went just to see the movie. And you insist on going to the Alcázar, as if the tickets were free, she tells me. Nevertheless, she thinks I'm very sweet and snuggles up to me ever more tightly in the twilight. But I can't. And those imbeciles in accounting are so jealous. What's your secret, stud? How do you manage to drive the girls crazy?

My secret, my tick, my life, is to look furtively toward the exit, amid the heat of the movie theater, where Carmen observes me mockingly, imitating the crunch of the mints I'm chewing, signaling to me that Aunt Malva is waiting for us to come to dinner. . . .")

Afterword

C ARMEN'S RUST arrived on the Chilean literary
scene in the mid–1980s establishing Ana María del
Río as a powerful voice within a unique narrative land-
scape.

Published during dark and violent years of dictatorship—years in which a multitude of infractions were
committed by the State against a targeted segment of the
population— *Carmen's Rust* offered, in an oblique way, a
matrix in which to situate the military regime's persistent
and manifold technology of control, discipline and
destruction.

Carmen is a character who is plunged into an
anguished and irreversible repression, the kind of repression that the powerful have often inflicted on women.

Her identity is marked by a creative, transgressive desire,
a will to celebrate her sensuality, to heed the demands of
her senses.

Nevertheless, her desire—which can be read as a literary expression of difference and power—is quelled by
the collusive machinations of her family. Only interested
in perpetuating traditional bourgeois power structures,
the dictatorial matriarchs subordinate her individuality to
mere functionality. To keep the family line untarnished
and intact, they must perpetuate the mediocre and con-
ventional existence of all of its members.

But there, amid an intricate web of bureaucratic
domestic vigilance, Carmen stands in contempt, as one
who—within the context of her incestuous desire—is
branded by the family matriarchs as inferior and weak,
the daughter of a lower-class mother. Carmen seeks the
kind of transgression and rebellion incest implies, and
her behavior signals the end of the family as a model for
social organization.

Because of her transgressive desires, institutional
forces lay siege to her in a relentless, severe and irreversible way. Like Franz Kafka's *The Metamorphosis*, the
novel depicts the crisis of a subject who rebels against

family convention, and demonstrates how rebellion leads to aberrant change, exhaustion, and death.

Carmen's Rust questions the way in which personal and political bodies are constructed. It questions the role occupied by the female body through the construction of a domestic microcosm. With intelligence and precision, the novel creates a confrontation among female characters, each of whom apparently possesses her own unique relationship to a feminine power that exercises in the private realm the same kind of vigilance that is exercised in the masculine (public) political order.

In the process, we are left with Carmen, one of the most disturbing and emblematic literary images in contemporary Chilean narrative.

DIAMELA ELTIT

TRANSLATED BY MICHAEL J. LAZZARA

A NOTE ON THE TYPE

The text was set in 12 point Centaur with a leading of 16 points space. Originally designed by Bruce Rogers for the Metropolitan Museum in 1914, Centaur was released by Monotype in 1929. Modeled on letters cut by the fifteenth-century printer Nicolas Jenson, Centaur has a beauty of line and proportion that has been widely acclaimed since its release. The italic type, originally named Arrighi, was designed by Frederic Warde in 1925. He modeled his letters on those of Ludovico deli Arrighi, a Renaissance scribe whose lettering work is among the finest of the chancery cursives. Arrighi was produced by Monotype as the companion for Centaur in 1929.

↬

Book composition by Charles B. Hames
New York, New York